Cities, Capitalism and the Politics of Sensibilities

"Emotions move cities and the world: this is the main lesson of this inspiring reading. Too often, emotions have been relegated to privatism and intimism. This is especially in today's cities, too often fragmented, commodified and anonymized, where sensibilities are either polarized or anesthetized. But emotions have also a cognitive and a conative component, strictly tied to beliefs and behaviours. Through a plural and transdisciplinary perspective, this book teaches that sensibilities have a purely social dimension and must be valued as a common good."
—Silvia Cataldi, *Department of Social and Developmental Psychology, Sapienza University of Rome, Italy*

"Drawing from a close dialogue with the sociology of emotions, this book brings an important contribution to urban studies, as these intertwine economic, social and cultural dimensions of seeing, feeling and acting, both from personal and collective perspectives. Warmly recommended."
—Joanildo A. Burity, *Pesquisador Titular/Lead Researcher Diretoria de Pesquisas Sociais/Institute for Social Research, Recife, Brazil*

"In this new and exciting book Project, Adrian Scribano, Margarita Camarena & Ana Lucía Cervio proffer an all-encompassing diagnosis which interrogates furtherly the life in an urban metropolis. To some extent, the radical transformations, which accelerated by global capitalism, has created different cosmologies revolving around "cities". Speaking about cities seems to explore the dense interplay among politics, ideology, domination and economic production. Doubtless, in this trailblazing book, editors continue a hot-debate originally initiated by De Coulanges, Lefevre, Castells and Sassen and always giving an innovative, fresh and multicultural insight. I have no doubt this is a seminal book which will stand the test of time."
—Maximiliano Korstanje, *University of Palermo, Argentina—CERS University of Leeds, UK*

"This edited volume brings together insightful analyses of the urban in late capitalism. It offers a transdisciplinary perspective ranging from the anthropological, cultural, economic, geographic political, psychological, sociological, and urban planning. Its strength lies in offering both a diverse and cohesive picture of cities in today's world."
—Geoffrey R. Skoll, *Emeritus Professor at SUNY (Buffalo), US*

Adrián Scribano · Margarita Camarena Luhrs ·
Ana Lucía Cervio
Editors

Cities, Capitalism and the Politics of Sensibilities

Editors
Adrián Scribano
National Scientific and Technical
Research Council
University of Buenos Aires
Buenos Aires, Argentina

Margarita Camarena Luhrs
Institute of Social Research
National Autonomous University of
Mexico
Mexico City, Mexico

Ana Lucía Cervio
National Scientific and Technical
Research Council
University of Buenos Aires
Buenos Aires, Argentina

ISBN 978-3-030-58034-6   ISBN 978-3-030-58035-3   (eBook)
https://doi.org/10.1007/978-3-030-58035-3

This Palgrave Macmillan imprint is published by the registered company Springer Nature Switzerland AG
The registered company address is: Gewerbestrasse 11, 6330 Cham, Switzerland

FOREWORD: THE EXPANDED AND DRAMATIZED EMOTIONS IN THE CONTEXT OF GLOBAL CITIES

SEVEN CHARACTERISTICS OF GLOBALIZATION AND THE GLOBAL ETHICS OF EMOTIONS

Defining Characters of Globalization

It is not easy to define the polyhedral concept of globalization, among other reasons because it is ideologically highly contaminated by the dominant influence of economic neoliberalism in today's world. However, a minimally rigorous approach to the term requires at least seven characteristics to be taken into account.

(1) The first, not without epistemological difficulties, consists in distinguishing between globalization and globalism (A. Giddens, U. Beck, R. Safranski y N. García-Canclini). The latter would be more determined by the exclusively economic dimension of globalization and by the ideological neoliberalism that is behind it, while globalization, in theory, would be a multidimensional phenomenon, with economic, ecological, social, cultural, scientific, tourist, communicative, warlike or terrorist character. In globalization, therefore, people, goods, values, information, ideologies, weapons, viruses, cultural products, ideas, concepts and emotions circulate.

(2) Now, certainly, the confusion between the two terms has brought about evident social unrest. And it is that, when we think about

globalization, we do it basically highlighting the evils rather than the benefits that it entails; benefits that have been substantial and not less significant than its negative consequences which have had them and not on a lesser plane. Hence, we fundamentally stress that the problems of inequality, poverty and hunger have not been solved (J. Stiglitz), but we forget that these were not solved in the stages prior to that of globalization either.

(3) This discomfort towards globalization has been accompanied by the fact that it has not become a global phenomenon; in fact, there is neither a world citizenship, nor a global policy, governance or ethics (U. Beck, Z. Bauman, J. Stiglitz and R. Safransky). In other words, there is no global political control—for example, over global warming of the planet, there is no political globalization—in spite of institutions such as the UN, the IMF or the World Bank; nor is there a world society, or rulers, or global citizens, or an ethic that inspires the way of acting and the civilizing course of the planet as a whole.

To this we must add that, on the economic level, that globalization refers more exactly to the trilateralization of the economy (U. Beck), which affects, above all, Europe and a part of America and Asia (China, Japan), plus Australia. This means that it has not reached, to its full extent, Africa, although it is rapidly transforming the continent due to the enormous Chinese investments in infrastructure. A similar pattern applies to large areas of Central and South America, where there are, ambivalently (García-Canclini), some fully integrated aspects of globalization yet in other dimensions not so much. Chile, for example, would exemplify this ambivalence in that, despite the fact that its economy is very open to the world, it has not managed to reduce the social distances between its citizens. Likewise, the indigenous claims, legitimate on the other hand, of the natives of the Amazon against the logging or mineral extraction companies continue to be closely linked to the old philosophy of "good living", linked to the Pachamama (or Mother Earth) and, consequently, they are very foreign to the modernization that globalization implies. The consequence of all this is that globalization has fostered growing inequality between continents, nations, regions and cities, between these and the rural world and, therefore, between the different citizens who inhabit them. This has meant that it is more "tangential" than "circular"

(N. García-Canclini), more imaginary than real, that only intellectuals or political and economic elites know and defend it. It is right that, in reality, globalization is something that big businessmen and some intellectuals normally think about, but not everyone meditates on it; moreover, it does not even reach all parts of the planet. In fact, those who do reflect on globalization do so tangentially, laterally, while globalization does not constitute the centre of their lives for the vast majority of the population. On the other hand, it is more imaginary than real, becoming for some—usually the most interested—a great ideal. Consequently, its scope is not total but rather fragmentary and, what is worse, instead of breaking the traditional social segmentation, it has become one more cause of it, one of the most important elements in the construction of a socially broken world (C. Castoriadis).

(4) Along with this, this globalization is a "frontier" (J. Arango), since, if in theory it should lead to the opening of borders, however, in reality, they have increased and have been built, precisely, in times of globalization: the wire fence of Ceuta, the wall that isolates Israel from Palestine, the fence between the USA and Mexico, the concrete wall in the Kurdish mountains that separates Turkey and Syria, and so on.

(5) This discomfort, this unequal distribution across the planet and its new frontiers, have not prevented globalization from being portrayed as a multidimensional phenomenon, insofar as it has led to multiple flows, variously economic, financial, material, cultural, ideological, informative, weapons and human. It is precisely the latter that are generating migratory currents, mainly concentrated in a series of "tectonic faults": from South to North, the Mediterranean, the Persian Gulf, the western shore of the Pacific or the border between the USA and Mexico. On their side, the same investors place their funds on the stock exchanges of New York, London or Hong Kong and tourists invade any corner of the planet. Also, it's easy to find a box of Coca-Cola inside the shack of a lost Masai town in Kenya, a McDonalds in Moscow or Beijing, a Chinese restaurant in Los Angeles, a paella stand in Manhattan, and skyscrapers in Chicago, New York, Dubai, Sao Paulo, Shanghai, Hong Kong and Kuala Lumpur. It is also very frequent that in theatres in India, Spain, Latin America, Australia or Egypt, there are Hollywood movies; or that in Romania there are groups of tango

fans, or in Tokyo there are flamenco lovers; or that, in the outskirts of Cape Town, children wear Barça shirts emblazoned with the name of Messi.

(6) It should be kept in mind, at the same time, that globalization is not an abstract phenomenon, since it affects, a great deal, our daily life and the emotions that unfold in it (A. Giddens). Indeed, the person with whom one is paired can be of a different colour and the children that they produce carry a "café con leche" hue. When you go to the doctor, the doctor may be of Cuban, Argentine, Chinese or Serbian origin, that is, of a race, ethnicity, language or religion different from that of the patient. People of gypsy, Latin American, Arab, Eastern European, Asian and Asian origin can live in the same building where we live. And all this means that, in the immediate future, we are basically faced with two options: either we live with the other, if it is possible with affection, or we generate disagreements, conflicts or battles with our global and daily neighbours.

(7) These two alternatives are also resolved in the tension existing between nation-states and stateless nationalities (S. Nair), a common problem in countries of the world as different as Spain, Italy, France, Germany, the Balkans, Hungary, China, Russia, Georgia, Ukraine, United States of America, Brazil, Philippines, Sri Lanka, Indonesia, Yemen, Somalia, Nigeria, Turkey, Syria and Iraq; or between the different ethnic groups, cultures and races that coexist in many of the contemporary states. Not in vain, Globalization has intensified the phenomena of local identity, localization, both phenomena constituting an indissoluble unity (I. Moreno). In this sense, it is often said that there are no local solutions for global issues (Z. Bauman), but there are also no global resolutions for local problems; that is, that we need "glocalization" (R. Robertson), which involves interdependencies and deep dialogues. For example, how are international issues ranging from migration, terrorism, drug trafficking, refugees (for example Syrians, Rohingya, Hutus and Tutsi, from Afghanistan or Venezuela) to regional conflicts (such as those in Syria, Yemen, Ukraine, Afghanistan and Libya) managed globally? How are challenges such as climate change and global pandemics tacked? We must not forget that, simultaneously, there are specific issues that

the great States cannot solve, such as traffic in cities, school administration, homelessness, the coexistence of villas and favelas, the accommodation of the homeless, etc.

The Global Ethics of Emotions

In summary, the complexity of the contemporary world is of such a calibre, the interdependencies so decisive, the dialogue so urgently necessary and the energies that must be brought into play so enormous, that we all need each other: multinational institutions, supra-state institutions, states, regional entities or local, citizens, experts, civic and social actors and companies (J. Tardif). And in this dialogue, what emotions do we put on the board, alongside each other's reasoning?

There is, therefore, the need for a global ethics of emotions. Indeed, ethics (Victoria Camps) cannot do without the affective or emotional part of human being because one of its tasks is to put in order, organize and make sense of emotions. This means that ethics channels emotions in the appropriate direction, in the trajectory of the encounter with the other, without forgetting that they possess, at the same time, a cognitive and sensitive substrate, which allows us to better understand the world and possess a greater empathy with the other. Not in vain, they can become a bridge between people's beliefs and desires, that is, between the image of the world they live in—their world map—and the goals and things to which they aspire, as well as between particular feelings of individuals and politics of sensibilities of public entities.

THE GLOBAL URBAN SPACE: NARROWING OR DILATION OF EMOTIONS?

Space Constrained by Globalization

Globalization has narrowed the spaces and distanced the distance. The first occurs because those spaces have become smaller, while communication has been made possible with people located thousands of kilometres away. And the second happens because each time one travels farther and, even, has gone so far as to leave the Earth itself. Thus, when one reflects on the concept of globalization, it is done in a narrow space; in one in which the distant is closer and closer; that it is more imaginary than real, and that it is neither thought nor felt by the majority as globalization. It is not surprising that globalization, to which we attach so much importance, is being devalued as a spatial concept because it is, above all, a product of the present, subject to the frenetic pace of merchandise and investment in securities, and, consequently, it is not a future project, a utopia that is going to change things. In other words, we are subjecting globalization to a time pressure that causes the world to "go wild" (A. Giddens), to commodify itself, to fetishize (C. Marx), to convert it more into an exchange value than a use value and, in short, it is devalued to the point that it is more dominated by time than by space.

This is related to a change in the means of understanding these latter categories and their fragmentation, which in turn affects various factors:

(1) First of all, there is a territorial crisis of the Nation-State, pressured from above by the supra-state entities (such the European Community and the Southern Cone) and from below, by the nations without a State (for example, Catalonia, the Basque Country, the Padania, Bavaria, Texas or Estado Grande Do Sul). This is giving rise to two interrelated phenomena: the appearance of transnational spaces and that of intercultural spaces.

Furthermore, the crisis of the State arises because there has been a tension between the global sphere of financial markets and the national sphere of politics, whose basic unit continues to be the Nation-State. And, although governments preserve the power to intervene in the economy, they are increasingly subject to the dictates of global competition for trade and capital. Thus, capitalism has been confronted with representative democracies, and this fight has entailed that the development of the global economy does not coincide with that of global society, and that the failure of politics and the discrediting of ideologies have occurred. Marxist, liberal and social democratic, as well as reformism and revolution (B. De Sousa), the Welfare State (S. Amin), traditional political parties and democratic institutions, have entered into a deep crisis of values and legitimation. In sum, it has become evident that the management of global capitalism has broken the requirement of "the market plus the State", something that had been one of the distinctive characteristics of capitalism, accustomed to historical coexistence and mutual dependence on two types of power—the private economic, coming from property and profit, and the coercive territorial power of the States (G. Ingham). Together, economic globalization has given rise to a world still fragmented into different nations and between rich and poor, as well as a revival of nationalisms and social struggles and the rise of ethnicity, a political response to economic globalization (S. Amin).

(2) Space is unobtrusive, which is linked to the triumph of uncompromising individualism (U. Beck, Z. Bauman, A. Giddens, and S. Lash), at least to the Western world, including Japan and China, as well like much of Latin America. This explains why the social space—the political agora—is reduced almost to nothing and that, consequently, the whole, the common is devalued, and only individual benefits are now deemed matters of interest. In turn, this is linked to the crisis of citizenship (Z. Bauman, E. Balibar) and institutions—such as the family (U. and E. Beck, Z. Bauman, A. Giddens) or work (R. Sennet, J. F. Tezanos), of social cement, of identity. It is also linked to being uprooted or not feeling anywhere, nothing, and even the desire to disappear from oneself (D. Le Breton). Globalization, therefore, narrows both the space that the bodies occupy, and the emotions that develop in the spatial interrelationships and inside our minds disappear.

(3) "Empty spaces of meaning" arise, which affects culture, or what is the same, "imaginary spaces" and "imagined communities" (B. Anderson) burst forth. As an example of this we have the Barcelona April Fair, held by Andalusian emigrants in Catalonia or the London Carnival, both exhibitions of trans-identitarian and trans-national spaces. There are also what we call "virtual spaces", such as Amusement Parks or shopping centres (J. Baudrillard, P. Virilio), and non-real or "decorative" ones. Las Vegas, for example, constitutes a very interesting sociological city, born in "the desert of the real" (J. Baudrillard) and which creates an urban environment with many gardens and abundant water. It is an artificial city powered by the power of money.

Global Cities and the Politics of Sensibilities

For a city to reach the definition of global, it must have financial centres, the presence of international corporate headquarters, the development of business and commercial management services, manufacturing centres, a well-developed transportation hub, international tourism, a considerable population size, a multicultural mix of national and foreign inhabitants and a concentration of artistic and scientific elites (N. García Canclini).

This is related to the fact that the global economy presents a great geographic dispersion and mobility and, simultaneously, a territorial concentration of resources for the management and provision of services. Therefore, the more companies globalize, the more their central management functions grow (S. Sassen), and the more they help the cities where they are installed to assume the label of "global".

For this reason, these types of global cities have actually been transformed into "megacities" (R. Florida), with 20 or 30 million inhabitants: Guangzhou, Tokyo, Shanghai, Jakarta, Delhi, Manila, Bombay, Seoul, Mexico City, Sao Paulo, New York, Cairo, Dhaka, Beijing and Lagos, On the other hand, there are the so-called megacity networks, for example, the east coast of the United States; in Spain we do not have these megacities, since Madrid and Barcelona are not that big, compared to other cities. In any case, these megacities concentrate the largest investments in securities and foreign exchange; the headquarters of the multinationals, which attract a whole network of service companies; also creativity with theatre, music, gastronomy, fashion companies, etc. In other words, they group a large part of the gross domestic product of the world. Even in the future, if these big cities wanted to be self-sufficient, they could be.

What consequences does this have, particularly for emotions? One of the most notable effects is that megacities need a lot of manpower, so they receive large migrations that are concentrated in ghettos in their suburbs—La Banlieue Paris or Lyon, the villas (Argentina), the favelas (Brazil), museque (Angola), callampa (Chile), slum (Colombia, Costa Rica and El Salvador), arripon (Cuba), hooverville (USA), sium (India), gecekondu (Turkey), and so on—and they make these cities, many of them located on the periphery of globalization, incorporate within them peripheries, peripheries of the periphery.

Other important consequences are that these cities become more multicultural and their identities are diluted. Along with this, social interrelationships increase quantitatively and qualitatively, and are not only reduced to the framework of rationality subject to ends, although they are filled with not a few conflicts and contradictory and complex emotions, in which the fear of the different, humiliation, disgust or shame ambivalently dwarf or intensify, devalue or dramatize. In relation to this, it should be borne in mind that, for the development of emotions, a narrow or intimate urban spatial environment is not the same as one that is dilated, globalized, as it is not one that is devalued and commodified than another in which what is at stake, above all, is survival.

ABOUT THE BOOK

Cities, Capitalism and the Politics of Sensibilities, is structured into two parts that articulate theoretical explorations and situated analyses of the metropolis. In total, it has thirteen chapters, dedicated to different topics in which, in general terms, cities are linked to the body, emotions and politics of sensibilities.

PART I: THEORETICAL APPROACHES TO URBAN SENSIBILITIES AND CAPITALISM

The first of the chapters, by Adrián Scribano, is dedicated to cities and emotions, and intends to present, in a synthetic way, three moments that can be observed in the presence of sensitivities in the cities of this century: the politics of senses, the shopping centre as a cathedral of consumption and the features of the city 4.0. The second, by Antonio Rafele, after reviewing an extensive corpus of studies and philosophical sources published during the nineteenth and twentieth centuries, points out how modern authors identified the ephemeral as the distinctive feature of the metropolitan experience and the visual media. The third, by Margarita Camarena, analyses how sensible interaction with the city provides exciting clues to follow bodyBodies/emotion perception and explores a dual socio-spatial plasticity: subject~bodies/emotions//city-city/object~bodies/emotions, which socializes the city as much as it embodies the social relations that classify its space. The fourth, by Mauro Guilherme Pinheiro Koury, discusses the notion of belonging, experienced in the processes of daily interaction, and it seeks to understand how the processes of construction of similarity and dissimilarity are formed and informed daily as an emotive culture, supported by the daily experiences of exchange and the formation of common bonds between peer. The fifth, by Tito Vagni, investigates the fusion between the expressive forms of the cultural industry and gastronomy, and proposes an analysis of the complex "effects" of electronic and digital media on food and gastronomic experience in cities. The sixth, by Charlie Mansfield, Derek Shepherd and Philipp Wassler, proposes a preparatory method for researchers and literary travel writers who are planning inquiry into a new urban space, with the French port city of Cherbourg, presented as a case study to illustrate this process. Using theory from Onfray, Bartlett and Patron, and travel writing from Ernaux, Barthes, Mann and Sebald the work develops the research instrument of the hexis for collecting and arranging knowledge discovered during archive searches and literary reading.

Part II: Cities Today: Situated Analyzes and Sensibilities

The seventh, by Lucía Carmina Jasso López, aims to analyse the (In)sensibility to the vigilance of others in Mexico City, initially focusing on the social effects of vigilance technologies in current cities, as well as in the implications of monitoring others. The eighth, by Edwin Catacora Vidangos, presents a theoretical-ethnographic study of the independent work carried out by Aymara traders in the main cities of Peruvian-Bolivian high Andean plateau (Juliaca, Puno, El Alto y La Paz), contextualized by profound local and global socioeconomic changes. The ninth, by Xiangnan Chai, discuss the sociodemographic and cultural contexts that influence the promotion of marriage and fertility in China After discussing the social phenomena that support and promote marriage, the author analyses how these phenomena reflect the politics of sensitivities in relation to traditional Chinese family values. The tenth, by Ana Lucía Cervio, engages in a dialogue with the contributions of Frantz Fanon and critically discusses the notion of racialization in relation to spatial configurations and urban sensibilities. After reflecting upon the links between the urban space and the practices of racialization, the chapter defines the dynamics of "racializing segregation" taking the figure of the *negro villero* in Argentina as the unit of analysis. The eleventh, by Jeanie Maritza Herrera Nájera, aims to understand the "inhabit" experiences of the residents of gated communities built in commuter towns in Guatemala City's Metropolitan Area. In this sense, this chapter analyses the intentions and motivations for the acquisition of properties in gated communities based on the politics of sensibilities and mechanisms of social support, identifying (dis)trust and fear as primary emotions. The twelfth, by Felipe Hernández y Ángela Franco, explores the effects of sustained violence on Afro-descendant and indigenous populations in Cali, Colombia. Based on empirical evidence, the chapter analyses the violence these groups suffer at the hands of right-wing paramilitaries and left-wing guerrilla groups who forced them out of their rural lands and into the city. Such suffering is enhanced by poor housing conditions, lack of governmental support, unemployment, aggression by drug trafficking gangs, and everyday exclusions by an inherently racist society. Finally, the thirteenth, by Adrián Scribano, Margarita Camarena Luhrs and Ana Lucía Cervio, is a three-part device that seeks to allow the reader to capture some fragments of the sensibilities of cities in the COVID-19 pandemic. The chapter has three sections that function as three "chapters". The authors have decided to claim authorship of each section separately, for having had the experience in different cities, for being impacted by dissimilar practices of being in the city, and for valuing how the collective does not eliminate the personal, hence the selection of the title of the chapter as a whole.

Coda

In short, this book represents an outstanding contribution to the study of bodies, emotions and politics of sensibilities in the context of cities and global spaces, focusing mainly on cities in the north, centre and south from America and in China. Undoubtedly, the impact of globalization on them is evident, but, moreover, they themselves help to build a globalization characterized by multiple fractures, separations, disaggregations and marginalizations. Only, on this occasion, the protagonism of the research focuses on peripheral globalization, and on the peripheries of that periphery, on the effects received and caused, which are as interesting and necessary to analyse as those of the power centres.

On the other hand, it should be borne in mind that they show the way in which globalization is precisely diluting that centre, or how polycentres, receptors and producers emerge. In them, on the thin line of global waves, the citizens of the world, their bodies and their emotions, try to live or survive their urban experiences, precisely following the energies of life, irrepressible, absolute, infinite and overflowing—as G. Simmel might put it. However, life, like the water that molds itself to its glass or bottle, it takes place in a precise environment, different from others, and, therefore, is experienced according to that particular context. Thus, in an increasingly expansive urbanization, emotions are also "stretched", expanded and, in doing so, are extreme and dramatized.

Therefore, it is possible that, with globalization, emotions, far from achieving harmony between the individual and society, between reason and feelings, today express more extreme individual suffering and intensify the incompatibility of the encounter with the different. It is not surprising that conflicts around coexistence increase and, at the same time, that lack of control or the possibility of managing politically and democratically the sensibilities increases. And, on the other hand, emotions—as the social and cultural constructions that they are—become as plural as their bearers and the situations in which they are involved; hence, they must be analysed with their nuances and differences and conjugated in the plural—fears, ways of loving, humiliation, shame, disgust and happiness.

All this, without a doubt, makes the emotional analysis of global societies more complex, while enriching and vitalizing it. And, perhaps, it makes more necessary than ever a comparative and transdisciplinary methodology—like the one presented in this book—that will obtain more universal results and that stimulates the sensibilities of researchers.

Juan Antonio Roche Cárcel
Alicante University
Alicante, Spain

Juan Antonio Roche Cárcel is Professor of Sociology at the University of Alicante (Spain). His publications include *Between the Mount of Apollo and the vine of Dionysus. Nature, Gods and Society in the theater architecture of Ancient Greece* (2016); *The Vanishing Society* (2012); *Transitions. The fragility of Democracy* (2016); *Spaces and Uncertain Times of Culture* (2007) and *Sociology as One of the Fine Arts. The influence of Arts and Literature on Sociological Thinking* (2013). He is also the author of numerous articles in specialized magazines in Spain, Europe, Latin and North America. He is professor invited in CUNY (City University of New York) and in universities of Argentina, Brazil, Colombia, Mexico, Turkey, France. He is currently Co-director of the Globalizaciones collection of the Anthropos, Barcelona.

ACKNOWLEDGEMENTS

A time is extinguished but not the song. A red wind hints at what can be transformed into a better world, to fire the black wind covering our lives with sad and desolate experiences. In these days that make clear the importance of feeling and not just knowing that we are alive, this book is dedicated to those who survived COVID-19 and those who have not. Many of her/his concerns are collected throughout the book, talking, feeling, looking for better cities, experiences and other horizons of coexistence.

If we begin by dedicating the book to the millions of people on the planet, especially those who face risks and threats caused by the pandemic, it is because at each step we also share the imperative to feel, think and do with the intention of dreaming a world better, that is, more egalitarian, fair, actively creative, sensible and happy.

This book is also completely dedicated to our families for their love and patience as always. To the authors who contributed passionately to this project, as well as the staff of Palgrave Macmillan, especially Anca Pusca, for their generous support. In this way, we appreciate the work and time of the reviewers who made a substantial contribution with their observations. We must underline the editing work carried out by Majid Yar, with his usual kindness and excellence.

Surely, we have not exhausted in this book all the connections between cities, capitalism and politics of the sensibilities, but we are sure that the critical discussion of these topics should remain a central axis of the Social Sciences in the times to come.

CONTENTS

Notes on Contributors

Margarita Camarena Luhrs is a political scientist and researcher at the National Autonomous University of Mexico (UNAM). She received his Ph.D. in Political Sciences and a Master's Degree in Economy, from the UNAM. She is titular researcher at the Institute of Social Research (UNAM), and professor at Urban Postgraduate Studies, Faculty of Architecture Social Sciences (UNAM). She is member of the prestigious Mexican Association of Sciences (AMC), and also a regular member of the Mexican Society of Geography and Statistics (SMGyE). In addition, she is member of the Editorial Comite (Books coordination) of de Social Research Institute (IISUNAM). Her line of research focuses on the study of common places in cities and between regions. Experiences of places, bodies and social sensibilities that organize practical and symbolic circulations of cities, regions and countries. Some recent collective publications produced within the framework of her research are: (2017) *Vida y vivencia en las Ciudades de hoy*, México: IISUNAM; (2018) *Aprender de las Ciudades*; (2019) *Experiencias colectivas en la Ciudad contemporánea*, México: IISUNAM.

Edwin Catacora Vidangos Doctor in Sociology, from Universidade Federal do Rio Grande do Sul (Brazil); Master of Sociology, from Universidade Estadual de Campinas (Brazil); and Master of Political Science, from Universidad Internacional de Andalucía (Spain). Associate Professor in the Department of Sociology at Universidad Nacional del Altiplano

(Peru). Research Field: Sociological Theory, Labor Sociology, Socioeconomic Development, Development Policies and Administration, Labor Relationships, and Social Policies. Last publications: Ethos del Mundo Andino: Organización y Manifestaciones Locales del Trabajo en los Territorios de Puno Perú y El Alto Bolivia (2019, *Norus*); Gobernabilidad en Crisis? (2018, *Revista Cuestiones de Sociología: Investigación en Ciencia y Desarrollo*); Ética andina: migraciones, trabajo y reconfiguración de los habitus en el Perú contemporáneo (2013, *SURES—Revista Digital do Instituto Latino-Americano de Arte, Cultura e História. Universidade Federal da Integração Latino-Americana*).

Ana Lucía Cervio is a sociologist and researcher at National Scientific and Technical Research Council of Argentina (CONICET). She received his Ph.D. in Social Sciences from the University of Buenos Aires (UBA). She is professor at Faculty of Social Sciences (UBA), member and researcher at Research and Sociological Studies Centre (CIES), member of the International Network of Sociology of Sensibilities (RedISS), and member of the Study Group on Sociology of Emotions and Bodies (GESEC) at Instituto de Investigaciones Gino Germani (Faculty of Social Sciences, UBA). In addition, she is the General Editor of *Revista Latinoamericana de Metodología de la Investigación Social* (Relmis) (www.relmis.com.ar). Her line of research focuses on the study of the connections between dwelling experiences, conflictivities and urban sensibilities, from an analytical perspective that articulates the social studies of the city with a sociology of bodies/emotions. Some publications produced within the framework of her research are: Cervio and Bustos García, *Confianza y Políticas de las Sensibilidades* (Estudios Sociológicos Editora, 2019); Afrodescendants, racialization and politics of sensibilities in Argentina (*Universitas*, Revista *de Ciencias Sociales y Humanas de la Universidad Politécnica Salesiana del Ecuador*, 2020); Scribano and Cervio "Distrust and Proximity. The Paradoxes of Violence in Argentina". In: Scribano, A. *Politics and Emotions,* pp. 193–219 (Studium Press, 2018).

Xiangnan Chai received his Ph.D. degree in sociology from the University of Western Ontario. Since January 2020, he has been working as a research assistant professor at Sociology, Nanjing University. His research interests include ageing and the life course, health and health inequality, marriage and family and, gender and sexuality, using both quantitative and qualitative methods. Among his latest publications, highlighted: Verdery,

Margolis, Zhou, Chai & Rittirong (2019). Kinlessness around the world. The Journals of Gerontology: Series B, 74(8), 1394–1405; Chai (2019). Living Alone: Five Decades of Change, and Its Implications for Health. Electronic Thesis and Dissertation Repository. 6462. Link: https://ir.lib. uwo.ca/etd/6462; Chai & Margolis (2020). Does Living Alone Mean Spending Time Differently? Time Use and Living Arrangements Among Older Canadians. Canadian Studies in Population, 1–16. DOI: https://doi.org/10.1007/s42650-020-00017-9.

Ángela Franco is an Architect, specialist in Urban Planning, MSc in Sociology and Ph.D. in Architecture. In 2011, she received the Hubert H. Humphrey Fulbright Fellowship Award to be part of the Special Program of Urban and Regional Studies at MIT. Currently she is an Associate Professor at the Department of Architecture of the Universidad del Valle in Cali (Colombia) where she also was Vice-Chancellor for Research. She leads the research group "Observatory of Contemporary Architecture and Urbanism" and her research and consultancy projects are mainly focused on urban marginality, informal settlements and planning and housing policies. One of her projects centred in socio-spatial impacts of urban renewal in Bogotá was awarded as the best academic research by the National Council of Architecture in Colombia.

Felipe Hernández is an Architect and Director of the Centre for Latin America Studies at the University of Cambridge (CLAS). He teaches architectural and Urban Design, while giving courses and seminars in the Theory and History of architecture and urbanism. Felipe has worked, and published, extensively on Latin America and other areas in the Developing World, including Africa and South East Asia. He is the author of B*habha for Architects* (Routledge 2010) and *Beyond Modernist Masters: Contemporary Architecture in Latin America* (Birkhauser 2009), as well as co-editor of *Marginal Urbanisms: Informal and Formal Development in Cities of Latin America* (CSP 2017), *Rethinking the Informal City: Critical Perspectives from Latin America* (Berghahn 2009) as well as *Transculturation: Cities, Spaces and Architectures in Latin America* (Rodopi 2005).

Jeanie Maritza Herrera Nájera Bachelor's degree in Sociology from San Carlos University of Guatemala (USAC). Studies in Master's degree in Research in Social Science at the University of Buenos Aires (UBA), and additional training in Public Policy, Gender, Human Rights and Social

Studies of Bodies and Emotions. She has publications on collective action, gender, social research methodology and social development. She is university professor of sociology at USAC, co-coordinator of the Working Group on Sensibilities, Subjectivities and Poverty of the Social Sciences Council of Latin America (CLACSO), member and researcher of the Research and Sociological Studies Centre (CIES-Argentina) and member of the International Network of Sociology of Sensibilities (RedISS). Her line of research is in the field of conflict, collective action and public policy from the sociology of bodies and emotions.

Lucía Carmina Jasso López Research Associate at the Institute of Social Research, National Autonomous University of Mexico (UNAM). Ph.D. in Public Policy from the Centre for Research and Teaching in Economics (CIDE) and Master in Political and Social Studies from UNAM. Her main topics and lines of research are: public security and public policies for crime reduction and prevention. Over the last 10 years, she has collaborated as postgraduate professor at UNAM, advisor to local and federal government, consultant to the private sector and researcher at non-governmental organizations on public security policies and crime prevention. Among her latest publications, highlighted: Crime prevention and technology: the installation of video surveillance cameras and alarms as a measure of protecting households in Mexico (2019); Towards the transterritorialization of public video surveillance policy in Mexico (2018); The demand for video surveillance in Mexico City. Analysis of citizen decisions in the Participatory Budget (2018); Disorder and incivility in public space: Approaches to public policy for its approach (2016).

Mauro Koury is Professor of the Graduate Program in Anthropology (PPGA) at the Federal University of Paraíba (UFPB), where currently serves as a Volunteer Professor. Member of the Brazilian Association of Anthropology, and *ad hoc* consultant to CNPq National Council for Scientific and Technological Development, CAPES Coordination for the Improvement of Higher Education Personnel, and the FAPESP Research Support Foundation of the state of São Paulo, among others. Founding member of the Josué de Castro Study and Research Centre. He has experience in the field of Anthropology, with an emphasis on Anthropology of Emotions, acting mainly on the following themes: photography and society, anthropology of emotions and urban anthropology, fear and society, sociology of emotions and urban sociology. He has several books published on the topics indicated, as well as numerous articles and book chapters. Editor of RBSE Brazilian Journal of Sociology of Emotion; and Editor of Sociabilidades Urbanas Revista de Antropologia e Sociologia, both from GREM. He is also editor of the Cadernos do GREM book series (Recife: Ed. Bagaço / João Pessoa: Editions of GREM).

Charlie Mansfield is Co-Director Heritage Research Centre, University of Plymouth, UK. He is part of the directorate leading the research centre for heritage at the University of Plymouth, he supervises Ph.D. researchers and leads Doctoral Study Days in innovative field methodologies for travel writers. In 2020 he was appointed to the Scientific Council of Research for Literature & Tourism at Lisbon University School of Management and the University of the Algarve. He was a stipendiary researcher at the CNRS Laboratory: LAMOP at the University of Paris, Panthéon-Sorbonne in Digital Heritage Management. His research focusses on city branding and cultural heritage tourism. He has published on literary tourism and has been awarded EU ERASMUS grants to develop Plymouth's research and teaching with its French partner universities in Nice, Nantes and Paris. In addition to being Programme Leader for the Masters for Travel Writers, he teaches tourism management on postgraduate and undergraduate degrees, plus French language and culture. Some of his main publications are: (2019) 'Les savoirs narratifs à partir de l'espace urbain Le cas de Nantes' in M. Lani-Bayle (Ed.) *Mettre l'expérience en mots. Les savoirs narratifs* (pp. 87–96). Lyon: Chronique Sociale; (2018) 'Les pratiques d'écriture pour la construction de l'espace imaginaire' In *Passage: The International Journal of Writing and Mobility*, 1(1) Algérie, Université de Boumerdès; (2018) 'Cultural Capital in Place-Making' *Journal of Hospitality & Tourism*, June, pp.1–17; (2017) 'Travel Writing in Place Branding—A Case Study on Nantes' Journal of Tourism, Heritage & Services Marketing 3(2)1–7.

Antonio Rafele is Professor of Communication at the University of Naples Federico II and Research Fellow at the CEAQ, University of Paris Descartes La Sorbonne. He received his Ph.D. in Sociology from the University of Paris La Sorbonne with a thesis on Walter Benjamin, and, later, he participated in two international research projects, in 2009 and in 2015, at the M.I.T. Mobile Experience Laboratory. He worked at the University of Turin (from 2009 to 2011), IULM University of Milan (from 2011 to 2013), University of São Paulo (2013–2015), University of Geneva (2017) and University of Lille (2018–2019). His research focuses on media and culture theory problems that have given rise to several publications, including two monographs: Representations of Fashion (San Diego University Press, 2013) and Replay. Calcio, vetrine e choc (Luca Sossella, 2018).

Adrián Scribano is Director of Research and Sociological Studies Centre (CIES- www.estudiosociologicos.org) and Principal Researcher at the National Scientific and Technical Research Council, Argentina. He is also the Director of the *Latin American Journal of Studies on Bodies, Emotions and Society (RELACES-* www.relaces.com.ar) and the Study Group on Sociology of Emotions and Bodies, in the Gino Germani Research Institute, Faculty of Social Sciences, University of Buenos Aires. He also serves as Coordinator of the 26 Working Group on Bodies and Emotions of the Latin American Association of Sociology (ALAS) and as Vice-President of the Thematic Group 08 Society and Emotions of the International Sociological Association (ISA).

Derek Shepherd Business School Accreditation Lead, University of Plymouth, UK. He worked as a professional economist for the National Farmers' Union and the Confederation of British Industry in London before joining the academic world in 1987. He teaches crisis and disaster management in the tourism, hospitality and events industries, business strategy for tourism and hospitality and tourism venture creation. He is also a visiting lecturer at the Czech University of Life Sciences in Prague and an experienced Ph.D. supervisor. His research interests lie in CAP reform and land management in the European Union. Some of his main publications are: Busby, G. and Shepherd, D. (2008) Disintermediation vs reintermediation—undergraduate understanding of e-commerce in tourism. *International Conference on Economic and Management Perspectives*, Famagusta, Northern Cyprus; Brunt and Shepherd (2004) The influence of crime on tourist decision-making: some empirical evidence. *Tourism*, 52(4), 317–327; Shepherd and Bouckova (2004) Czech agriculture in the post-communist period: the story so far, *Journal of the Royal Agricultural Society of England*, 165.

Tito Vagni is Research Fellow at the Centre d'Études sur l'Actuel et le Quotidien (CEAQ), Paris Descartes University. He was lecturer at IULM University, University of Macerata and Istituto Marangoni. He was visiting fellow at the EHESS in Paris and at the ATOPOS international research centre of the Universidade de SãoPaulo (ECA-USP). His research interests concern media theory, cultural studies and the mediatization of food. The last book is *Abitare la TV. Teorie, immaginari, reality show* (2017).

Philipp Wassler Senior Lecturer in Tourism and Hospitality, University of Bournemouth, UK. He holds a Ph.D. awarded at the School of Hotel and Tourism Management, The Hong Kong Polytechnic University. Research interests include philosophical issues in tourism, with a particular focus on phenomenology and host–guest relations. In August 2018 he was awarded Newton funding to participate in the research leadership network: Innovation in Inclusion in Heritage Tourism with the University of Birmingham in Phuket, Thailand. Some of his main publications are: Wassler and Kuteynikova (2020). Living travel vulnerability: A phenomenological study. *Tourism Management*, 76, Wassler, Nguyen, Mai and Schuckert (2019). Social representations and resident attitudes: A multiple-mixed-method approach. *Annals of Tourism Research*, 78; Wassler and Kirillova, (2019). Hell is other people? An existential-phenomenological analysis of the local gaze in tourism. *Tourism Management*, 71, 116–126; Wassler and Schuckert (2017). The lived travel experience to North Korea. *Tourism Management*, 63, 123–134.

LIST OF TABLES

PART I

Theoretical Approaches to Urban Sensibilities and Capitalism

CHAPTER 1

City and Emotions

Adrián Scribano

INTRODUCTION

In the analyses of the city, from the classics to the present day, emotions have played a fundamental role, an example of this is the structuring of the narration offered by Fustel de Coulanges:

> As to honest and scrupulous men, the perpetual dissensions which they saw disgusted them with the municipal system. They could not love a form of society, where it was necessary to fight every day, where the rich and the poor were always at war, and where they saw popular violence and aristocratic vengeance alternate without end. They wished to escape from a regime which, after having produced real grandeur, no longer produced anything but suffering and hatred. They began to feel the necessity of abandoning the municipal system, and of arriving at some other form of government than the city. Many men dreamed at last of establishing above the cities a sort of sovereign power, which should look to the maintenance of order, and compel those turbulent little societies to live in peace. (Fustel de Coulanges 2001, 318, our emphasis)

A. Scribano (✉)
National Scientific and Technical Research Council, University of Buenos Aires, Buenos Aires, Argentina

© The Author(s), under exclusive license to Springer Nature Switzerland AG 2021
A. Scribano et al. (eds.), *Cities, Capitalism and the Politics of Sensibilities*,
https://doi.org/10.1007/978-3-030-58035-3_1

In terms of the modifications of the municipal regime, disgust, rejection, revenge, desire, pomp, dreams and a peaceful life intersect to describe a modification in the politics of sensibilities that implies the transformations in the management of the city.

In another time and on the other side of the Atlantic, one of the founding fathers of North American sociology, Robert Park, analysing the relationship between feelings and interests as structuring axes of social relations of coexistence in cities, wrote:

> The existence of a sentimental attitude indicates that there are motives for action of which the individual who is moved by them is not wholly conscious; motives over which he has only a partial control. Every sentiment has a history, either in the experience of the individual, or in the experience of the race, but the person who acts on that sentiment may not be aware of the history. (Park 1915, 558)

It is easy to understand why Park, crossed by the debate on intentionality and rationality of action, is presented with the structuring force of feelings as one of his suggestions for investigating human behaviour in cities.

Returning to Europe and getting back to one of the great classics on cities and metropolises, we find Simmel who summarizes in a forceful way:

> The psychological foundation, upon which the metropolitan individuality is erected, is the intensification of emotional life due to the swift and continuous shift of external and internal stimuli. (Simmel 2002, 11)

Later, in another recent classic work, Karp, Stone and Yoles argue for the importance of emotions in analysing the structure of cities:

> Unless we consider the use, the meaning, the symbolic significance, and frequently the sentiments and emotions attached to various features of the city's topology, we shall incorrectly understand patterns of interaction in the city, and by definition, therefore, incompletely understand the city's social organization. (Karp et al. 1977, 65)

In his classic work on the production of space, Lefebvre highlights the place of emotions in people's perceptions:

> The disentanglement of these impressions from knowledge allows another code or reading –the symbolic one– to come into play. Meanwhile, 'Ego'

is bound to feel some emotion: he may have been here before, long ago, or always dreamt of coming; he may have read a book or seen a film - Death in Venice perhaps. Such feelings are the basis of the subjective and personal code which now emerges, giving the decoding activity the musical qualities of a fugue: the theme (i.e. this place - the Square, the Palace, and so on) mobilizes several voices in a counterpoint in which these are never either distinct or confused. (Lefebvre 1991, 161)

Emotions are codes that connect us with the processes, spaces, times, objects and living beings that cities imply; cities are the result of an "emotional stratigraphy" that implies history and the social made body.

From a different perspective, but it can be said along the same lines, Manuel Castells wrote in his well-known work "The Urban Question":

In each case, demand is created by ideological pressure, in accordance with the form of housing made socially and economically necessary. Thus, the ideology of the pavilion exalts good citizenship, security, the feeling of being at home, privacy and the feeling that one is away from it all; the ideology of the city exalts the pride in consumption of the elite, which has become the master of the spatial centre; the philosophy of social housing puts the accent on the practical side, with an invitation to look back to the badly housed and forward to a rural utopia, lived in a mythical way and sustained as a bait for social mobility. (Castells 1977, 168)

The ideological strategy of accepting socially necessary housing is based on practices of feeling—the city is a network of ways of feeling that is translated into politics of sensibilities.

In the context of this ancient and close connection between city and emotions, between cities and sensibilities, this chapter sets out to present, in a synthetic way, three moments that can be observed in the presence of sensibilities in the cities of this century: politics of senses,[1] the shopping centre as a cathedral of consumption, and the features of the city 4.0.

In various places, we have written about the coloniality of contemporary cities, about the mental walls, racializing segregation, the enslavement of security politics, the geopolitics of hunger, accounting for the multiple facets of poverty and unequal distribution of nutrients

---

[1] It is preferred to keep the expression 'politics of sense' here and leave political sense aside to emphasize that they are a set of actions aimed at an end and not only the politicization of the senses.

(Scribano 2017, 2018). Here we are interested in configuring an approach to the moral imperatives of feeling nested in the politics of the sensibilities of a city understood as the centre of normalized societies in immediate enjoyment through consumption.

Cities are woven with emotions and sensibilities because they connect/disconnect sensations and this process are created from and with the senses. Touching, smelling, tasting, listening and seeing are the traces that characterize what is universal and particular in cities. Within the framework of the centrality of consumption as a vehicle for enjoyment, there is a pedagogy of consuming through the senses that can be grasped by analysing the "place" of shopping centres today. Senses and consumption converge in a direct way towards the current transformations of society 4.0, which ultimately implies the creation of a "sensibility of platform". A "sensibilities of platform" emerges in this 4.0 society that is immediate in three senses: (a) in the vehicle the action resides (it is the feeling of always being "on line"), (b) it is a society that "is during use", "between", "in passing" and (c) is pure presentification (here/now). Much of digital work has the same characteristics and, in this direction, the political economy of morality consecrates this way of "feeling the world".

In this context, the following argumentative strategy has been selected as the narrative structure: first, the connection between the politics of the senses and the structuring of the city is presented schematically; second, a "re-description" of shopping is offered as the founding space of the political economy of the morality of the city and thirdly, the central features of the city 4.0 and the elaboration of a sensibility of platform are outlined. The chapter ends with a reflection on the city as a place for utopia.

POLITICS OF THE SENSES AND THE CITY

The contemporary city has mental walls that are embodied and that spatialize racialization. The bricks, these walls, are composed of the set of inequalities that are separated from each other in new geometries of the bodies. These bricks have multiple inequality as raw material, which implies gender, age, ethnicity and class. These bricks are made from the mud of distance, labelling and embodied history. These cemented bricks come together through prejudice, rejection and devaluation.

The work exists at distance from a politics of touch where the other cannot be touched and must be avoided for being the object of a brand that infects and threatens. Distance is defined by appearance and face the other becomes an object interpreted by what he has on, by what appears to be, by what is socially said to be. The other is condemned by the face, is valued because it seems dangerous. In the city you learn to value by looking at the face, you learn by just looking that the other can be a threat. The city teaches labelling, naming, making the prejudiced gaze performative.

The city is reached from the limit, it is assumed from its edges and inhabited in relation to its margins, as expressions of sensibilities that read its disposition of "place" as a result of eyes, noses, mouths, hands and ears socially elaborated as compasses and as storage containers for embodied social history.

The "bodies-in-contact" assemble the schematics of the plots of the senses turned into emphatic mediators of the contacts, the touches and the pacts. The city is (and will be more and more) the spatialization of that special combination of past, present, future and presentification.

Being with another through sound, smell, image, taste and bodily folds can unfold as a condition of possibility of social relationships.

If the marks, lines and thickness are followed; if one pays attention to the landscapes, settings and contexts whose limits, borders and margins they draw and colour, a series of connections can be grasped between different dispositions of the city in its intersections with the politics of bodies and sensibilities. Some of them are as follows: (a) the policies of the entry, accumulation and circulation of food structure and order the provisions of the city's forms; (b) the policies of origin, circulation and uses of water are pre-conditions for the survival of the inhabitants in terms of the axes of nutrients, classes and bodily geometries in the form of differentiated habitabilities; the policies of the social forms of management of sunlight distribute, attribute and impute the capacities of order, displacement and visibility of the agents made bodies, (c) the structures of selection, management and accumulation of waste imply policies of administration of odours and redefinition of the "possible predation climate"; (d) the multiple "routes" of transfer, visualization and contact affect and are "pre-designed" according to class, age, ethnicity and gender and (e) the distribution structures of energy sources for eating, sheltering, moving and communicating are the knots of a network hatched around its accesses and possession.

The tensions between the multiple experiences of eating, of the hours and diagrams of natural and artificial light that are accessed, of the differential and unequal distributions of water, of the modes of movement and the points of contact between which they inhabit the city, are based on and are a fundamental part of the politics of bodies and emotions in force. The aforementioned tensions are what "make" a city and place it in that spiral process between its particularity and the universality of "every city".

It is the "social bodies" that guide, locate and accompany the movement through and in the city; it is the sensory regulation devices that "use" as a reservoir of possible orientations to these social organs. The lives of citizens are experienced as existential ways of presenting, in and by the body, conflicts and affective encounters in the context of the diversity of sensibilities.

The forms of predation, especially those linked to the expropriation of bodily and social energies, take shape in urban plots and locate/de-locate the subjects involved in them. From this perspective, the city provides time-space for the surplus expropriations that performatively make expropriator and expropriated look, smell, touch and listen through the politics of sensations.

In this context, some of the vectors with the most "weight" in the consequences of mimetic consumption on the structures of sensibilities appear, namely: the politics of the gaze, the politics of the mimetic image and the politics of instantaneous enjoyment. Precisely these three politics are shaped around the obliteration, avoidance and evasion of what is conflicting in the colonizing ways of life. The Mobesian group from which they depart, branch and twist is the unnoticed, naturalizing and inadvertent situation of conflict between the expellers and the expelled, segregators and segregated, colonizers and colonized. The multiple intermediate "locations", interposed locations and blurred positions that are built in the folding and re-folding processes of the three aforementioned politics are those that guarantee, testify and endorse the opposing tensions that generate them.

The politics of gaze(s) are designed in the torsion produced by *being willing and disposed* for classificatory observation, seduction of what is seen (and re-seen) and the face labels. The one and the other, the fears and the aggressions are made (in principle) from the "distance" of the look(s) that narrate(s), produce(s) and/or eliminate (s) the other from the vision, perception and imputation of threatening/friendly traits, proper/improper, close/foreign, impacting on (the) possible (im) socia-bilities. In other words, it is about the provisions of a classification and taxonomy of *what is*, *what can be expected* and *how far* the observer can approach without care, without defences, without barriers. Along with this, there is a practice of producing the individual "to-be-seen", as the axis of a permanent state of *seducing for acceptance, recognition or at least "non-rejection"* which is based on *appearing as must* to circumvent the "scanner" of multiple classifications. This is where the face emerges with force as a "seat" of the gaze that consecrates difference, inequality, differentiation and distance. Labelled faces, typical faces, "ethical" faces identified, selected, ordered, consumed and "circulated" as axes of the current political economy of morality. It is in this context that a look in our cities can cost one's life, allow access to enjoyment or (im) enable displacement.

From the base of the second twist described in the politics of looks (the individual "to-be-seen") the possible bands of the politics (es) of the mimetic image (s) are opened (s). In its plots of limits, edges and margins, in the city scenarios, landscapes and contexts of a life are consti-tuted to be shown/hidden. The dialectic between body, skin, image and movement is resolved and promoted as "practices-for-others". In the same tension, the experience of the city appears as multiple windows, stained glass windows and walkways directly related to consumption. The mimetic image is a consequence of the differences and inequalities in the consumption of bodies and emotions as objects, as a source of labile, contingent and context-attached "identities". Every city worth its salt has possible detection, classification, selection and imitation routes. These are the processes that will make viable and liveable a habitability valued and valued according to the material conditions of selection of each one of them.

In the meanders of the connections between the politics of the gaze and the mimetic images, that is, in what is common to them with consumption, the politics of instant enjoyment are created and designed. The spatialization and production of the means of enjoyment is carried out today in and through the city. Instant enjoyment underscores the range of temporality acquired by a set of practices "dependent" on spaces, and especially on which limits, edges and margins are performed.

Instant enjoyment is characterized by being a parenthesis "here-now", thanks to its claim to be continuity in time and by the subjective removal that it allows and demands. Enjoyment is made as a circumstantial, contingent, fleeting, but "absolute" and radical "here-now". Enjoyment is an act with the pretence of totality that suspends the flow of life every day, which is why it is "done", produced, performed and is the result of a teleological action. It is enjoyed to continue enjoying. In reality, everything in life is taken and consumed with (and according to) relation to enjoyment. This form of enjoyment dissociates the subject from its context: the one who consumes/enjoys is not "is-that-subject", it is only an enjoyer. Subjective unpinning is done through the primacy of the object of enjoyment that varies according to quantity/quality, volume/density and forms of access/denial to it.

These entanglements between the politics of the gaze, the politics of the mimetic image and the politics of instantaneous enjoyment make visible the distances and proximities between the marks on the edges of the autonomy/heteronomy game, the lines of the limits of the dialectic between expulsion/dismissal and the thickness of the margins.

What is, is put and is put in (and through) the limits, edges and margins are practices of feeling that stabilize, fluidize, coagulate and mobilize the "logic of occupation" of the city. Whether these are objects, subjects or relationships, they are all subject to the operation of sensibilities that are produced in the sensation regulation devices and social support mechanisms that nest in these forms of being that the city has. For this reason (and in this), the emergence of a colonizing city is verified, which, by *occupying, expropriating*, enabling the *inhabiting of the time-space of another* and *having the power to decide on the lives of others* expands its effects and consequences "beyond". The world in general, but particularly in the Global South, is viewed and viewed from the performative consequences of the limits, edges and margins that make the politics of emotions cut to the size of the politics of the gaze, of the mimetic image and instant enjoyment. The differences and inequalities in the capacities to design, apply and live the politics of the sensibilities lie in the measurements, densities and volumes that the material conditions of existence give to the brands, lines and thickness that the city creates.

One of the structuring axes of consumption as the backbone of contemporary societies normalized in enjoyment are the spaces and times to consume. Shopping centres and shopping malls occupy a central place in the elaboration of the political economy of morality at present, and the intention of the next section is to show the central features of said policy.

SHOPPING AS A CATHEDRAL

For Western cities in general, and very especially for those emerging in medieval Europe, cathedrals were central. They were not only very important religious references, episcopal seez, formations of the clergy, ceremonial centres, places of pilgrimage, etc.; but also places of high commercial and political importance.

This section tries to make evident, through a metaphor, how the features of the shopping centres of the twenty-first century are similar to those of such cathedrals in reference to the political economy of morality that is in force (Panofsky 2007).

Display Case and Stained Glass

In shopping, in the shopping centre, in its relationship or in synonymy with the cathedral, you can find the connection between the showcase and the stained glass.

In the medieval cathedral, the stained glass served as a vehicle for catechesis. In the contemporary shopping centre, the showcase served as a vehicle for shopping knowledge.

Thus, the stained glass recounted the history of salvation, the life of Jesus Christ, the great evangelical events and the life of the saints. Today the windows tell us about the bodies, about the sensations, about the stories, about the accepted and acceptable ways of being a human being; today, the showcase is prepared, designed and elaborated as an opportunity where the fantasy of being another is narrated by obtaining and mimesis with the object. Today the shop windows are the point of reference for the walk through the shopping centre, just like the stained glass were used by this logic of the evolution of the cathedral of its central nave, of the transept, of how the form connected with what was narrated. That history of salvation, the history of passion, the way of the cross, serves as a form of movement between the history of religion and God-made man; in this sense, shopping malls have become cathedrals. Shopping malls are precisely the places where you have to go to buy and sell, but more specifically to learn how to buy and sell, and more especially to learn how you should be in the world. It is clear that today this is combined with the mobile phone, with the applications with the world that is surrounded and structured from delivery, from home delivery, from the immediacy of the purchase. But this is one more twist of what the shopping centre has transformed into support, as a logic where what is searched for on the internet and is found in the shopping centre, one more twist in learning how to buy. From childhood the family outing is to go to the shopping centre, and going back to the analogy, with the cathedrals the architecture was the one that delivered lessons, it was the one that taught life; in the shopping malls those big buildings and those big urban interventions are in their own forms, in its architectural logic, in its aesthetics, the message to be taught: life is a shopping trip.

Place of Socialization

The shopping centre is also today as the churches and cathedrals were once a space for socialization; the shopping centre is a meeting place, of knowledge, of exchange of glances, of the opportunity to share food, of the opportunity to play games; the shopping centre is a place of entertainment formerly built around churches and cathedrals, this space is constituted as a centre of interrelational activity, as a space where the other came in proximity, as a place where one systematically attended outside hours and the workspace. Today, the shopping centre, that no place, but also that no space, that no time, is the scene of a future that allows us to put a parenthesis around the life of work. But, on the other hand, this socialization also has to do with ages, with gender, with classes, with ethnicity, why these shopping centres approve or disapprove, allow or restrict access for some and not for others, for those that can go to look, for those who can go to buy, so that what they are going to go around, but who do not really participate in the exchange, what they are going to do is to look and to be looked at. In any case, the shopping centre currently performs the functions of the Sunday mass in towns in remote places, where one would go in order to socialize. This is why in the shopping centre there are offers of practices and of objects, according to ages, genders and races, according to possibilities, and that is why the supply is segmented and the demand for sensibilities is built. That's why the shopping centre is the best way to introduce children to a consumer society; that's why the commercial centre comes the space where adolescents gather in conditions of protection, in conditions of enforcement by the police; that is why the mall is the main element that cities have so that parents can let go of children, adolescents and young people. The shopping centre is in some way the socialization space where the rules for consumption, the appropriate ways of consumption are social-ized are learned, distributed; they elaborate that, if you want to be a good consumer, you have to go to the mall when you are a child, when you are a teenager, to learn how to buy and therefore to be able to call yourself a good buyer; it is an obligatory place where you have to go.

THE MARKET AND THE TEMPLE

The effectiveness of the shopping centre is to see together the charac-teristics of the market and the features of the temple. On the one hand, the shopping centre is a space where the various forms of commercial exchange are produced and reproduced: in this way we can buy and sell what is necessary, what we want and also what we wish Large shopping malls are home to supermarkets, fashion stores, jewellery stores, gyms, food courts, movie theatres and many more variations of entertainment and the commodification of life. Those who offer the goods that are included in this dialectical relationship between preferences, needs and money meet in the shopping centre; these great spaces of objectification build and elaborate the reflection of the distance and proximity between what we need and want. Wanting, possessing practices and desiring prac-tices are moulded from the possibility of class position and condition. The big shopping malls are, in short, a city on such a scale that the only thing we cannot do is sleep; we can eat, buy, that is, consume and mediate consumables. For this reason, from the market perspective, the rules of merchandise govern, for that in these temples of consumption govern the rules of supply and demand. But without a doubt, shop-ping malls are the architectural way of instantiating, on the one hand, the morality of enjoyment and, on the other hand, the neocolonial reli-gion. The shopping centre has become a temple of commodification, its corridors are a metaphor for how someone must be to appear to be, how human beings blend with objects and, far from being people, individ-uals are transformed into actors of written scripts to be represented in the temples of consumption and entertainment. The conjunction between the morality of enjoyment, a demand for instantaneousness and indeterminate forms of satisfaction are the new rules that make the shopping centre a temple where the religion of consumption is officiated.

That is why it is possible to maintain that the shopping centre is one of the bases of practical aesthetics and political instantiation of a renewed Moral Political Economy: read that it makes immediate enjoyment through consumption the aesthetic, ethical and political key of the cities of the twenty-first century.

Now, not only is the city made up of a shopping centre, it is also true that the logic of work, the logic of production, and the logic of public infrastructure are central parts of these new ways of linking dependent economies to structures of emotionalization. Among many other aspects to make the panorama more complete we must pay attention to the times and modality of the displacement. Subjects must rest and also produce in a relative and also marginal proximity with the heart of the city as a node of global consumer networks. Therefore, in order to be able to complement what we have just analysed with respect to shopping centres, we must refer to the pedagogies of the transfer, the transfer times and the displacement vehicles.

CITY 4.0 AND SENSIBILITIES

The gaze on the city as a Moebius strip takes us to the present time and to the recent "crossing" between the city and the so-called 4.0 revolution. The cities of the last 15 years across the entire planet have been modified for various and multiple reasons. Here we will only refer to three of the greatest changes: (a) economic modifications, (b) changes in the coordination of action processes and (c) the consolidation of a special politics of sensibilities.

a. Society 4.0 is associated with Industry 4.0, which is understood as a stage of digitization of the manufacturing sector, driven by four modifications: more data managed by industrial companies, powerful and cheap computers, greater analytical capacity and developments in interactions between people and machines, from artificial intelligence to androids and robots to production through 3D printers. The reduction of costs, the improvements in the production lines, and the use of new databases are some of the central results derived from such modifications.

In this context, the

Fourth Industrial Revolution,... can be characterized by the consolidation of at least three factors: (a) the appearance of Big Data as a resource for social diagnosis, (b) the Gig Economy as evidence of the growth of deinstitutionalization and, (c) the Internet of Things (IoT) as a new form of production and "management of sensibilities". (Scribano and Lisdero 2019, 5)

As has been happening in capitalism since its inception, the modifications in the productive system, labour management and the social relations that this implies have a direct impact on the structures of cities.

Much has already been written about Smart Cities. For example, Lom, Pribyl and Svitek argue that:

> The main purpose of the Smart City Initiative is thus ensuring the sustainability of cities, improving quality of life and safety of their citizens, and providing maximum energy efficiency, all of those in the six key areas: economy, environment, mobility, people, living, and governance, with the contribution of the latest technologies. (Lom, Pribyl and Svitek 2016, 2).

Recently, So et al. (2019) have found the following characteristics in the different narratives about the Smart City: ICT technologies, improvement of civil functions, environment and climate change, social interaction and inclusiveness, economic growth, quality of life, civil service and governance.

Another widely used concept has been that of the Creative City, which many have also linked to technological transformations. An example is Roche Cárcel, who maintains:

> Economic globalization and creativity therefore go hand in hand, since the former has facilitated the emergence of creative cities (...) in which economic growth has not been driven by specialization, but rather by innovation and flexibility, along with geographical location, an essential factor in the global economy. This importance of the place, linked to its personality, is consequently what brings wealth. (Roche Cárcel 2019, 185)

As it is easy to see, the city of the twenty-first century is undergoing a redefinition of its role in the new production scheme, in the planetarization of new ways of managing work, and the appearance of "new" economies.

b. Another factor that has transformed social life in cities is the appearance and consolidation of social networks as a vehicle for interaction and coordination of action. From Facebook, through WhatsApp and Instagram, to Tinder and Twitter, knowing, finding, meeting, loving and hating other people is done digitally/virtually. PPPs and platforms enable us to produce, locate, send, pay and consume everything from food to medicine, from drinks to sex, from religions to the management of births, marriages and deaths.

Basically, what was previously only done in squares, bars, restaurants, theatres, schools, stadiums, parks, chapels, cemeteries, etc., today can be done in and through the mobile phone, Tablet, PC or all kinds of digital devices.

The twenty-first city is, in this sense, a digital socialization city where beliefs, social norms, rules of courtesy and laws have changed as well as crime, threat, violence, harassment and so many other forms of aggression, discrimination and injustice.

These new sociabilities also imply modifications in the experiences and sensibilities that we will see in the next section, but for now let us pause to reflect on a few modifications of these sociabilities.

First, the criteria of the public and the private are modified as two dimensions of social practices and the structure of cities precisely based on the distinction and definition of these two aspects of social life. Houses, public buildings, companies, transport terminals, all facilities in the city are designed with free and restricted access areas, with private and public areas all associated with physical barriers. It is precisely these barriers that have been eliminated, at least partially, today through social and digital networks.

Secondly, the criteria of far and near, of near and distant are transformed. One of the features of the Gig Economy, the C2C economy and the platform economy in general is that by typing the location and using "light" cargo transport, products and services can be ordered and shipped irrespective of distance, also counting, in some cases such as food, the preparation times.

Third, the notions of what is fundamentally known and unknown are modified to be, transit and interact in any city—what were previously referred to as maps, published references, indications of the city government, councils of friends, etc. Today all smartphones have a virtual assistant, a GPS, and internet access, whereby it is very easy to find organized by hierarchies and types of activities, opinions, evaluations, photos, videos and direct interaction with government offices, restaurants, international companies, transport terminals, etc. There is no city activity that does not have a virtual/digital correlate.

Fourth, the aesthetic criteria for cities have been modified. Monuments, streets, avenues, walks, museums, theatres, galleries, artistic works in public places, squares, churches and cemeteries were considered emblems of cities, for their beauty, their antiquity, their size, for the materials with which they were built. Today it is the "likes", the times that your photos have been reproduced, the number of people who have seen your web pages, the number of times that your videos are downloaded from YouTube, the photos that appear on Instagram, etc., which serve to define what is considered as an attractive, beautiful, "visitable" place.

The ways of coexistence, production, reproduction and distribution of livelihoods have been modified in cities and this process will surely become increasingly global, complex and comprehensive.

c. In cities 4.0, politics of sensibilities have also been modified, creating a "sensibility of platform". Elsewhere we have addressed the direct relationship between digital work, planetary structuring process and political sensibilities and the emergence of sensibilities of platform (Scribano and Lisdero 2019).

A politics of sensibilities

> (...) are understood as the set of cognitive-affective social practices aimed at the production, management and reproduction of horizons of action, disposition and cognition. These horizons refer: (1) to the organization of daily life..., (2) to the information to order preferences and values..., and (3) to the parameters for time/space management. (De Sena and Scribano 2020, 40)

In this context, the city 4.0 more than the transformations already mentioned involve, among others, two central features that constitute "sensibilities of platform": one around the experience of the house and another around connection to general consumption.

House 4.0 can be understood as a "total institution" where everything can be done: working, eating, entertaining, expressing various forms of eroticism, educating children, creating, writing, do physical activity, literally everything. The internet of things (IoT) connects all our devices through APP and/or administration programmes; home working allows us to be part of a production process that may be happening at another time and in a different region of the planet; the hundreds Platform companies from which we can order and pay for their products with our electronic wallet live connected to customers to know what they want; we can try on a dress without leaving the living room of the house. So, from virtual sex, studying in a very important University, doing yoga and seeing a concert or an opera, all of this is possible indoors. All of which transforms at least three things: what it is to have an experience; what it means to "be-in-a-place"; and what is public/private. These are the basic questions to elaborate on an organization of life, an order of preferences and parameters of time/space management. In other words, a "sensibility of platform" is built as part of a city 4.0-specific sensibility policy. The city is the home, or whatever we call from here on the "place" where we produce/consume.

The other founding feature of a sensibilities of platform is our relationship with consumption as a vehicle for knowing and making life, now mediated by virtual, digital and mobile technology. It is possible to emphasize here "seeing is touching", "consuming is asking" and "now is here".

A day in a city and in a house 4.0 begins on the mobile phone: calendars, time management apps and virtual assistants are made accessible by touching a device; to open your eyes is to touch. It is not just the world in the palm of your hand, it is the knowledge in a click—by touching I see the time, the weather, the news, the activity of loved ones, the obligation structure of the day, week and month, just for starters. Crossings are seen on a virtual map, accidents, incidents and normalities are seen on devices that are used by simply touching. Swiping, pressing, "colouring" become digital touching skills that open the door to the applications and information associated with viewing.

The experience of digital consumption is specified as a process, how to do, and the practice of asking. Companies, churches, states, NGOs, and families develop or purchase an app to improve the connection between desire, need, product and consumption. It is possible to select colours, flavours, smells and textures of foods, objects and experiences that we wish to have. It is possible to compare, evaluate and "visit" stores, factories, stores, shopping centres in and through thousands of apps that give access to the elaboration, production and sale of the objects, processes, or practices that are desired. It is possible to view and explore online catalogues, videos, photos, power points covering everything from shoes, ice cream, houses, cars, to trips, museums and theatrical events. In this context, the search for what will be selected becomes consumption in itself and anticipates the practices of feeling associated with the enjoyment of the satisfier. An alteration in the forms of consumption is occurring where seeking is already having.

Finally, a third feature of the sensibility of platform of the city 4.0 is the conflagration, the time/space shock where the here and now are facets of the variables of the experiences that both producers and consumers must guarantee. It must arrive now: the consumer is informed when the order arrives at its place as part of the consumption process itself. The distance measured in time between the payment of the provider and the purchase arriving at the place of the person who has paid is part of the sensibility of digital consumption: security, speed, quality of what is received and ease of the process are some of the perceptibility features that the provider must guarantee so that the consumer feels good. Just as the State has shifted from assuring well-being to the role of assuring good feeling, the founding pillar is "feel-in-consumption". Immediate enjoyment through consumption is by definition here/now.

The modifications in the experiences of the home and consumption generate a special sensibility of platform that the State and the Market use and manage as a fundamental component of the city 4.0.

Although it is true that the view that is operated here from the politics of the senses, passing through the place of shopping in the political economy of morality until reaching city 4.0 and its sensibility of platform, offers a panorama far from respect for the other and fair living for all, we believe we can re-meet with the utopian gaze from the city.

STARTING AGAIN: THE CITY AS A UTOPIAN SPACE

The great utopias were written in a setting of cities where the common became a springboard for happiness. Just to mention some of the most important ones: in 1516 Thomas More wrote *Utopia*; Tommaso Campanella wrote *The City of the Sun* in 1613; *Theory of the four movements and the general destinations* of Charles Fourier appeared anonymously in Lyon in 1808 and Ettiene Cabet publishes *Travel and Adventures of Lord William Carisdall in Icaria* in 1840.

It is not possible to finish this chapter without mentioning the city in its potentiality as spaces of co-presence, fraternity, sorority and humanity.

Nor is it possible to end this chapter without at least mentioning the place and importance of all living things and all species in the constitution of cities in the twenty-first century.

On the one hand, the city is crossed by the coexistence of species, by the coexistence of the diversity of biological origin of which the cities inhabit; it is not only houses, streets and human beings, but also trees, rivers, fish and all kinds of other animals. It is in this direction that a different look at the common, that a different path for happiness in coexistence must be thought, and must be experienced from respect and consideration to all of us who inhabit the city. From this perspective, the city ceases to be a mere container of objects, including all the animals that inhabit it, but rather a space of proximity and encounter.

On the other hand, the city is a space of co-presence of and for human beings, that is, of an existence that acquires meaning with the other being there. Co-presence is clearly a being with others, it is a shared presence, it is an experience in reciprocity referenced by the encounter. Along these same lines, the city is also an opportunity for brotherhood, for fraternity for the collective constituted from equality. A utopian view of the city requires thinking of it as a structuring locus of connections between equals. But also, the city, today more than ever, is the space for sorority, solidarity between women, for sisterhood among women to grow. Thus the city, its institutions, its facilities, ceases to be an opportunity for abuse, inequality and slavery of women and become a plaza, an open space for the reconstruction of the relationship of multiple genders based on the strength of that collective feminist horizontality. That fraternity and sorority are co-present, they constitute the angular figure of a reconstruction of the human that unfolds in the city that is born, grows and becomes effective; a humanity that is transformed into the practice of the common, of co-experience and happiness.

References

Castells, M. (1977). *The Urban Question a Marxist Approach*. London: Edward Arnold.

De Sena, A., & Scribano, A. (2020). *Social Policies and Emotions. A Look from the Global South*. Cham: Palgrave Macmillan.

Fustel De Coulanges, N. D. (2001). *The Ancient City. A Study on the Religion, Laws, and Institutions of Greece and Rome*. Kitchener, ON: Batoche Books Kitchener.

Karp, D. A., Stone, G. P., & Yoels, W. C. (1977). *Being Urban: A Social Psychological View of City Life*. Lexington: Heath and Company.

Lefebvre, H. (1991). *The Production of Space*. Oxford, UK: Basil Blackwell.

Lom, M., Pribyl, O., & Svitek, M. (2016). Industry 4.0 as a Part of Smart Cities. In *2016 Smart Cities Symposium Prague (SCSP)* (pp. 1–6). Prague. https://doi.org/10.1109/SCSP.2016.7501015.

Panofsky, E. (2007). *Arquitectura gótica y pensamiento escolástico*. Madrid: Siruela.

Park, R. (1915). The City: Suggestions for the Investigation of Human Behavior in the City Environment. *American Journal of Sociology, 20*(5), 577–612.

Roche Cárcel, J. (2019). An Approach to Creative Work in the Global Economy of Risk and Uncertainty. In A. Scribano & P. Lisdero (Eds.), *Digital Labour, Society and Politics of Sensibilities* (pp. 169–190). Basingstoke, UK: Palgrave Macmillan.

Scribano, A. (2017). *Normalization, Enjoyment and Bodies/Emotions: Argentine Sensibilities*. New York: Nova Science Publishers.

Scribano, A. (2018). *Politics and Emotions*. Houston: Studium Press llc.

Scribano, A., & Lisdero, P. (2019). Introduction: Politics of Sensibilities, Society 4.0 and Digital Labour. In A. Scribano & P. Lisdero (Eds.), *Digital Labour, Society and Politics of Sensibilities* (pp. 1–17). Basingstoke, UK: Palgrave Macmillan.

Simmel, G. (2002). The Metropolis and Mental Life [1903]. In G. Bridge & S. Watson (Eds.), *The Blackwell City Reader*. Oxford and Malden, MA: Wiley-Blackwell.

So, J., Kim, T., Kim, M., Kang, J., Lee, H., & Cho, J. M. (2019, April). A Study on the Concept of Smart City and Smart City Transport. *Journal of Korean Society of Transportation, 37*(2), 79–91. https://doi.org/10.7470/jkst.2019.37.2.079.

CHAPTER 2

The Ephemeral and The Metropolis: A Study on a Philosophical Idea from Romantic Aesthetic to Media Theory

Antonio Rafele

INTRODUCTION

Traditionally conceived as opposed to the lasting, the eternal and the necessary, *ephemeral* indicates a dimension of existence that is characterized by the sequence of ultimately irrelevant moments, which seem to not produce strong effects in self-building processes. In the Platonic formulation (Plato 2003) the ephemeral is interpreted in opposition to the strict and strengthened habits, emerging thus as a vector of individual and social disaggregation. In the humanistic tradition, its fundamental elaboration about the canon and memory as lasting domains (Asmann 2012), able to survive the instant of reading or consumption, assumes the ephemeral as an antipodal concept. Between the twentieth and twenty-first centuries,

A. Rafele (✉)
University of Naples Federico II, Naples, Italy
e-mail: antonio.rafele@unina.it

University of Paris Descartes La Sorbonne, Paris, France

A. Scribano et al. (eds.), *Cities, Capitalism and the Politics of Sensibilities*, https://doi.org/10.1007/978-3-030-58035-3_2

a third tradition arises which this paper intends to delineate and reconstruct, one that connects Romantic aesthetics (Leopardi 2013; Novalis 2007; Wordsworth 2000, Kierkegaard 1980) with the deepest insights of media theory (Simmel, Benjamin and McLuhan): a *corpus* of philosophical texts in which the concept of the ephemeral frees itself from any negative implication. By reviewing these sources, this chapter will underline how, in this tradition, the ephemeral structures *a unique constellation of the deepest problems of the self*, starting from the following key identified terms: *Time* as discontinuity; *Media* as forms of experience; *Attention and Distraction* as essential functions of perception; *Desire and Pleasure* as the structure of imagination; *Displays* as modes of consumption; *Lifestyles* as individual identity; *Habit, Addiction and Narcosis* as ways and configurations of daily experience and as fragments of psychic history; *Memory* as a representation of the moment; *Aloneness* in its double meaning of exclusion and immersion; and *Opinion* as the display that shows, in a multitude of refractions, individual and collective time.

Working from this set of issues, the study develops a constellation of concepts by crossing them with the set of authors, while tracing the genealogical paths between pairs of authors-concepts, to make the ephemeral into an analytical tool to understand and connect the modern and contemporary experiences of media and metropolis. At the same time, this framework should underline and unveil some of the operative modes of the contemporary individual, exposed to an acceleration of time which represents one of the fundamental traits of urban life in the twenty-first century, and one of the pillar concepts of media consumption in the 20th.

This paper builds on several authors who have worked on the theme of the ephemeral in different disciplines, such as media studies (Abruzzese 2003; Baudrillard 1988; Morton 2010; Hansen 2006), aesthetics and literature theory (Gumbrecht 2004; Lombardo 2003; Casetti 2008; Moretti 1996), social theory (Maffesoli 1990; Cerulo 2018; Campbell 1987; Pecchinenda 2018), communication history (Peters 1999; Schivellbush 1992) and media archaeology (Huhtamo and Parikka 2011; Ebeling 2012). Most of all, it is concerned with those that have recognized this relationship between the ephemeral and modernity and extended it to contemporary media. Compared to these studies, this paper aims: first, to trace a genealogy, both historical and theoretical, between the authors of the metropolis in the twenty-first century and the media researchers of the 20th; second, to construct a constellation of the ephemeral, providing these disciplines with conceptual lines to understand their relatedness and a framework to enable empirical inquiry. Both these novelties are necessary to attain the two main objectives of the chapter: (1) to study the relationship between the ephemeral and the construction of the self in its details, proposing but also questioning the ephemeral as a constitutive trait of modern and contemporary experience; (2) advance the idea of media as the form and substance of individual experience, investigating its origin in the modern ephemeral, and its implications for the study of individual and historical processes: the point of view, made explicit by McLuhan and the Toronto School, of considering the aesthetic, psychological and sociological through the prism of the dominant media of their time.

I intend to create a procedure of history and genealogy of culture, through the interpretation of a *corpus* of philosophical texts. This interpretation will follow the framework of the analytic indications provided by the deconstructionist school, and, more in detail, the framework presented by Paul de Man (1979, 1983, 1984) within his *Allegories of Reading*. The main contents of this framework underline that: (a) the philosophical text has to be considered as literature because in both emerges an essential convergence between rhetoric and thought; (b) such a formal analysis allows us to approach at the same time issues of aesthetic, sociological and psychological order; (c) the centrality of reading in the reconstruction and updating of the text. I proceed with such a formal and thematic analysis of the corpus, constituting a reading-updating process organized towards the building and employment of the constellation of terms. The research will also adopt two complementary methodological principles: the dialectical image, elaborated by Benjamin as a peculiar relationship between the present and the past of the thought, and the mosaic of fragments, theorized by McLuhan as a means to expose and construct a research path. In addition to the known strengths of each of the above approaches, adopting this methodology shall enable important intuitions from twenty-first-century aesthetics to enhance the reading and interpretation of authors such as Simmel, Benjamin and McLuhan, while, in turn, let the works of these authors shed new light on romantic aesthetic thought.

FASHION AND HABITS

The metropolitan type rests on the following psychological premise: "[T]he intensification of emotional life due to the swift and continuous shift of external and internal stimuli" (Simmel 2010, 103). The number, frequency and intensity of the stimuli available and alluring in the metropolis are much greater than in the provincial town. Such seemingly insignificant variants as quantity and speed cause a qualitative leap in individual experience: the self is projected into a new techno-sensorial world, which challenges its previous mental balance. In order to adapt to the new rhythms of life, the self strengthens one particular organ: "Instead of reacting emotionally, the metropolitan type reacts primarily in a rational manner, thus creating a mental predominance through the intensification of consciousness, which in turn is caused by it" (Simmel 2010, 104). This organ, which occupies the upper strata of the mind, can be defined as the most adaptable of our inner forces. In order to adjust itself to the shifts and contradictions in events, it does not require "the disturbances and inner upheavals which are the only means whereby more conservative personalities are able to adapt themselves to the same rhythm of events" (Simmel 2010, 104). The response to stimuli is moved to a malleable and dynamic psychic zone, able to sense and neutralize as many stimuli as possible. As a means of absorbing and processing stimuli from the outside, emotionality is overcome and becomes a mode of the past, consistent with provincial life, but totally inadequate for metropolitan life. If the provincial town is a *medium* that requires distinct practices and forms of organization, the metropolis is a *medium* that stimulates new strategies of aggregation. The technological difference between the provincial city and the metropolis reflects itself in the difference between a *moral* and an *allegorical* intention, between a mode characterized by the preservation and repetition of habits, and one which instead tends to build and undo them rapidly, thus acknowledging that habits are ephemeral and illusory. The metropolis weakens pre-existing boundaries between subject and object by conferring to the medium, rather than to the self, the power of originating historical and social processes. The advent of a new medium deviates and regenerates the course of time, by creating a new mental condition, and the potential for new modes and possibilities of living. The self is pure energy, the vital and inviolable structure that justifies the presence of things because things exist only insofar as they are being used;

but the self is also a mere reflection of the outside, the ever-developing product of the pressures coming from society.

The individual proceeds as if suspended and daydreaming in the middle of thousands of "shocks" or stimuli. While being seduced by lights, posters, gazes, passers-by, noises, colours and shop windows, the individual is able to let all these stimuli quickly glide away. In other words, the individual wanders through the streets of the metropolis *distractedly*; an organ is strengthened, one that is light, resilient and dynamic, halfway between consciousness and unconsciousness, capable of neutralizing any new stimulus or prompt from the outside. Distraction does not represent a degraded form of experience; it is an active and effective device: it allows an individual to keep pace with the rapid and fast dispersing rhythms of the metropolis without inner upheaval, and it allows millions of people to live side by side, putting up with, and ignoring one another. From a different perspective, distraction creates a problem far from easy to solve: is it possible to make this multitude of stimuli meaningful? Is it possible to obtain a clear and distinct image of the self, of one's characteristics and of one's potential? Distraction is a broad perception but can only glide over things. As does everyday life, it flows rapid, light and uninterrupted. Consciousness can only surface by rending the veil of this *continuum*, by suddenly and momentarily interrupting the flow of experience, allowing the subject to leap to a higher mental level offering a sharper representation of the self. A continuous interplay or a to-ing and fro-ing between distraction and attention comes about, where the former serves to live with a life populated by stimuli that leave little space for thought, and the latter serves to register a quantitative and initially indistinct series of events, later to be transformed and elaborated into self-consciousness. The life of the self unfolds in a *pars construens*, which is swift, conscious and unconscious, and in a *pars destruens* which is slow, lucid and entirely dependent upon the former. Indeed, it is only possible to deconstruct something once experienced, and then, only by working on it. To deconstruct means to mortify, to treat living things as if they were dead objects, but also to enhance the experience, to cast light on it: the individual follows a life in a "reverse direction", focusing on details, on interferences and gaps in the narration, on those parts in which a clear and linear sequence leaves room for additions, for sudden interruptions and turns that modify and recreate the event experienced. The self makes a leap to a higher mental level, and, in this kind of transfiguration, reaches a "high observation point" from which to look back and gain a distinct, although provisional, image of its own characteristics and potential, of its own strengths and weaknesses. In this moment of self-awareness, the self is lifted towards a liminal dimension, halfway between life and death, a dimension which grants a "better and deeper perspective", but which also numbs the senses. Consciousness appears to be essentially tactile, a reflection of experience, but also, automatically, a distancing from it: it is a prosthesis of experience, as well as a weapon against it.

Money, allegory and a multiplicity of stimuli produce an unprecedented psychic phenomenon: "The essence of the blasé attitude is an indifference toward the distinctions between things. Not in the sense that they are not perceived, as is the case of mental dullness, but rather that the meaning and the value of the distinctions between things" (Simmel 2010, 106). On the one hand, money causes a levelling of the difference between values and objects, the public and the private, interiority and exteriority; on the other hand, the speed at which different experiences follow each other makes them appear a mere prosthesis of the everyday. The excitement produced by the multiplicity of different situations encountered turns into its opposite: the feeling that all experience is ephemeral, vain and illusory. A circular and potentially infinite process aimed at its own self-reproduction originates within the self: illusion and disillusion, renewed illusion and renewed disillusion. Free from morals and a sense of duty, the individual lives life in the real or imaginary pursuit of *pleasure*. Pleasure is not derived from achieving a goal, or from preserving and safeguarding given values; it rather derives from a psychic condition of openness and alertness, nourished by illusions and disillusions related to things, people and experiences. The persuasion that illusions will materialize one day is the drive of individual life. However, it is not the realisation of illusions that matters; rather it is the tension that generates around them: the idea of *being able* to realize them (Campbell 1987).

At a symbolic level, the proliferation of lifestyles paves the way for a radical change in the relationship between history and nature: "The decisive fact here is that in the life of a city, struggle with nature for the means of life is transformed into a conflict with human beings, and the gain which is fought for is granted, not by nature, but by man" (Simmel 2010, 109). The metropolis replaces what was once the "struggle with nature" with a new "struggle with man", whereby everyone strives to prevail over others via distinction and originality. This competition is made possible by the proliferation of styles, each with something new to exhibit and display. What is at stake is a success, but it is an end in itself, completely subject to the mutability of public opinion. Consent and dissent, enthusiasm and surprise, or, vice versa, boredom and indifference, measure the success or failure of an individual. Individuals live a life, which, as it were, is glued to the present and flattened into the general way of feeling; the deeper self is almost emptied and is affected by the tastes and judgements of others. Social life revolves around egoism and opinion, the former guarantees its functioning, the latter reflects approval, disapproval or justification. It unfolds as a virtual narration whose protagonists do not stand in opposition to the things of the world, but rather, via an uninterrupted dialogue with them; they adapt to these things, as if to distract themselves from nature, and from the vanity of life and things, to shun the view of "bare reality". The whole of these daily practices changes the existing relationship between history and nature and causes the former to dominate over the latter. If in its ancient form history reproduced the sense and limits of nature by imposing a precise social conduct, in its modern form history and nature drift apart, configuring themselves as two perfectly parallel worlds. Nature is a smooth and empty flow, mute and indescribable, while history is a succession of habits, stimulating exchanges or conflicts among individuals. Any sense of truth, utility and necessity withers from human things, which become mere *stimuli* to ever-new and better-targeted desires. Illusory, vain and transient things are necessary to measure out everyday time; the subject recognizes them as the sole traces of life available, fragments of the psyche, and tools for action. Nature becomes a phantom or a projection, a residual image compared with the habits, and the countless habituations that cross daily life. From a distance, social life acquires the features of a *game*, a *drug* or a *second nature*. It produces an achronic and aimless movement, circular and self-referential, mindless of anything beyond its own repetition and perpetuation. Meanwhile, the processes of social life fold in on themselves; their meaning is historically redefined by those actors who operate a negotiation, and through devices, which establish a continuity between forms of the past and forms of the present, such as quotations, recovery or denial.

Media and Images

In its role as the first *medium*, photography offers scenarios, situations, beliefs and practices directly dependent upon its technical and expressive potential: "Are not all great conquests in the field of forms ultimately a matter of technical discoveries? Only now are we beginning to guess what forms—and they will be determinative for our epoch—lie hidden in machines" (Benjamin 1999, 155). Its model of fruition differs from that of the Renaissance which implied cultural distinction on one hand, and, on the other the conception of art as a sensorial experience, whose duration and existence transcend fruition. With photography the medium itself by its very power activates content and sensorial responses and does so independently from explicit ideas and desires. The medium generates habits that the self metabolizes and repeats, while its duration coincides with its consumption. The spectator becomes integral to the medium because the latter exists and lives only insofar as it is being experienced.

A new and *ab nihilo* creation, the photo can encapsulate fragments of time, things and people in a detached and all-comprehensive view, almost from a position of superiority By crystallizing moments in time, photography differs from classical sculpture, which aspired towards dura- tion and a-temporality. Each snapshot automatically becomes past and *dead*; for this reason, looking at a photo of oneself involves relating to the experience of death and what has passed.

> If we open a 1938 copy of *Life*, the pictures or postures then seen as normal now give a sharper sense of remote time than do objects of real antiquity. Small children now attach the phrase "the olden days" to yester- day's hats and overshoes, so keenly are they attuned to the abrupt seasonal changes of visual posture in the world of fashions. But the basic expe- rience here is one that most people feel for yesterday's newspaper, than which nothing could be more drastically out of fashion. Jazz musicians express their distaste for recorded jazz by saying, 'It is as stale as yesterday's newspaper'. (McLuhan 1994, 196)

Each photograph is the representation of a moment condensing a piece of world history; there is no linearity or progression between one photo and another; only intermittence and discontinuity. Life unfolds as a sequence of moments that "have just happened". It is as if a straight line were continuously cut into small and discrete segments, each holding within it an entire period of time. These changes translate into a new percep- tion of existence: a succession of immersions and resurfacing. Something is experienced, and once that experience is over, it is considered in retrospective. Immersion, resurfacing and retrospective thinking characterize our relationship to things, from which experience, memory and knowledge are drawn. In the light of a retrospective view, the things of the world will be perceived as illusions, clothing and habituations, only temporarily absorbing and occupying the time of the self. Death irrupts into everyday life, not in a biological form, an unspeakable, marginal experience compared to our infinite distractions and habits, but through the experience of the ephemeral. Things simultaneously show their two sides: vitality and ruin where vitality blends with the desolation of ruins, and together they seep into the time of the self. The circularity of life and death overrides the opposition between them; this opposition implies a rigid separation of the two, with a central role given to the myth of immortality. In the circularity life-death, the value of temporal duration is weakened and displaced, so that memory offers the only resistance to the corrosive and destructive action of time.

The birth of a new medium corresponds, in individual consciousness, with the multiplication of ideal images, in which the individual and the collective attempt to remove imperfections from the product and any defects in the social system.

> Corresponding to the form of the new means of production, which in the beginning is still ruled by the form of the old (Marx), are images in the collective consciousness in which the new is permeated with the old [...] At the same time, what emerges in these wish images is the resolute effort to distance oneself from all that is antiquated – which includes, however, the recent past. These tendencies deflect the imagination (which is given impetus by the new) back upon the primal past. In the dream in which each epoch entertains images of its successor, the latter appears wedded to elements of primary history < *Urgeschichte*> – that is, to elements of a classless society. And the experiences of such a society – as stored in the unconscious of the collective – engender, through interpenetration with what is new, the utopia that has left its trace in a thousand configurations of life, from enduring edifices to passing fashions. (Benjamin 1999, 4)

The novelty at first seems to be an *angelus novus*, a circumstance soon to become a daily practice, yet is still shapeless and nascent. During this phase, the new has two sides to it. It appears as a reflection and a derivation from the old: early photography recalls painting, cinema literature, the metropolis, the municipality, and the web of television. Paradoxically, however, the new also raises expectations and desires, a political and social potential that asks to be made manifest, and, if necessary, destroys the ties and divisions posed by the old system. At an imaginary level, a breach between "present" and "recent past" is thus created. This breach feeds the need typical of every generation to take its distance from the immediately preceding epoch: "to each generation the one immediately preceding it seems the most radical anti-aphrodisiac imaginable" (Benjamin 1999, 64). In order to impose its difference and originality, the new elaborates a series of discourses that push individual and collective imagination back to a remote past, to the fantasy of an original society, without social bonds, class divisions or social actors. These discourses represent man in an idyllic condition, full of humanity, but completely immaterial and decontextualized. Such discourses temporarily suspend experience and the social equilibrium, and they correspond to the sensation or illusion that the need for a social equilibrium can be finally overcome. Utopias are only apparently detached from the present, while, in fact, they constitute an extension of it, if not a defence. They do not aim to realize their project, but to perfect novelty: "to give machines a more human face". Utopias pertain to a dormant or subconscious phase, lasting only until the new has entirely taken over in everyday life. Novelty transforms into a "working machine", capable of combining its original objectives—commerce, wealth and consumption—with the human needs that have developed meanwhile. The transformation of *myth* into *habitus*, of a blind and instinctual force into a clear and neat situation inseparable from action, entails a simultaneous redefinition of the functions, values and powers of the various social actors.

The shift from myth to habit also manifests itself when we divert from the general level of social life to the particular one of individual microhistories: "[W]hereas the education of earlier generations explained these dreams for them in terms of tradition, of religious doctrine, present-day education simply amounts to the distraction of children" (Benjamin 1999, 388). In both cases, social life and the individual, the metropolis is the cause of the whole process, the space that fills the existence of individuals and the collective with infinite events that are discontinuous from each other and disconnected from past experiences. Under these circumstances, identity coincides with the infinity of situations experienced and is led purely by chance, far from any image of perfectibility. As a result, the individual feels deeply estranged from the structures and institutions that used to protect an identity that was both individual and collective. Growth is fragmented and takes place in solitude as the individual progressively recognizes the traces left by experience on his current behaviour. Recognition happens at those moments when time is suspended and the *continuum* of existence is interrupted. Thus, individual existence becomes populated with fragments, figures and images that layer upon layer, over the course of everyday life, have stratified and merged with the self. In an instant, there is a kind of leap from a latent preconscious and distracted level to a lucid and conscious one. The potential, characteristics and circumstances determining everyday action then appear clear and distinct, even though they remain provisional.

The growth coincides, on one hand, with the events experienced by the self, and, on the other, the way in which the self elaborates these events (Pecchinenda 2018). Previously separate, growth and knowledge now merge: every single piece of new knowledge will add a further peg—vital to one's personal growth, yet replaceable. This means that self-knowledge is indissolubly linked to the experiences that produced it, and to the self. It also means that self-knowledge is left to chance because nothing ensures that the self will ever gain self-knowledge. The "collective self", once immediately guaranteed by the family and the church, now redefines itself only partially through a self that elaborates experience and relates it to others. Knowledge and memory can no longer be considered as chronological systems of objective experiences, but become ephemeral and discontinuous processes, dependent on the self and the experiences that made them possible. Should new media, capable of stimulating different reflections and memories, replace the historical experiences of the metropolis and the media in the organization of everyday life, their whole body of critical materials will inevitably be destroyed or decay. Knowledge and the medium form a system at once close and chaotic: *close*, because only a specific medium originates and seals in a distinct organization of knowledge, *chaotic* because a medium can bring infinite variations and possibilities of knowledge even to a single individual.

The isolation of the self and the consequent loss of any sense of the finality of time bring everyday life centre stage. The *everyday* becomes the matrix of all experiences, but also a system of modes and practices whereby the self reassesses the value, function and sense of ongoing events. Before becoming a habit, every single event presents itself to the individual as a potential narrative. In this phase, it is experienced as a myth or a daydream, as a blind and instinctive force that demands to manifest itself. Daily use, repetition, and self-observation transform that potential into a familiar *habitus*, circumscribed and perfectly recognizable.

A repeated experience becomes absorbed and integrated into behaviour, one more fragment of the history of one's psyche. The sense and meaning of the various experiences come together in the self only a posteriori: things do not have an intrinsic or autonomous value. Their meaning only surfaces when the self makes an image of them, when it recognizes and relativizes them as a prosthesis of everyday happenings. The crucial question here is not, what does that specific event mean? Rather, what does that event mean for me, what is its impact on my daily life, and how does it stand in relation to the previous experiences I have interiorized? On this premise, the self experiences and interprets even great social structures, such as religion and politics, not as holistic systems, but as small fragments or details "stuck" between the folds of clothes and daily actions. The self appears to itself as a system always *in potential*, eligible for sudden reconfigurations, but constantly aiming towards illusory or concrete pleasure. The self is a dynamic singularity that cannot be pinned down; its action is justified by its relation and communication with other singularities. Interaction with people is unavoidable, yet justified by mere interest (not in the sense of personal benefit). People spend time together for the sake of pleasure, aesthetically, in the original sense of the term, and in order to enjoy themselves, not for political or ideological reasons, or for a distinct purpose.

Objects and Pleasure

Acknowledging that pleasure is the key motive, the driving force behind individual will and action, implies the following: external objects are perceived as prosthesis or stimuli, boxes to fill and empty, *circumstances* that can simulate desires and emotions, illusion and disillusion. When objects are produced it is with the expected uses the consumer will make of them in mind. The pivot of a sophisticated game revolving around the dynamics of attention and seduction is the consumer. This applies to exhibitions and art nouveau, but also to early nineteenth-century novels: "World exhibitions are places of pilgrimage to the commodity fetish. [...] They open a phantasmagoria which a person enters in order to be distracted" (Benjamin 1999, 7). The mass "comes centre stage in the role of the customer": it lets itself become entrapped in a complex labyrinth of mirrors and windows where it participates in a roaring world of illusions. This manipulates individuals by taking their attention away from the alienation of factory work. Objects are miniatures of the exhibition as a whole and they correspond perfectly with the nature of metropolitan stimuli; mere prompts, distractions, and *shocks*. The exhibition has an essentially ludic character and is conceived for the visiting public. Maps, glass buildings (Crystal Palace, 1851), the testimonial (Queen Victoria, 1851), and retrieval of past aesthetic experiences such as the museum and the basilica, all contribute to seducing, attracting and entertaining the passer-by and the potential customer. The consumer exploring the various sections of the exhibition experiences them as an opportunity for leisure, entertainment and distraction. The instrumental or communicative side of the experience is therefore allowed to prevail over the historical and aesthetic.

Objects are produced and consumed *distractedly*: what matters is not the profound value of the experience, but the ever-changing desire for objects, their allure and magnetism, and, of course, their enjoyment.

> I prefer commencing with the consideration of an *effect*. [...] I say to myself, in the first place, "Of the innumerable effects, or impressions, of which the heart, the intellect, or (more generally) the soul is susceptible, what one shall I, on the present occasion, select?" (Poe 2007, 5)

As with photography and exhibitions, the work of art loses its cultural nature and simply becomes a *medium*, the device for communication between author and reader. The author is a particularly inspired technician, a professional whose instruments come from the stores of memory and the stylistic archives of literary history, while the reader *gets into* the text and is the mental operation through which and for which the text comes alive. In *The Raven*, the choice of the rhetorical circumstance, and the combination of its various elements (length, topos, characters, refrain), and its invention, writing, re-reading, revision and refining, is created by imagining the possible reactions of the reader. Thus, the literary tradition is broken down into parts, reassembled and re-read, and the aesthetic experience acquires an essentially ludic character both at the level of creativity and of reception. The literary work transforms itself into a very refined game to attract and distract the reader. The author, on the other hand, draws his techniques from the *intérieur* and the *bricoleur* and establishes a tactile and factual relationship with the text, similar to that of the tailor with fabrics.

These changes give the shadow of an idea of the way that the literary critic needs to go in order to interpret a text. The role of the author, and that of the critic overlap: they represent two complementary and dialectic moments: the *pars construens* and the *pars destruens* of the text. The text is "core" to both, and both draw on the same tools, i.e. the corpus of literary tradition. But while the author outlines and builds the narrative action, the critic is like a detective breaking down and separating its parts until the components that made it possible can be identified. In simple terms, the author gives life and appeal to dead elements, whereas the critic transforms living words into dead objects. By getting a comprehensive vision of the work, the critic might also detect any eventual flaws or defects in the narrative fabric. These passages are very important because they call for an interpretative *surplus* that can transcend the simple text, and pave the way to further possibilities of reflection that may be latent in the text.

The value of the object is not measured by its content, or by its story, but by its capacity to stimulate in the passer-by a daydream, a fantasy that will remain alive until replaced by a new object that can trigger the same process all over again. Meanwhile, content fades away and reveals its mere material, vain and illusory nature: enjoyment lasts but an instant, and all that remains, after all, is the experience of pleasure:

> In order to express the indefinable effect that the odes of Anacreon have upon us, I can find no better comparison and example than a passing waft of fresh breeze in the summer, fragrant and refreshing, which all at once restores you in a way, and seems to open your lungs and heart with a kind of gaiety; but before you are able to fully satisfy that pleasure, or study its quality, and understand why you feel so refreshed, that breath has passed [...] for that indefinable sensation is almost instantaneous, and if you want to study its quality, it eludes you, you no longer feel it, you return to reading, only the dry words remain in your hand, that little breeze, so to speak, has vanished, and you can barely recall, confusedly, the sensation that the same words before your eyes had produced just a moment before. (Leopardi 2013, 42)

Pleasure gives way to the desolation one feels when in front of ancient ruins, the perception and awareness that the pleasure granted by the text is temporary and false and is actually like empty, dead, dry and extinct matter. Pleasure coincides with the moment of reading ("[it] all at once restores you in a way, and seems to open your lungs and heart with a kind of gaiety"); once that magic rapture is over, beauty and pleasure are also gone. When it is re-read and analyzed, the text resembles a landscape of ruins, an aggregation of dry and empty words: that "passing waft of fresh breeze" has vanished. The time of the self and of the work coincide: the work of art swallows up the reader, but at the same time its existence rests upon the use the reader makes of it. Nevertheless, the self needs the work of art to build imaginary worlds that can distract from the boredom and vacuity of existence. This process turns the object into a filter that distances the self from the vision of reality, hence from itself. It is rather like the hedge of the *Infinito* hindering a view over the real landscape, causes it to be replaced by an imaginary one; as its threshold, the hedge itself ambiguously belongs to it. In both their infinite number and the infinite possibilities of "coinciding with individual experience, *circumstances* are an extension and repetition of the principle of the hedge: each of them limits an experience that opens the door to the imagination" (Colaiacomo 2014, 91).

Time as Discontinuity

The sense and historical meaning of innumerable experiences can only be made a posteriori in the researcher's mind. This builds a "high point of observation" from which to obtain a clear and distinct image of our "now-being", and to place that image, alongside others history has already made readable or visible.

> Its founding concept is not progress but actualization [...] It's not that what is past casts its light on what is present, or what is present its light on what is past; rather, image is that wherein what has been comes together in a flash with the now to form a constellation. In other words, image is dialectics at a standstill. For while the relation of the present to the past is a purely temporal, continuous one, the relation of what-has-been to the now is dialectical: is not progression but image, suddenly emergent. – Only dialectical images are genuine images. (Benjamin 1999, 460)

On the basis of experiences lived and observed, the researcher offers an image of our now-being related to those fragments of the past that seem to have desired, anticipated and prompted the present. The image the present builds of the past, of remnants of the past that survive as a present and living memory, is their current interpretation and actualization. The past does not merge linearly with the present, but this breaks down the past and only the fragments perceived as closest to it, are retrieved and transfigured. The historian only pays attention to the relationship the present establishes with residues of the past; a line of continuity "internal" rather than "external" to historical processes is thus created. History is legitimized by its own creations, and justified by its own mechanisms. The relationship between present and past confirms the operational mode of the present in its distinct way of connecting to the past; it also unravels the constants, needs and sense (or insignificance) of human action in general.

History and conscience mirror each other: they appear as a series of infinite discontinuities that in crystallizing, offer a reconfiguration of parts of a pre-existing system or the recuperation of elements long cast aside or denied: "Each time, what sets the tone is […] the newest, but only where it emerges in the medium of the oldest, the longest past, the most ingrained. This spectacle, the unique self-construction of the newest in the medium of what has been, makes for the true dialectical theatre of fashion" (Benjamin 1999, 64). The present is a new turn of history retrieving for its own use and consumption pieces of the past that it finds useful, necessary or close. Closeness is not only chronological but, consistent with fashion, also stylistic.

The forms of history are not independent of one another, but always prone to sudden reconfigurations. A new event may bear a deep impact on the whole system, or on parts of it. When novelty appears, it resembles a phantasmagoria able to fuel desires, expectations, and new and distinct possibilities of expression that existing forms may no longer satisfy. The unstoppable advance of the new, with its everyday life and its diffusion, automatically turns the old forms into ruins, forcing them to compete in a way that will either marginalize them or exhaust their expressive potential. At a social level, the individual and the community experience novelty as both desire and fear; desire reflects the wish to dive into the new in search for new feelings of pleasure, while fear reflects anxiety about the changes the medium will bring to the existing equilibrium. Fear and desire characterize the initial phase of interiorization; they are like figures the self creates to give a name to the outside world. The following phase is day-by-day habituation: the social body enters the medium and becomes numb following its rhythms and features, constructive or destructive as they may be until it accepts and exhausts it.

History appears to be a potentially infinite sequence of moments, which are "present" but also "have just happened". Single events do not stand in linear progression but jump about, and this lack of continuity is directly proportional to the technical difference separating them. Novelty marks the advent of a new fragment of history, but also of a new and irreparable rift in it: "In the same way a translation, instead of resembling the meaning of the original, must lovingly and in detail incorporate the original's mode of signification, thus making both the original and the translation recognizable as fragments of a greater language, just as fragments are part of a vessel" (Benjamin 1996, 259). Fragments are essentially isolated, they follow each other discontinuously and will never become a whole: the original vessel does not exist, rather we have no awareness or knowledge of it, nor access to it. The original creative moment does not coincide with a hypothetical original fragment or matrix holding all the others together, but with the sudden flash and leap of a new event. When novelty appears, it generates history and action immediately; it thus moves towards the experience of the sacred, not in a dogmatic religious sense, but in the sense of an event capable of breaking the course of time, and of inaugurating new possibilities of life.

A view of history based on the idea of it as a sequence of events and habits excludes any sense of finality and end; in fact, it recognizes that pleasure or the will to live is its sole and essential drive. Events offer a lifestyle; pleasure holds and justifies their infinite proliferation. As a mirror image of *fashion*, history enacts a circular time, infinitely extensible:

> Where they impinge on the present moment, birth and death [...] considerably restrict the field of play for fashion. This state of affairs is properly elucidated through two parallel circumstances. The first concerns birth, and shows the natural engendering of life "overcome" <*aufgehoben*> by novelty in the realm of fashion. The second circumstance concerns death: it appears in fashion as no less "overcome," and precisely through the sex appeal of the inorganic, which is something generated by fashion. (Benjamin 1999, 79)

The self's experiences preserve and overcome birth and death only through *illusion* and *disillusion*, projections that recall, transfigure and simulate their rhythms. A bifurcation separates biological from historical time. History appears as a creation of the self, a dimension existing in parallel with nature, simulating its mode of functioning, but essentially artificial and illusory. History evolves by creating, via past and present media, many different *virtual worlds*; it is a kind of *second nature* that attracts and distracts the self from the otherwise empty and homogeneous flux of natural time. As an infinite and intermittent succession of events, *history* becomes an uncontrollable system, with no single viewpoint because each historical moment corresponds to irreducible configurations and mental states.

Viewed from above, history coincides with the countless *histories* of the self, of its habits and habituations. Since internal elements of the self and external techniques are factors that operate within the self as habituations and potential means of expression, an equivalence between them is created. The crucial issue occurring, again and again, is the individual's need, and search, for self-expression. Depending on the existing balance, the individual's potential will emerge from this process with varying intensity. All creations make sense solely and exclusively within the relationships the self establishes with the other; they are re-read not as an ideology or an absolute truth, but simply as prosthesis, organized and provisional systems. This "communicative" perspective corresponds to the profound historical consciousness, to a feeling of emptiness and despair coming from the infinite through insignificant possibilities it offers:

> Whoever has learned to be anxious in the right way has learned the ultimate. [...] [T]he more profoundly he is in anxiety, the greater is the man – yet non in the sense usually understood, in which anxiety is about something external, about something outside a person, but in the sense that he himself produces the anxiety. [...] Anxiety is freedom's possibility, and only such anxiety is through faith absolutely educative, because it consumes all finite ends and discovers all their deceptiveness. [...] Whoever is educated by anxiety is educated by possibility, and only he who is educated by possibility is educated according to his infinitude. Therefore possibility is the weightiest of all categories. [...] [W]hoever has truly been brought up by possibility has grasped the terrible as well as the joyful. [...] [O]ne certainly should not be in anxiety about men and about finitude, but only he who passes through the anxiety of the possible is educated to have no anxiety, not because he can escape the terrible things of life but because these always become weak by comparison with those of possibility. (Kierkegaard 1980, 155)

Anxiety is at once a product of, and a detachment from, history: the sense of possibility that comes from the incredible accumulation and acceleration of historical habits, merges with their vanity and illusiveness. The distracted gaze of everyday life adds to another vision, one that frustrates and overcomes things while recognizing that they are indispensable for the existence and affirmation of the self.

References

Abruzzese, A. (2003). *Lessico della comunicazione*. Roma: Meltemi.

Asmann, A. (2012). *Cultural Memory and Western Civilization: Functions, Media, Archives*. Cambridge: Cambridge University Press.

Baudrillard, J. (1988). *America*. London and New York: Verso.

Benjamin, W. (1996). *Selected Writings, Vol. I: 1913–1926*. Cambridge: Harvard University Press.

Benjamin, W. (1999). *The Arcades Project*. Cambridge: Harvard University Press.

Campbell, C. (1987). *The Romantic Ethic and the Spirit of Modern Consumerism*. Oxford: Basil Blackwell.

Casetti, F. (2008). *Eye of the Century. Film, Experience, Modernity*. New York: Columbia University Press.

Cerulo, M. (2018). *Sociologia delle emozioni. Autori, teorie, concetti*. Bologna: Il Mulino.

Colaiacomo, C. (2014). *Il poeta della vita moderna. Leopardi e il Romanticismo*. Sossella: Roma.

De Man, P. (1979). *Allegories of Reading: Figural Language in Rousseau, Nietzsche, Rilke, and Proust*. New Haven: Yale University Press.

De Man, P. (1983). *Blindness and Insight: Essays in the Rhetoric of Contemporary Criticism*. New Haven: Yale University Press.

De Man, P. (1984). *The Rhetoric of Romanticism*. New York: Columbia University Press.

Ebeling, K. (2012). *Wilde Archäologien 1: Theorien der materiellen Kultur von Kant bis Kittler*. Berlin: Kadmos.

Gumbrecht, H. U. (2004). *Production of Presence: What Meaning Cannot Convey*. Stanford, CA: Stanford University Press.

Hansen, M. B. N. (2006). *Bodies in Code: Interfaces with Digital Media*. London: Routledge.

Huhtamo, E., & Parikka, J. (Eds.). (2011). *Media Archaeology: Approaches, Applications and Implications*. Berkeley: University of California Press.

Kierkegaard, S. (1980). *The Concept of Anxiety*. Princeton: Princeton University Press.

Leopardi, G. (2013). *Zibaldone*. New York: Farrar, Straus and Giroux.

Lombardo, P. (2003). *Cities, Words, Images. From Poe to Scorsese*. Basingstoke: Palgrave Macmillan.

Maffesoli, M. (1990). *Au creux des apparences. Pour une éthique de l'esthétique*. Paris: Plon.

McLuhan, M. (1994). *Understanding Media*. Cambridge: The MIT Press.

Moretti, F. (1996). *The Modern Epic: The World-System from Goethe to García Márquez*. London: Verso.

Morton, T. (2010). *The Ecological Thought*. Cambridge: Harvard University Press.

Novalis. (2007). *Notes for a Romantic Encyclopaedia*. New York: State University of New York Press.

Pecchinenda, G. (2018). *L'essere e l'io*. Meltemi: Roma.

Peters, J. D. (1999). *Speaking into the Air: A History of the Idea of Communication*. Chicago: University of Chicago Press.

Plato. (2003). *The Republic*. London: Penguin.

Poe, E. A. (2007). *The Philosophy of Composition*. München: Grin Verlag.

Schivellbush, W. (1992). *Licht, Schein und Wahn: Auftritte der elektrischen Beleuchtung im 20*. Berlin: Ernst.

Simmel, G. (2010). The Metropolis and Mental Life. In G. Bridge & S. Watson (Eds.), *The Blackwell City Reader* (pp. 103–110). Chichester: Wiley-Blackwell.

Wordsworth, W. (2000). *The Major Works*. Oxford: Oxford University Press.

CHAPTER 3

Plasticity of Bodies/Emotions in the City: Socialization Places, Embodying Social Relations

Margarita Camarena Luhrs

INTRODUCTION

As some experiences of those who live in the city are often reversible, it is known that they are then experienced as advances-reversals of facts, practices, expressions and feelings, which return to their referents from the usual place from which they occurred. It only needs to be noted that there are limits to such plasticity of the bodies/emotions that articulate the city. Because, in other less plastic ways, or even completely inelastic, there is an experience of change in the city that makes it impossible for some displacements of their dislocations to return to their previous positions.

Next, an attempt to answer the question is made: why are the actions and perceptions that socialize the city so attractive? This is assuming that there are perceived actions through which it is possible to (ir)reversibly

M. Camarena Luhrs (✉)
Institute of Social Research, National Autonomous University of Mexico, Mexico City, Mexico
e-mail: margarita@sociales.unam.mx

© The Author(s), under exclusive license to Springer Nature Switzerland AG 2021
A. Scribano et al. (eds.), *Cities, Capitalism and the Politics of Sensibilities*, https://doi.org/10.1007/978-3-030-58035-3_3

43

(re)incorporate previous positions of the bodies/emotions that have lived in those moments and places in the city. For this, effects of adjustments in the adaptive experiences of social relations in cities are highlighted, with emphasis on those that are reversible or that are, otherwise, irreversible—without plasticity—because they have crossed the limit that makes it impossible to return to the locations, identities and perceptions based on the orders, arrangements and landscapes of the original places.

It is about suggesting that those who make the city do so with a peculiar feeling, managing capacities that put it in tension. Feeling and knowing about the city, can either deform it or make it recover—or not—, its original form: the way of looking and feeling it. In other words, the social, economic, political and cultural relations of the social subjects, who socialize the city in these ways, can't stop being relations that are given in a precise space, place, territory, landscape and time, from which the bodies/emotions that have built them are embodied.

The class imprint that is fixed in a certain way to the places in the city, according to how it acts, works, experiences, perceives and represents, maybe a constant (re)construction of the city as a geographical physical space, which is read separately although it occurs inseparably from the embodiment with which the city itself imbues the socially related subjects who build it and live it day by day.

Socialization: incorporation processes (experiences of socializing, as well as of acquiring the city or incorporating in it), with which the city is socialized in classist ways—homogeneously asymmetric and irreconcilable, not convergent—produced from the social relation that, however, can't stop socializing the city, even if it were exclusive, even if it were like that since it was built from each of the moments in which its physical spaces were used, reduced or expanded, as (ir)reversible, as fixed/mobile, showing in each deformation and remnants how their elastic limits are reached.

Classified Sense of the City

This work ponders the social relations, those of subject-object, the bodies/emotions that are embodied by acting in the city, incorporating it as an integral part of their own existential and sensible dimensions. And when acting this way, they are, at the same time, endowing it with a dominant/dominated class content to every place lived.

These incorporated, spatial, sensible characteristics are built at the same time as the subjects interrelate with their bodies/emotions in uniquely classified ways in the world-historical continuum that takes shape in the common places of the cities, as well as in the extensive globalities in which they operate as, dislocated and indiscriminately, the financial capital of the contemporary world.

As the city classifiably edifies its centres/peripheries, its accesses and physical connections, tangible and intangible, the social class differences are embodied in the spaces of the city, and they are learned by integrating the experiences in an internalization process of norms and values set by the dominant ideology.

The fixed and flexible of the city are classified and thus, the social relations of the bodies/emotions are embodied; not only because iden tity signs, behaviours, languages, signs and inseparable understandings of the times and places from which they are emitted and received, have been incorporated into the bodies/emotions, but also because they are socialized communications in (from) the "wanted" place that selectively and classificationally goes through, towards (and as far as) the subjects who cross it as it is embodied corporately, emotionally and expressively throughout various parts of the city.

In this way, the social, economic, politic and cultural relations that these subjects establish between themselves are given in precise spaces, places, sites, territories and landscapes. From imprints (signs, footprints and marks) already classified, they are embodied at the same time to mark affiliation to one class or another, and one or another style of its pref- erences for living in a built place, for moving through this and other sites.

Thus, social subjects in their reciprocal relations arm the city, according to political power, according to the strength of needs. Therefore, next, an attempt is made to highlight the limits of the plasticity of that double socio-spatial: subject/city-city/subject, which socializes the physical city- space, as a scene of confrontation and struggle, both due to its own social relations of opposition to capitalism, from which it is constructed because, at the same time, the city is produced as an enclosure that imbues this embodiment through all the social relations of its inhabitants.

In this frame, the bodies/emotions of the social subject, intersubjec- tive and *ad hominem,* that live in the city, turn out to be as rigid and as plastic to the contradictive adaptative process in which the Mexican and Latin-American cities grow and reproduce. Between the huge tensions contained in those social relations incorporated in the city (and by the city of the subjects, thus mutually constructed), the bodies/emotions embodied are key to the investigations about social life in general, as well as those about, in particular, Mexico, North America and Latin America.

In today's society, at the dawn of the twenty-first century, it is no surprise that capitalism keeps these irreconcilable class relations in and through the cities, precisely through these common-places, in a way that such social relations and capitalist cities manage to prevail in the middle of continuous critical, economic, ecological, social and cultural collapses. This happens so frequently that it is not known in which of all the following critical episodes it will end up being unable to reconstitute (Streeck 2017, 291).

A key to understanding this systemic resilience, in general, is the constitution of social subjectivity, emerging from the objective materiality of flesh and bones, of the social emotions and feelings that, contained by the bodies/emotions, turn out as spontaneous as decisive for the social structure. Therefore, the plasticity or displacement of the relocations of the city may be central, through which the limits of the reversibility of actions and social intentions of the social subjects that appear conjugated as soon as the subject is particularized, are reached or crossed, even when unlimited utopian cities were planted in its extent (Narváez Tejerina 2008, 87).

Accordingly, as soon as the adaptive plasticity of the bodies/emotions in the city becomes visible, it is clear that they socialize the city, just as they carry an inevitable—albeit unconscious—embodiment of social, economic, politic and cultural relations, with which they can become (in)visible bearers, more or less creative-destructive, expressive-repressive makers of the city of advances/setbacks of life in the city.

Hence, the common thread of this reflection is the plasticity that there is and can be in the displacements of the dislocations of subjects/objects of the city, which socialize it with actions from which a peculiar "feeling that is knowing" that does not need more definition than any feeling is embodied, so immediately defined because for all people it is as evident as feeling in the proximity of a loved one, as in a love of the city such that it was only another form of happiness.

Bodies/emotions are embodied in social relations with which they become the city by constantly socializing it. It is in such a way that this double simultaneous process of socializing unfolds: embodying, making it possible to live incorporated by and in the same city—even with its unusual class crashes, irreducible tensions of histories, times and places—in the middle of a space subject by constant oppositions and violent class contradictions.

In this regard, there are very different academic and political perspectives since the capitalist structure prevails, because the development of social relations in cities is not only different in each place, but is particularly unrepeatable at each moment and because, in different ways interstitial, other forms of pre-existing coexistence between all of us are already anticipated.

In this way, the ideas presented below seek to take advantage of some advances in world cosmopolitanism inspired by the ideas of a global city; as well as taking into account certain approaches to smart cities, favoured both by practices in the development of information and communication technology (ICT), and inspired by sustained eco-technological development.

Even so, the central idea is the one proposed by Adrián Scribano's (2010, 2013) school of thought about the Global South and developed by himself and his colleagues and collaborators, on the need to visualize, with increasing urgency, the challenges that it raises about the centrality of the bodies/emotions, especially those embodied in today's social relations (Scribano 2010, 206), which do not cease to socialize, but contradictorily, continue to shape the appropriate places in the middle of the unfolded and multiple (dis)connected spaces in the heart of urban space.

In the described context, the undeniable role of emotions is present in the most diverse scenarios of world city dominance, crystallized peculiarly in continental America—Hispanic, Anglo, Lusitanian and Francophone—as hegemony and especially as a world alternative, with the very varied links and differences with which all of this, together with the nascent twenty-first century, alerts us the dawn of another era of real history.

Faced with the need for critical, multi—and transdisciplinary approaches, which face the difficulty of working with the multi-scalar complexity of the socialized city through the bodies/emotions in which the embodied (in the best case, citizenized) objectivity of the social relations within the urban body—in the wide display of social relations incorporated by the city and turned itself into city—, its plasticity needs to be responsibly intervened. That is, to previously intend the displacements that occur in its dislocated joints, in so violent an adaptive effort that it could only announce the opening of a franker coexistence based on the principles of reciprocity. But will it be possible to do so?

Therefore, this chapter tries to offer the reader an approximation to the binding urban bond, the object of the urban social relation, considered as a powerful force for change, which, if it becomes common consciousness, can serve to better guide the increasingly predominant life of the social urban (in)sensibilities, the repetitive expression of that which is "socialized" in the city and inevitably "embodied" in the dominant social relations of the contemporary city itself.

Social Relations, Subject-Object of the Bodies/Emotions in the City

Inhabitants of the world of social relations, that is the place and time embodied by every one of us at every moment, observe rather unconsciously social structures and processes that involve the most diverse activities. As well as the urban processes that interconnect inhabitants, there are the different scales of the local, regional and global, displaced flows that dislocate people, capital, merchandise, information and influences to achieve the ends of the world market.

Reaching this degree of incorporation is possible due to historical changes that have maintained the capitalist structure through constant adaptive changes in society, the economy, politics and especially in what makes the physical bodies and territories of the city as their own doers, those who are the hundreds, thousands and millions of bodies/emotions embodied in and by their constituent subjects.

From this perspective, society as the city can only be changing and complex. But, it is especially in the embodiment of social relations that social subjects crystallize, put bodies/emotions into action to avoid the uncertainty and chance that make so questionable not only the type of city and the way of life with which we make ourselves daily in and out of it, but to the ecological and vital costs with which we have built both. And, above all, with a view to the future, to foresee what would be plasticity of urban coexistence, possible and desirable to build for this twenty-first century.

There is a clear need for urban planning that seeks other new forms of understanding, designing and building the contemporary urban space in which it is also created and transformed, with full awareness and from previously stated intentions, that work continuously from the identity of citizens and from their own needs and perspectives, to propose the best of urban spaces, integrating them coherently in all their extension and implicit complexity.

For this reason, Latin-American urban planning needs new ways of thinking and executing public decisions that make it possible to consult with the inhabitants, users, neighbours, actors and experts of all kinds, the decision-making processes that affects them, linking with them (Ascher 2004, 84), more than progressive and participatory, in an autonomistical way.

Also, it is known that theoretical and practical proposals are necessary for urban planning in the twenty-first century, especially because cities take on special relevance in the financial reproduction of capital but, more precisely, because social subjects immersed in unsolvable class contradictions are not capable of succeeding more than through the dominant subjects, subjected in turn, as slaves to their predatory ambition, to the generation-expropriation-dispossession of the neo-capitalist surplus profit of the cities-bodies-emotions-market, or by the different degrees of (in)submission caused by the forced transfer of sovereignties.

Of course, as long as it is the same structure of the time, the possibilities of other integral, sustainable urban-architectural practices that take into account the real needs of social subjects, as a whole, are less than impossible. However, since the city is a historical social product, that is, a changing one, it must be borne in mind that the city-state-market is not eternal, neither are its subjects-social objects, nor it is socially battered and wasted bodies/emotions that make and support it. Such trends in urban change suggest that:

> urban spaces acquire importance by incorporating precise characteristics and meanings (historical, social, economic, political, cultural) for the community that ultimately inhabits and socializes them, being marked in the popular imagination as places with meanings, history and memories (personal or collectives) that are traditionally transmitted from generation to generation... This is part of their identity, without forgetting that the moment we are living generates a multiple, complex and fast-moving world and, therefore, "ambiguous", "entangled" and plastic", uncertain, paradoxical and even "chaotic" (Bauman 2007: 34). (Reyes-Guarnizo 2014, 2)

In such a way, it cannot be forgotten that appropriate spaces and places in the city are more than the physical support of the activities that their classified societies want to undertake on their territories. Cities are socio-cultural supports for their subject-objects, bodies/emotions, that give them their substance and senses. The city is inevitably its "sociocultural expressions (Alva and Aldrete 2011) and its collective imagination, which influences living and development conditions for all its inhabitants" (Reyes-Guarnizo 2014, 2).

In these conditions, the challenge is not less since it involves an in-depth study of the correlation of forces in the fight for the power of the city and to exercise the right to make the city—which should assist everyone equally, only for sharing the same location and their life of inter-relation in common—so under these conditions, changing the relational life between asymmetrically bodies/emotions is essential for any change in the way of socializing what is understood, it conceptualizes and designs to make the spaces of the city achieve a constructive effect that is neces-sary, that is effectively realistic and understandable for those who occupy it.

Embodied Social Relations vs. Socialization of Class Contradictions in Contemporary Cities

The city is a momentary experience that feels complete. Something external to other regulations that impose forms and distances, situations and inci-dents that, nevertheless, open interstices through which other practices of feeling escape. These embodied signs show purposes and means with those that the city is more than solitude, a way of making us part of it with what can only be part of us. (Salgado and Camarena 2018, 87)

Our own and the others' presences in each situation make us find a subjec-tivation of the social relationships that the embodied bodies/emotions carry in the city of the present. The difficulty is that this finding of its plasticity is capable of breaking the chain of its foreseeable futures, an inseparable way of verifying in its materialization, its subjectivation.

Putting limits to the place of the time of change that maintains these social relations incorporated by, for and from, the financial city of neolib-eralism, is a way of facing what is currently happening and anticipating its possibilities in advance. It also means to register what is changing in the objectification—involuntary—and with the subjectification—volun-tary and intentional—of the social subjects incorporated in (from, for) the city, through their emotional-corporalities, of its excitedly embodied inhabitants.

Since contemporary cities are made up of experiences that rather erase corporeality, it has become normal and natural to cultivate this way of eliminating the perceptual, emotional and sensorial register of what it is to inhabit. In conditions of living in oblivion—and more than the commodi-fication and financialization of the bodies/emotions of the social subjects embodied in and by the capital of the city—the urgency is to deny the nonsense of: feeling just on the brink of absence; to live without contacts and without taking care of life; of going from one pause to another, with hardly having a suspicion of the other; in conditions that embodied bodies/emotions do not stop sending signals of how needy they are to socialize their love.

As in the contingency and ambiguity of the present, a particular embodiment of the social (dis)encounter is woven. It is not that the social subject is lost or that it returns as if from an imaginary rescue of antiquity or the ethnographic New Age, but that it is about a subjectivity that is not only visible, but is recognized in all its harshness in every possibility of anticipating the construction of another egalitarian, free, solidary and just society.

What embodied bodies/emotions do, is what make them. Desires change, realizations change. If this is today, who knows if tomorrow other longings for caresses change the present of the connected city, of its displaced access and of its dislocated centres that increasingly lead to the social (dis)encounter. This is one of the moments in which the citizen conceives its city, free; he makes a discovery that is remembering, an innovation that seems to ignore having forgotten what has been lived, which presupposes what is hidden, which jointly makes that city-like way of becoming citizens that pre-existed in us, with a provisional feeling of reaching full experience.

There are unimaginable transfers of times and place. They were seeds of the historical development of the same life of social relations of the city making it possible for them to take substance as body-emotions in each city, in each of its limiting moments, just with the increase of the exchange and growth of modern pre-state forms, which were initiated with the bureaucracy and the guilds of antiquity and of which the city is made itself, no longer feudal but capitalist, was repeated plasticity that until now had been able to return its causal effect to its original position.

Now financial rents and profitabilities colonize social subjectivities, via perfectly calculated materialistic controls, carried out from the highest sense of commitment to the "ethical obligation", to constantly expand financial (and fiscal) profitability to the advantage of a few. It is categorical imperative that drags social sensibilities, which is surely determined by an ingrained—religious—ethic of capitalist utility. There, subjectivities for which the sense of a philosophy of "making money" is already something so extremely ambitious that conventional individualism no longer serves it, it is inoperative and incapable.

Although this structural historical persistence does not make it possible to suggest a long vitality to the order of things (Streeck 2017, 14), the unusual thing about the city's present history is that it is the millions of bodies/emotions that inhabit it, that sustain it in the face of the enormous number of collapses, crises, wars and setbacks of which, however, these plastically incorporated social-emotional-corporalities have made it possible to continue to move forward in and from cities.

Although there are enormous discrepancies around this discussion of the future of capitalism, and of the same globalized capitalist city that will be dominant in some decades, it is very interesting to witness what happens to try to intervene in these accelerated processes of re-objectification of the objective materiality of bodies/emotions that hold the city socially objectified in physical, tangible, perceivable, affordable, profitable, financialized and functional ways. These are processes that remain a matter that further limits the ungovernable management of the contemporary city.

To this we cannot fail to add the bidirectionality of the interactions of the world role of the city concerning the urban, rather than politically urbanized, of the city that has become a world of worlds. In other words, its performance as a node of the "network space/flow space/socio-cyber space", of a possible:

> networked humanity" more connected and interdependent, [although] it does not necessarily imply a reduction of tensions or a collaborative approach. On the contrary, it could be said that interdependence has become a currency of power. Even the Internet is used as a "weapon", which is fragmented and used for security concerns or to avoid such inter-dependence. The society of the 21st century is faced with a constant redefinition of power, a power that is easier to change hands but also to be lost (Naim 2014). (de Torres 2016, 3)

Connectivity in which, at the same time as the global function of the financialized "global" city is deployed, the form of a city-state is adopted with a trans-territorialized domain, both today and for the future, in which the possibility of incorporating/exciting the best of the mediatizing dimensions that could be in the current world market, that could even be transformed into perhaps autonomous and truly cosmopolitan resources, is still distant.

WHAT DOES THE PLASTICITY OF BODIES/EMOTIONS THAT MAKE AND ARE MADE IN THE CITY ANTICIPATE?

By 2050, two-thirds of the world will live in cities. Ideas and practices of coexistence facing this forecast are important from now on. For this reason, it may be useful to advance on those who could substantiate this accelerated process of world urbanization. As the experiences of internationalization of the various scopes of the cities from which they take their positions in the current interconnected world, they overcome contradictions and dichotomies of their own/other, internal/external, local/global, territoriality/virtuality, etc., critical perspectives on these modalities of expansion—constant and growing—of the capital that organizes the world urban concert are necessary.

Other realities, another predominantly urban era, are frequent in the emphasis given to the ideas of transit and historical transition to which the current narrative pays some attention. Super communication, super computation, super processing of large volumes of information, the simultaneity of complex processes, greater interdependence, intercommunication, interconnectivity and interaction, diversification of markets, acceleration of the circulation of financial capital, the intensity of the rotation of financial capital, greater efficiency, efficacy, sufficiency and responsibility in the care of the production processes, logistics circulations or marketing, are characteristics of contemporary financial expansion.

What is sustained with other social practices, through the adaptive plasticity of the bodies/emotions? The same structure with other highly developed expressions of the enshrined social relationship is evident only when we take into account that by 2020, the vast majority of the world population has indiscriminate access to a cell phone, hands and mentality, tremendous capacity for data processing, communications, perhaps unimaginable to another consciousness even a decade ago.

Such accessibility, centrality and connectivity of globalization are not neutral. They cause, among other effects: (a) a vast concentration and centralization of wealth, that is, a much more inequitable distribution of wealth and opportunities, with which, (b) at the world level, it is "ahead" of the central economies, strengthening the mechanisms of its centrality; at the same time that it "lags" further on the peripheries, dislocating the emerging sectors of their economies, and that it (c) causes enormous tensions due to the breaking of the chains of scientific-technological invention-innovation, with the obvious consequences, positive and negative, in the transport and communication networks, in the uses and consumptions of energy and in the new exchanges of all kinds of experiences through digital platforms and the Internet, which, (d) not only crystallize greater absolute and relative conventional intensity of the exploitation of labour, but, above all, that provide guidelines for the most diverse and implausible ways of generating, capturing, expropriating, dispossessing, that is, of financing/profiting the appropriation of their surpluses to legitimate producers or possessors who embody some bodies/emotions and not any of them; rather, it triggers them, (e) enormous destruction of their own bodies/emotions, of the habitat and of the social fabric that had sheltered them, particularly of the habits of relation and coexistence in the city, thereby increasing situations of insecurity and violence, conflicts that destroy identity bases of cohesion and social norms of coexistence.

And, with which, at the same time that it erodes, dents, intoxicates and destroys the sovereignty of the subjects of the city, it turns out that bodies/emotions struggle to open interstices with alternatives that populate the urban horizon with possibilities of realizing improvement, democratization, citizen empowerment, but it is terrible that they still do not succeed in establishing, lasting and changing the status quo. You may wonder why.

More connections and more interdependence are not equal to more collaboration. Social tensions increase in the city. However, the power struggle that these new social "controls" provide certainly polarize much more the inequalities. Connectivity, centrality and accessibility are used to secure some people, groups, goods or information, even to manipulate this interdependence, even to break social bonds.

It must be taken into account that it is the social relations that support and nurture the social bodies/emotions that make the city, which transmit such tensions. The current context is such that, in addition to the inherent uncertainty of capitalism, it can be seen that "that system could come to an end in the not too distant future—even without the existence of a regime that succeeds it insight—as a consequence of the unfolding of its internal contradictions" (Streeck 2017, 13).

For this reason, it is necessary to appeal to these incorporated-and-excited social relations that are constantly being regenerated and recovered from what they have done to the city. Summon (a) conscious attention, that is, to feeling that it is knowledge learned by feeling the city itself through city bodies/emotions, appealing to the collective sensibilities that animate lives within (b) not only to its identity landscapes and recreational beauties, but to all those responsible for the action of the city, in terms of (c) the physical spatial system of buildings classified by their uses, functions, heritage, history and inheritance, type of public/private management to which they are subject, individually/collectively; and, mainly, concerning (d) social norms that integrate as much as they separate and segregate spaces, sites, places as accesses, uses and functions of the habitat, through which it is necessary (e) to identify, interpret and addressing such emotional-bodily issues of the inhabitants who can no longer be merely a spectator, expectant, but claim to be treated as necessary actors and participants in this set of interdependencies.

"What We Do, Makes Us". Plasticity of the Social Bodies/Emotions that Make the City

In this context, two-thirds of the planet's population as a whole will live in cities in the next 35 years, the force of such inertial/intentional change is embodied by the enshrined bodies/emotions, which we know from their urban condition of inhabiting cities. But, if the easiest thing when referring to the multiple subjects of the city is its inseparable presence, position, corporality, sensibility, its identity crystallizes in buildings and streets, when perceiving its smells and aromas, listening to its noises, feeling the footsteps of passers-by, walkers, travellers, to the degree that without place there is no identity.

The built city is perceived by its mass, size, landscapes, commonplaces and private places. The city is material, there it is, it is solid and rigid in its buildings, flexible and intangible movement, with more or less balance, sufficiency, saturation or congestion, it is and is in space. As for its social relations from which it is built-in socialized oppositions, the city acquires very different dimensions. There are these objective material dimensions, the result of the actions of and among the social classes that physically and sensorially construct what is perceived. But, above all, other emotional bodies are superimposed on it in a constant, endless transition, which anticipates and confirms, pulls pasts and shelters even immaterial future capacities.

To appreciate the bodies/emotions that make the city, which are the lived city as extension, roof and floor, streets and sidewalks, made of rods and bricks, of materials and spaces that are permanent bodies of the city. Permanent bodies, which are also the protection of the roof, the security of their own soil, the so enjoyable livelihood of coexistence nurtured by the common, appropriate, shared place in the house-plaza-market-temple-school-field. These city emotion-bodies are also the different places of the government-company, the physical body places of the city that are non-permanent or that are less necessary such as those of informal groups, clubs, places of little use and few users and so on.

Apart from the mass, weight, size, colours, shapes, structures, morphologies and functions of the city, it is made up of all the bodies/emotions that make it changeable, that live it differently at every moment, that enjoy it in its equality or that, on the contrary, as it happens for the big cities, suffer it in their inequalities, deficiencies, abuses, absence of liberties, lack of respect for their civil and social rights, the exclusion of other classified bodies/emotions and, therefore, excluded from there yes, being sovereign, yes being powerful, if they can be as accepting of differences as they can to transmute perceptions of their living the city into colours, shapes, sounds, stories, words, fables of beauty.

It is not so easy to add the city dwellers, alike, because they are not the same but in terms of their social class differentials, although it would certainly be possible to involve them perceptually and reflexively in all the modes of habitability that have occurred and that they massively produce us (Mercado 2015, 5). The truth is that perhaps they are only similar in their class differences, possessors: dispossessed-expropriated-segregated.

However, their social relations cannot only be of marginalization, because they have competed through the classified bodies/emotions that the exclusionaries carry, the two exclusionaries at each step and in each of their differentials. In reality, there is no other way of relating or relating socially to make a particular city.

It is a practical, active and political plasticity of human bodies/emotions of being mutually moulded in their particularities as in their differences, there are limits, there are fences, borders and edges, there are impossibilities within the framework of the historical structure of capital like any other. In the (dis)encounter, the (dis)connection, the social differences are so brutal that they seem to occur in separate worlds. Mutuality is impossible in the context of these oppositions, and even so the plasticity of ideological subjectivity also connects and dominates everything equally. But not in the same way; some social classes and others are forged in their interrelation, they are related so that they take resigned forms, both extremes, even until they change their character to remain subdued.

Under these conditions, the bodies/emotions that are the city have a great innate adaptive plasticity, even though they have their own limits. The capacities of expression and vitality, the ideation of attempts and intentions, that they contain is part of something like a social intelligence that is sensible and intuitive, in which we feel as well as know. But, in the city, this plasticity is about the centre that is encounter, and that is shared. A centre that, if it can be multiple shared centres in infinite ways, a reversible and elastic moment that does not replicate geometrically as two halves or many halves distributed, but is a non-dispersing centre-centraliser, which in dance or music is felt and it is known that it is well known, and with which the city is conceived as free.

This conjunction of two is in the voice that speaks to the other, excited. More in laughter, also in crying, in the basic emotions of surprise, disgust, fear, joy and sadness and anger, which are innate adaptive capacities. As the human substance is social, that is, naturally the result of the relations, of social interaction, the countless body/emotions, feelings and mental states that are the city, are reached by proving a willingness to live in common. Sensibilities, evolutionary inheritance, the adaptive means of the human species, humanize the social bonds (not of marketing) and to all the material that supports it, that is, to the entire physical body of the city, built by and as shelter and sustenance to the bodies/emotions that by inhabiting it, make it an appropriate city in a new way, at every moment.

CONCLUSIONS

The spatial city, socialized by the bodies/emotions, is a materiality that embodies the same social relations that enshrine and socially classify the bodies/emotions. It is a city, socialized, embodied, that is overtly inclusive because it gives-takes away and recognizes-ignores the place of the social subjects, intersubjectivities and people who live it, thereby organizing it. More than a stage, it increasingly incorporates and emotionalizes socio-cybernetically, its infra/superstructures of relations, learning and knowledge.

Even without detaching from the historical structure that founded it as a market city and that now financializes it without limits, its radical enclosure can't fail to combine unstoppable socialization with what it combines in its materiality, other novel forms of objectification and subjectivation of the social relationship of the financial imperative weighing on the constitution of their bodies/emotions.

This presence of the bodies/emotions is felt. From what has been suggested, plasticity—as an (ir)reversible displacement of its dislocations or elasticities of these bodies/emotions in the social life of the city—provoke and testify, transformations of what is continually being received—and—giving to and from the complex world that is the city.

Among the interesting questions are the following: how do the bodies/emotions of the cosmopolitan citizen "feel, therefore, they know"? In what ways does this incorporation/excited direct the most sensible transformations of cities? What is the function of the most sophisticated financial ICT that is intended to serve the citizens? What effects do investments in fixed urban infrastructure have: land and its various uses such as housing, work, consumption, education, care and recreation; and flexible: transport and communications in and between cities? Or, by whom and why are some technological solutions being promoted? These may be some questions whose answers serve to inform what the socialized and embodied body/emotion city is currently about, and what this moment holds for the long transition followed by cities.

These guiding questions of this reflection lead to highlight the interstices that make their way in the midst of this polarized process and that are aggravated by practising, albeit momentarily and fleetingly, other possible states of life relations that synthetically support the bodies/emotions in cities. What has been mentioned happens amid enormous tensions that are giving way to other possibilities for development.

If what arises in front of the bodies/emotions of the urban expansion promoted by financial capitalism only elicits fleeting experiences that fail to prevail, they nevertheless do not cease to prove themselves as anticipated advances of other better possible worlds of the urban life of tomorrow, as it has been called by the authors of descriptions of urban expansions characteristic of the city in Mexico, and generally across Latin America.

An attempt has been made to point to situations in this city that are anticipated in their contemporary operation, which are presented as advances that already work because they condense and shorten the distances-times of the exchange with which the beats of the financial materiality of capital expand for all the bodies/emotions that inhabit, live and build the Latin-American city.

Bodies/emotions have a transitive capacity with which they probably cross all the centres of the cities—which operate from the control of socialized futures—and they do so, in the effort to disappear the space, socializing the accesses, embodying the centres, at the same time as expanding and multiplying the connections. With which, although they manage to shorten times, they can't avoid implanting another relation of speed that makes the bodies/emotions (in)visible, makes their reversibility to the previous positions impossible and, thus, injures or destroys the plasticity of their original identities.

The same goes for the wills of social subjects, crystallized through their constant intersubjective communication, via cell phones and digital platforms that are directly activated by their bodies-minds-sensibilities, which "adjust" the objective materiality: involuntary, impersonal, incorporeal and without feelings of the economy and political-financial power—that is, updating the original separation of doing and the fact that founds the capitalist social relations—, what it achieves is to reproduce itself without personality or place, without headquarters or spatial identity.

Until the financial capital that founds the city and makes its structure contemporary, especially after the 2008 crisis, manages to prevail as the practical base—also symbolic—of this digitized era, streets and squares are places of identity, a shelter of emotions, reasons of meaning to its (in)materiality. The subjects have been torn from their places and identities, in the way they made-and-recognized bodies/emotions themselves, according to their position within the place.

The exalted acceptance of differences, even of oppositions of social relations, grows as enriching nutrients of coexistence based on mutual respect and consideration for the other. Internal and own, external and foreign, lose meaning, giving way to very different cultural, political and practical areas of the multifaceted, multiple and diverse, with which participatory proposals are encouraged and the use of technical resources to choose sizes and functions, preferences and conditions of the common city, move to something like the conscious city (smart city), precisely because of the excited participatory incorporation of its inhabitants. This could mean that, even unequally, it was put at the service of the groups that share it, that other possibilities of alternative relations were made present, that the subject subjected their own relations in the common interest, that they were left behind, as unfeasible and contrary to life. These are bodies/emotions that have been forced to be embodied, incorporating in their own self an enclosed separately in a city that consumes and rejects them. Feeling to be, knowing how to be in the city, is an adaptive plastic force of the bodies/emotions that, in the cities of the present century, alerts us to continue through another sustainable way that is encouraging of the dignity of the encounter, of the strength of reciprocity in urban coexistence.

References

Alva, B., & Aldrete, F. D. (2011). Identidad urbana en San Luis Potosí a través de la percepción social en el añlo 2011, en Ruiz H. (et al.) (Coords.), *Diversidad cultural, identidades y territorio: adscripción, apropiación y recreación.* https://www.eumed.net/libros/2012a/1149/indice.htm.
Ascher, F. (2004). *Los nuevos principios del urbanismo.* Madrid: Alianza.
de Torres, P. (2016). Ciudadanos cosmopolitas en red: la dimensión internacional de las ciudades. *II Congreso Ciudades Inteligentes: Grupo TECMA RED.* https://www.esmartcity.es/comunicaciones/ciudadanos-cosmopolitas-red-dimension-internacional-ciudades. Accessed 2 February 2020.
Mercado, P. (2015). Cuerpo y ciudad: el habitante. *Blog Letra Urbana,* incluido en Espacio Urbano, edición 13. Buenos Aires. http://letraurbana.com/articulos/cuerpo-y-ciudad-el-habitante. Accessed 30 July 2019.
Narváez Tijerina, A. B. (2008). La ciudad red y la utopía: el surgimiento de un imaginario hegemónico. *Iztapalapa Revista de Ciencias Sociales y Humanidades, 64–65*(29), 63–91.
Reyes-Guarnizo, A. B. (2014). De los imaginarios colectivos a la apropiación del territorio: Un recorrido conceptual. *Revista Bitácora Urbano Territorial, 24*(1), 1–21.
Salgado, S. M., & Camarena, M. (2018). De la unión a la expansión generalizada de los "otros". Mismidad y recentramiento interurbano. In M. Camarena Luhrs (Coord.), *Aprender de las Ciudades* (pp. 82–112). México: Posgrado en Urbanismo, UNAM.
Scribano, A. (2010). Filosofía de las ciencias sociales y estudios sociales sobre los cuerpos. In C. Hidalgo & V. Tozzi (Comp.), *Filosofía para la ciencia y*

la sociedad. Indagaciones en honor a Félix Gustavo Schuster (pp. 205–220). Buenos Aires: CICCUS-CLACSO.

Scribano, A. (2013). Cuerpos, emociones y sociedad. *Revista Latinoamericana de Estudios sobre Cuerpos, Emociones y Sociedad, 4*(10), 93–113.

Streeck, W. (2017). *¿Cómo terminará el capitalismo? ensayos sobre un sistema en decadencia.* Madrid: Edición Traficantes de Sueños.

CHAPTER 4

Emotive Culture and Belonging: Sensibilities, Fears and Moralities in an Urban Context

Mauro Koury

This article bases its central argument on the notion of belonging, experienced in the processes of daily interaction of the insertion of individuals in the city and among themselves, as a set of selves constituted in the intersubjective process in situations of exchange with others close and generalized (Mead 1934), in diverse and continuous contexts, tense and conflicting, pregnant with common fears, in the contemporary urban experience. The idea of belonging here is embedded in the more general conception of what I call emotive culture (Koury 2017, p. 13–30).

Emotive culture is defined as the continuous process of exchanges and confrontations between individuals and groups in everyday situations, which allows the establishment of bonds or their opposite, distancing and conflict. This concept of emotive culture is close to what Simmel (1908, 1910) calls *sociation*, Geertz's notion of *ethos* (1978), and what Peter Berger & Tomas Luckmann (2005) define as *symbolic universes*—multiple arenas of cultural signs that shape the codes of experience. Arenas

M. Koury (✉)
Universidade Federal Da Paraíba, João Pessoa, Brazil

© The Author(s), under exclusive license to Springer Nature
Switzerland AG 2021
A. Scribano et al. (eds.), *Cities, Capitalism and the Politics of Sensibilities*,
https://doi.org/10.1007/978-3-030-58035-3_4

63

are always expanding and subject to a multiplicity of interpretations of contextualized situations.

Emotive culture is the process of setting up an action towards the other and experimenting with it, as in Simmelian sociality (Simmel 1908, 1910)[1], which allows individual and collective experiences to be carried out in situations where they are felt, translated and shared in the communicational game in action. Emotive culture, like a shared network of experiences, allows the individual and his/her peers to feel integrated or part of a place. This place is lived as an environment of belonging, in which the world is lived and experienced as a lived world.

The sense of belonging (Goffman 2014), as the feeling of being part of the place, concerns the community of affections generated as an emotive and belonging culture, as an urban locus. This article analyses part of the material collected during the fieldwork in the city of João Pessoa, capital of Paraíba, Brazil, for a research project on common fears (Koury 2002a)[2]. It seeks to understand how processes of construction of similarity and dissimilarity are formed and are informed daily as an emotive culture, supported by the daily experiences of exchange and the formation of common bonds between peers. And they give meaning to a common emotive and moral set and, based on the affirmation of a feeling of belonging, the ways of overcoming the fear of the other and the daily strategies used in the affirmation of personal and group dignity as recognition. This statement is in relation to the civilizing offensives (Regt 2017) coming from the official city, and the stigmas and threats to which they are subjected daily, coming from the local media, or the prejudice about the community of belonging and its residents.

It analyses the processes felt as opposed and complementary in the actions and affirmations socially disposed of in the permanent process of building new meanings of belonging. It tells a little about the history and current events of one of the oldest neighbourhoods in the city, the Varadouro neighbourhood, from the perspective of its residents[3], exploring the issue of belonging, solidarity networks and everyday social fears faced by the resident population, whether in relation to the

---

[1] Also close to Schütz's (1974) notion of the *lifeworld*, as an experienced intersubjective world; and the Arendt's (1993) conformation of the *common world*.

[2] Umbrella project in development at the GREM Grupo de Pesquisa em Antropologia e Sociologia das Emoções (*Research Group on Anthropology and Sociology of Emotions*), under the coordination of the author.

[3] The names of the interviewees used in this article are fictional names to guarantee their anonymity.

commonplace of their existence, either in response to themselves and to others about how the city sees them, as a neighbourhood and as a neighbourhood pointed out as containing high levels of violence and poverty.

It is an ethnographic account in which the interviewees lend their voice in defining the thematic contents and in constituting a problematization of their neighbourhood and their relations with it, and with what the city thinks about it. Categories such as emotive culture, belonging and solidarity networks are considered here because they are presented in the interviewees' narratives as constituting the present world or as nostalgia for the past (Halbwachs 1995), alongside categories such as fears and violence, as interfaces of their view of themselves and their peers as residents of a neighbourhood, and the city that imposes stigmas, impressions, notions and fields of planning and control on them.

It is not a study on memory, although it is based on life stories and the interviewees' memories. It is, rather, a study of fears, not only the great fears that make up the current Brazilian and Western urban culture, but, above all, the common fears, where the interviewees can oppose themselves to other residents, making up an emotive culture and a moral nucleus, and with the city, and reflect and revive possibilities of belonging and solidarity, as well as redefining the contents imposed on them by the official city[4], as a violent, dangerous neighbourhood, and resizing the maps of solidarity and tension to which they are exposed and that make possible the constitution of their daily lives.

The article starts from the reconstitution of the neighbourhood today, emphasizing its population of residents and regulars, to understand how they elucidate living in the neighbourhood. It brings up the discussion that belonging is a notion lived in the tension between yesterday and today, between self and other, between solidarity and fear and, finally, between situating themselves and situating others, similar or dissimilar, and being situated by them.

---

[4] *Official city* refers to the moral instances represented by the governmental and administrative institutions of the city, as well as of other instances such as the media, churches and local power groups, instituted or in institution.

Introducing the Neighbourhood

The Varadouro neighbourhood, bordering the Sanhauá River, is a point of reference and birthplace of the capital of the State of Paraíba, Brazil, and where commerce and local politics were concentrated until the end of the nineteenth century and the first decades of the 20th. It is part of the so-called lower city and the city's historic core.

Today it is a run down neighbourhood, and it survives as a point of commercial establishments for the low-income population and services, with mechanical workshops, graphics, construction and office supplies. It houses a poor population in its narrow streets and decaying and poorly maintained buildings, along with a large informal market, consisting of street vendors, bars and places of prostitution. It also hosts a fluctuating population of workers who live from cargo transportation and alternative urban transport to the neighbourhoods of the capital and other cities in the interior of the state and neighbouring states.

In the narrow strip between the Sanhauá River and the railroad line, small plots of simple houses extend with a population composed of unemployed and underemployed people, mostly from the interior. They live off the informal trade and fish for seafood and crabs in the vast mangrove of the river.

Varadouro is also home to the capital's bus and train stations, and most of the city's bus lines converge there. The bus terminal for all neighbourhoods in the city and municipalities in the metropolitan region of the capital is close to the bus station, which facilitates the coming and going of residents, as well as the circulation of city dwellers. Thus, there is a huge influx of people who do not live or work in the region, but who are attracted to it, either by the popular commerce that dominates the place or by the bus terminals and urban and inter-municipal and state trains.

Along the narrow streets of the neighbourhood, next to many abandoned buildings, destroyed or in the process of being destroyed, there are inns and cheap hotels that shelter both a population that comes from the interior to the capital, as well as sexual links with local prostitution. In Varadouro, on a walk through its streets, it is possible to notice bars, with doors and balconies, or with a lounge where chairs and tables are arranged, extended at night to the sidewalk space, many functioning as houses of prostitution: besides the living room where the bar is situated and where women are waiting for customers, there is a corridor with rooms to serve them. Many women live in their own houses of prostitution, while others, in greater numbers, live in rented rooms in the neighbourhood or other neighbourhoods and attend the place professionally. The local market, next to the bus stops that give access to the municipalities, concentrates a mobile population of people who work in the capital and come to it for study, business, or sightseeing. It also congregates a considerable number of snack bars and bars close to the bus stops and facing the market that serves this population, alongside prostitutes, street vendors, workers and local residents.

Varadouro is a central district of the city, with a lot of movement, despite its evident decay. The movement is guaranteed by the state, interstate and municipal bus terminals and the city's railway line, and by the concentration of diversified street commerce, cheap accommodation, a varied public market and the concentration of cheap prostitution in the capital.[5]

Varadouro extends further along a strip of land located between the banks of the Sanhauá River and the railroad, and crosses the Porto do Capim Community. In it lives a needy population, in simple houses in a kind of street. The place is celebrated as the first attempt at a port in the capital: Porto do Capim.

The Porto do Capim Community is an easily demarcated place in Varadouro. The simple houses make a kind of street between the railway line, the mangrove, and the Sanhauá estuary, opening onto the other

---

[5] Since the end of the 1990s, the Varadouro neighbourhood has been the subject of discussion about its revitalization. Today it is part of the so-called historic centre of the city. This process plans to recover the historic site of the neighbourhood and establish a tourist and leisure hub for the city. The fact is that this that will change the profile of the neighbourhood and its inhabitants. Many of the local residents, street vendors and participants in low-income sex market in the neighbourhood, gave uneasy testimonies about the possibility of their gradual eviction from the area. In the 1990s, a first stage of revitalization was inaugurated, concentrating bars and cafes that have become a leisure centre for young people and intellectuals in the city and a tourist spot for the most acclaimed. At the beginning of the twenty-first century, however, the place went into serious decline and the consuming public went back to the seafront (in the upscale neighbourhoods of Tambaú and Manaíra) and the 'university' neighbourhood in the south (Bancários). As of 2016, there was a new impetus concerning the revitalization of the historic centre and an offensive towards the expulsion of residents and 'regulation' of street commerce and local sex. This is a reality that has been experienced with apprehension by the residents and local workers, but has also been accompanied by a movement of struggle and solidarity from the city's intellectual sectors in the sense of supporting the conservation and maintenance of local residents and preserving the historic site.

streets of the neighbourhood. These are streets where a low-income population lives, in houses and buildings in a poor state of repair, sharing the space with informal commerce, mechanical workshops and services, and bars and houses of prostitution.

Porto do Capim, in Varadouro, was once an important centre for the entry and exit of goods from the city, in its origin. Much of the goods that supplied the city were unloaded there (Tavares da Silva 1997). In the 1930s, a vast project for the construction of a modern port was aimed at the place where there was traditionally an anchorage called Porto do Capim, not made possible by technical and political issues (Joffily 1983). The work was embargoed and later put aside, and its funds transferred to the modernization of the seaport of Cabedelo, the city that makes up Greater João Pessoa.

The transfer of funds, according to Agamenon, caused "… the abandonment of the neighbourhood… and now… only unemployed people, houses all falling down, and people turning around as they can … and the weakening of the place…" Martina informs us that, with the diversion from the port to Cabedelo, "… the city began to turn its back on the river and started towards the sea… And in that, as always, the rich got along… they moved on until they reached the beach, the remedied poor were forcibly moved to the *brenhas* (remote location)… And those who had nothing like us, the way was to stay, when he no longer had an address, he raised, at the back of another little house, a covered front and we stayed there. I have two kids myself, see, one for my daughter with two boys of hers and the other for my boy who was funny with a lady and brought her here to live with him. Everything is tight, but it's the way."

In the old and deteriorated buildings, or even in those already destroyed, a poor population lives. Many of these properties are rented at low cost and many others have been transformed into rows of "rental rooms", or small conglomerates of huts among the ruins of the older buildings. These are ruined buildings, shacks, tenements, mixed with ruins of old factories, warehouses and small workshops. In Varadouro, the simple houses are permeated by old warehouses close to the berth, all of them almost unused, and small mechanical workshops that manage to survive. The houses and shacks are located, in turn, between the edge of the mangrove and the end of the old buildings.

The current population is made up of people from the countryside, as well as those "born and raised" in the capital. The neighbourhood had been more populated before when it was important for the city's general commerce. With the closure of warehouses and factories, there was a dispersion and interruption of investments in the area, which is no longer economically attractive.

It's Good to Live in Varadouro

Despite the interviewees' homesick and sentimental comments about the neighbourhood of yesteryear, compared to the neighbourhood's decay today, it is good to live in Varadouro. They claim that the neighbourhood, because it is central, makes life easier for those who live in it, either through the formal and informal commerce that thrives around it, allowing proximity to the place where they live and work or because there are local bus terminals, which makes it easy to get to any part of the city with just one ticket; or even by the river estuary that allows crab fishing, as well as being close to cheap leisure areas such as the *Bica* and the *Lagoa*.

The big question posed in the neighbourhood by the residents is its decay, although they know they are still in the neighbourhood because of it. The revitalization movement in the 1990s divided the opinions of the informants. Some saw the city's interest in rebuilding the neighbourhood as benefiting it and local living. Others, the majority, saw the revitalization as another threat to the residents of the neighbourhood.

The extension of the revitalization process, for the latter, will increase the cost of housing and displacement to areas far from the centre. The discussion slowed down, towards the beginning of the year 2000, due to the weakening of the process that had made a lot of noise at the end of the last century. Occasionally it surfaced, and it accelerated from 2016, when the revitalization project was discussed again and official eviction policies began to run,[6] increasing the residents' fear.

---

[6] Since 2010, a Movement for the Permanence of the Porto do Capim Community has reinforced the movement of residents. Local artists, intellectuals, academics from different areas (anthropologists, architects, sociologists, social workers, psychologists, among others) from the local universities, reinforce the need to preserve the community, its antiquity in the place, its livelihood which depends on the surrounding environment, as well as the historical importance of the area to the city. Not long ago, at the end of 2019, an eviction order was suppressed by the movement's solidarity and struggle through the occupation of the district with shows and events, petitions and intensive mobilization of social networks on the "absurdity" of the official eviction act, and technical arguments that overturned the official arguments, suppressing (or postponing) the eviction order.

Cruz, who has lived in the neighbourhood for fifty years, speaks of attachment to the place and the differences between the past and the present. She indicates the departure of your neighbours at different times to other locations in the city, at the time of housing developments, and also to rental houses in other neighbourhoods and slums in the city. She informs us that: "The neighbourhood is gone... Now there is one or the other that we are intimate with. I talk to everyone... but I no longer have that thing of going to the house, having a party on the street, talking on the sidewalks. Now everything that is in your house, when there is still a house because when it is not a workshop, it is a whore establishment. The neighbourhood is no longer what I knew, but it is still a good neighbourhood to live in: close to everything and easy to go anywhere." The feeling of loss is evident in Cruz's speech.

According to Robério, the Varadouro that "was once the most important neighbourhood in the city... now, it is just chagrin! Where I live is still cool... but it's a great mix. I have small children and I no longer let them live on the street. First: a lot of movement, people who come and go that you don't control; then, the easy-living girls and their audience; decent residents are almost gone... Last year I lost a friend who lived here... had to leave due to the increase in rent. Now he is far away, in a horrible place... The place he left here is now a workshop... What makes people who still live here? It is already used and the proximity to everything. In my case, because of the workplace, because a few blocks ahead and I'm already there setting up my tent..."

When asking if Varadouro is a dangerous neighbourhood and what you are afraid of, the answer is dry and clear, "we are not afraid of anything". What seems to contradict the afflictions about the decay of the neighbourhood, the gradual expulsion of its residents, the fact that they can no longer let their children play on the sidewalks, living with the houses of prostitution in place, etc. The word fear, for residents, is associated with urban violence as discussed today by the media: Varadouro as an area of thefts, murders, drugs and drug sales points, etc., and not because of the public's differentiation, scarcity and loss of links between residents, as there were in the past. The answer that "nobody has to be afraid here" emphasizes the statement that, "despite being poor", Varadouro "is a peaceful place".

Belonging and Feeling of Discrimination

The emphasis on the tranquillity of the place responds to the stigmas of the city that qualifies the neighbourhood as a dangerous environment: thieves and drugs.[7] The media publicizes the place as a problem neighbourhood: a violent and dangerous area. Undoing this image is a constant concern: Varadouro and its poorest nucleus carry the image of danger that a large part of the people who live there do not agree with and reject. The image is seen by residents as "mounted": by the media, by the official city and by the people of the city, to denigrate the already battered feelings of dignity and local recognition, turning residents "into suspects", "because we are poor and weak".

The image created by people in the neighbourhood, however, is the opposite or inverse to that of the media. They advocate the neighbourhood as a calm, peaceful and good place to live, and "the place where the city was born".

Residents face the stigma of being deemed *dangerous*: for Euclídia, "we are poor, clean, honest and God-fearing, we are not marginals! The people here are good, they know each other, they are workers and they struggle to survive". Euclídia's statement demonstrates how much these people share the social, moral and emotional pressure on them, and how much they suffer from trying to respond positively (they are *good people*), and contrary to the images of danger and violence that hang over them and the neighbourhood.

José adds: "we miss the improvement, the work for us... many are leaving for this reason and we no longer have the same partnership as before with the neighbourhood that was scarce. But we who live here are all good people. I don't see anyone bad around here, only if it is the people from outside who come here to do evil and we take the blame."

Another item in the discussion about fears among the interviewees, when confronted with the issue of the neighbourhood's image by the official city and reinvigorated by the media, is that, if there is violence in the neighbourhood, it is not from its residents, but from *people who come from outside*. It is the *outsiders* who denigrate the image of the place, not the residents.

---

[7] In GREM's survey of print and online newspapers, blogs, and television and radio news in the city, between 2000 and 2019, Varadouro appears frequently in news reports on policy issues, with a particular focus on: theft, delinquency, and the consumption and sale of drugs.

Respondents present Varadouro as a quiet and good place to live, despite the emptiness and visible decay, and not as a dangerous area, as the media claims. They explain that violence, if it exists, comes from outside: "by the trade movement, with the arrival and departure of people of all kinds and from all corners; for local prostitution; or along the *border roads* with other neighbourhoods where the bandits come from outside, make a mess in here and tarnish the neighbourhood's credibility in the city", as Antonio said.

Common Fears

The question about the feeling of fear analytically has a mosaic that portrays a problem of different fears of the daily sociability in the neighbourhood, and the neighbourhood in relation to the city. One of the items that gives consistency to local fears talks about the city's view of the neighbourhood. Residents feel discriminated against as city dwellers because they live in the neighbourhood. Therefore, there is a need to combat the vision of "problem neighbourhood", with that of "quiet neighbourhood"; and to present violence as an action by *outsiders*.

Another item speaks of the fears of a visible threat, in this case, the process of revitalizing the neighbourhood, and the attempts to expel the residents: and they identify it as violence *from outside*, which persecutes and afflicts them. Affliction is present in Vitorina's narrative, "... at any time we can be thrown out... Today the neighbours are scarce, and we live in the middle of haunted houses, everything falling... There is no more than good old climate... more is my place, good to live. In a square not even dead... but I'm scared of *men* (referring to the official city) to put me here to run..."

This mosaic satisfies the meaning structure (Geertz 1978) set in the everyday plots of sociability that make up the local meaning networks. In them, fear appears as the main fibre of the braided fabric in the current daily lives of residents, in relation to themselves and in relation to the neighbourhood and the city. It is a fibre that disturbs the local emotive culture, in the intertwining of individual and collective memory between past and present time.

This fibre exposes residents tensely suspended between what has been lived and now as a commonplace of suffering, but also tensions for every resident who lives the problem unevenly. The situations of fear and threats cause distress, shame and embarrassment in everyone, and a feeling of failure (Koury 2019), loneliness and moral and emotional fragmentation. These are situations where fears arise in social relationships and are felt by people who experience them through the idea of personal failure (Koury 2002b).

The insecurity to which they are exposed, as poor or as degraded, causes them, on the one hand, to deny stigma, confronting an opposite view and, on the other, to face stigma as fatality (Koury 2018). In both possibilities, fear, the feeling of risk, or the evaluation of others is considered through the emotion of shame (Elias 1993; Scheff 2016; Koury 2003, 2017).

Shame seems to delimit the structures of the meaning of the place and mark the residents as dissimilar from those who inhabit the other neighbourhoods of the city. A feeling of fear pervades them in the face of the modernizing offensives of the official city and their consequences for each one of their lives (Koury 2008). Among the fears felt, in addition to the fear of being expelled from their homes, there is concern about work, the fear of losing it or of not finding it again. Working, having the means to support the family, and providing conditions for their children's studies, form a part of the informants' concerns:

> "We know the fate of those who don't have a job, right? It is worse than the street of bitterness", said Josefa. Pedro, unemployed for almost two years, already almost 60, reports that "... the life of the unemployed is hard. After a while the colleagues avoid you, the children look at you differently and even the woman doesn't want to do the wedding duties anymore... we... become shit!...I make beaks: seeing popcorn; carrying shopping; I wash the car; I do everything for my family to have something to eat. But not having the right, not having a profession like the one I had... makes us lose respect with ourselves and everyone in relation to us." Being employed is one of the guiding points of interviewees' inner security. The loss of a job increases isolation: colleagues disappear, self-esteem and confidence are lost. It also reflects in the comparison of the current neighbourhood with that of "the old days".

For Eufrásia, "today we no longer find the comfort we had with the neighbourhood." She refers to the solidarity network of the past among the residents of the neighbourhood. With the emptying, the neighbourhood is unrecognizable. The houses left are abandoned or turned into sites of commerce or services. With the emptying, the neighbourhood networks were broken; there is no longer a solidary exchange or affection, nor the parties and sharing of old. Now there is no one else, and whoever remains is dispersed: "one here, another there, with no common life", adds Marquinhos.

The emptying of the neighbourhood and the growing number of ruined and empty buildings, together with commerce, provoke not only the feeling of breaking ties of solidarity, but also another type of fear: the presence of *outsiders* who invade unoccupied neighbouring buildings to sleep, and said Isidro, "to do something that sucks."

The fear about those who look for a place to sleep and do "what is not good" is associated, according to Isidro, with the "males and girls from *outside*, who look for the neighbourhood for *things* and melt the name of the place in the city and that of the residents: our and honest people", but also with the personal fear of having the house invaded by those who wander among the ruined buildings, increasing insecurity.

Eulália follows Isidro's path and affirms fear with a particular fact. She reports that her land was invaded by young people from another neighbourhood to play football, and that they abuse her when she was going to complain. She tells how she was woken up at night by noise and found that two couples were setting up shacks to live in at the back of her house. "I screamed, my son and I went out, me with the broom, and we put the *invaders* to run... But we are unsure of what will happen tomorrow! What if they come back, what if there's something else and I can't contain it? The neighbours are few and we don't have the same approach as before. The houses are abandoned or are of recent invasion. I live near Pedro, but he is old and sick..."

Pedro, who lives close to Eulália, adds: "we no longer have peace. The people come by the railway line and invade everything, steal the coconuts, bananas and that's why. It's all personal from the outside..."

The fears are of *outsiders*, who cross the railway line or who arrive from I don't know where; but the fear remains from a diffuse feeling of nostalgia for the "past", which speaks of the progressive emptying of the neighbourhood. Today, in this diffuse configuration of fear, there is longer a feeling of collectivity present "in the past"; not because they changed the residents, but because they left! With the absence came isolation, relationship difficulties, but also the feeling of ageing.

About Ageing

There is no longer the sharing of yesteryear, living in Varadouro is today synonymous with isolation and fear of what will come. There are almost no neighbours to talk to, the empty buildings are occupied by commerce or by "people who arrive at night and stay for a few days" and use the space to "do things...", and only increase, according to Ernilda, the bad reputation of the neighbourhood in the city.

This feeling of loneliness increases over the years and reaches the ageing consciousness of those who stayed in the neighbourhood. The children have grown up, some of them remain in place in *puxadinhos* (self-construction) in their parents' houses, but not for long: when they can, they move in with their new family. Or, in Cruz's case, the house serves as a shelter for daughters, grandchildren and sons-in-law, when one of them, without a husband, works outside the home, or when the husband of one of them loses his job and can no longer support a home.

However, Cruz's solidarity arrangements that serve as support to the family when in financial or emotional crisis are also felt as provisional. The house, which houses them all, becomes a kind of isolated unit in the neighbourhood. The neighbours are gone; there is no more the affective exchange, of favours, the security of the collective of before. Today Cruz says she does not know "almost anyone in these parts". She points out one house and another where people considered close live, with whom he exchanges "some ideas", but, "there is no intimacy". Old age arriving increases the feeling of loneliness. You no longer have partners for confidences[8]; "We get more and more alone, look around and no longer have friends..." They all left, some inland, accompanying the children who grew up, and others scattered throughout the capital's neighbourhoods. "Once in a while, we meet... but each one's time is different now, and we keep reminiscing about the past and soon go back to chores and deal with it daily and spend a lot of time without seeing each other."

"The neighbourhood is no longer the same", continues Cruz. "It used to be better, but it's the neighbourhood where I live... I don't want to leave. Here it is close to everything: we walk to a lot of places, life is

---

[8] Cruz refers to children as great children; they have the closeness, intimacy and trust of a close family that she thanks "every day to God for giving me this happiness". But, she adds "...children are children. They are more concerned with receiving support... and, certain things that an old woman like me feels, no matter how open and secure the relationship between us may be, there is no way to talk to them...".

cheaper and easier to live... although, less safe. We are in solitude, with a desire for the proximity of yesteryear, for camaraderie and warmth in difficult times, for friends, neighbours, one covering and welcoming the other in need, one seeing the other's house and helping to protect...".

Socorro extends Cruz's narrative and states that "...we get old and become insecure: we see the children grow up, we see the grandchildren arrive, but it gets more alone... And we are afraid: with an enormous fear of feeling pain, of dying and having no one with us; of not recognizing the things where we live, with the *news* that appears here... of looking for old acquaintances and only having one or the other... and we are left alone and making everything strange. If a new neighbour appears, we find it strange, if we see the boys from the other neighbourhood around here; we are suspicious, afraid that they will do something with us... But this is all about old people... the corner where I live is my corner, I just leave here for the cemetery...".

VIOLENCE COMES FROM OUTSIDE TO INSIDE

The neighbourhood is still quiet, according to the informants. They try to undo the image of a violent neighbourhood that the media and the official city insist on maintaining. Violence comes *from the outside to the inside*, by emptying the place it allows other people to use the empty spaces to seek shelter or to commit illegal acts: but it is not the neighbourhood, it is the *outside*. The departure of former neighbours, comrades, isolates the residents ever more: the neighbourhood no longer has the coexistence of old, which increases loneliness and insecurity, but this is attributed to *old age*.

The fear of ageing is what favours insecurity, for Amaro, "the older we get, the more afraid we are... This is the *thing* of old people alone! But, if I leave here, I die much sooner than God wants, because my whole life is here, and I can remember; and outside, what will be left to me, except a house, perhaps better, more sure, worse, and I in the least of my sentimentality!"

Amaro has lived in the same place for 75 years. It has many memories in place: of the *cachaças* partying with friends; the *many* girlfriends; employment at the Matarazzo factory; the wife now dead; his parents; brothers, children and grandchildren; and neighbours. He lives isolated, insecure, afraid and, mainly, homesick. But, unlike other feelings, for him, ambivalently, homesickness "is a damned good feeling from a good time, full of difficulties as it is a full life, but there was never a shortage of food, like now... I always had a job, raised my children, saw the neighbourhood sink, with the residents leaving in search of a better or more affordable place, and I stayed and watched everything change, and it remains my song. I know everything here, every stone, and every fallen piece: it is my corner..."

Augustina, speaking of her fears, describes the changes in the neighbourhood in the more than 40 years she has lived there. She speaks of ageing; she talks about the children who are leaving; she speaks of "*outsiders*" and reports invasions of homes; she talks about young people today who play ball in her backyard and make fun of her and don't respect her; but, also, she recalls the "old days". She recalls the solidary neighbourhood; remembers the beautiful trees in her backyard; of the small community garden behind her house, and she misses it. Longing that soon turns into fear of loneliness and insecurity of not having anyone else to turn to.

She speaks of her fear of having her home invaded again, or of being robbed. She says that the neighbourhood today "has a lot of bad people" and she, alone, is "cowering for fear of being robbed and even killed". The fear of thieves, of evildoers, she knows, is the result of the stories she hears on the radio "all day", says that she does not know any case nearby, except "the pranks of the boys and these people who invade our place." She associates fear with loneliness and the "outsiders who invade our place", and what the radio says happens all the time in the city and "here in Varadouro."

In the neighbourhood, the fear is directed at the "outsiders" who inhabit the empty buildings, or who wander in the silence between one ruin and another. They are the sniffers, the stoners, and the bad people (os *safados*), among other local denominations. There is also the fear of the police, due to the brutality with which they deal with the situations which they are called upon to resolve: the fights of couples, the theft of fruit from the backyards, to contain one or another drunk, etc.

Lack of work and lack of perspective are situations that cause anxiety and fear. The idea of personal failure and weakness generates personal and collective discomfort and refers to a feeling of intimidation towards the future.

The fear of being affected by unemployment creates anguish. They all have stories of neighbours, family members, if not of themselves, in the difficult periods of lack of work and the lack of hope of "life-improving".

Whoever has a business, like Ermelindo, is afraid of going bankrupt. He is afraid of not selling enough to replenish the stock, and not being able to support the family. Ermelindo talks about the fear that "...it scares us all the time because we who live on our own know that things have gotten much worse, but what to do but keep trying... But the chill in the belly has been constant... when we think like now about tomorrow..."

Conclusion

Banal situations fill the daily lives of residents of Varadouro. These situations are interspersed with a sentimental vision of a past in which there was a greater number of inhabitants, a better quality of life, and greater solidarity between neighbours. It was a place of cordiality and affection in social relations, and solidarity in different situations such as: preparing parties at one or the other's home; the celebration of children's birthdays and weddings; collective preparation of street parties; festivities of São João and São Pedro; and in dramatic situations: like job loss, illness or death of one or another resident.

The decay of the neighbourhood; fear of expulsion; the anguish of personal ageing and the deterioration of the place; the inability to be able to support themselves and their family gives rise to insecurity and the feeling of social exclusion. Ambivalent feelings that compound the struggle for the permanence and defence of the neighbourhood against the stigmas of the official city that portrays it as violent, live side by side with the feeling of helplessness and the intimidation of others (from outside, from the official city, from the media) that do not stop "disturbing us, here".

Varadouro, in the comparative ambivalence of yesterday and today, is remaking the comprehensive bases and structures of meaning about the residents and the neighbourhood as a whole. Fears and their confrontations—seen towards the future, as a permanent threat; or, towards the past, filled with sentimentality—compose the scenarios of loss and fragmentation of the local emotive culture, increasing personal and collective fears about the now and the near future, and shaking the sense of belonging, by breaking and pulverizing the network links of solidarity remembered and lived in the past. This is what exacerbates the tense relations with the official city more, and increases the feeling of loneliness and isolation of the inhabitants of the neighbourhood, who observe themselves as outsiders in the place that they insist on calling their own.

REFERENCES

Arendt, H. (1993). *A dignidade da política*. Rio de Janeiro: Delume-Dumará.

Berger, P., & Luckmann, T. (2005). *A construção social da realidade* (25a ed.). Petrópolis: Vozes.

Elias, N. (1993). *O processo civilizador*. Rio de Janeiro: Jorge Zahar.

Geertz, C. (1978). *A interpretação das culturas*. Rio de Janeiro: Editora Jorge Zahar.

Goffman, E. (2014). Sobre o resfriamento do marca: alguns aspectos da adaptação ao fracasso. *RBSE Revista Brasileira de Sociologia Da Emoção, 13*(39), 266–283.

Halbwachs, M. (1995). *Les cadres sociaux de le mémoire*. Paris: Plón.

Joffily, J. (1983). *Porto político*. Rio de Janeiro: Civilização Brasileira.

Koury, M. (2002a). *Medos Corriqueiros: a construção social da semelhança e da dessemelhança entre os habitantes urbanos das cidades brasileiras na contemporaneidade*. João Pessoa: Edições do GREM.

Koury, M. (2002b). Medos Corriqueiros: em busca de uma aproximação metodológica. *Cronos, 3*(1), 94–101.

Koury, M. (2003). *Sociologia da emoção: o Brasil urbano sob a ótica do luto*. Petrópolis: Vozes.

Koury, M. (2008). *De que João Pessoa tem medo? Uma abordagem em Antropologia das Emoções*. Coleção Cadernos do GREM, v. 6. João Pessoa: Editora Universitária UFPB/Edições do GREM.

Koury, M. (2017). *Etnografias urbanas sobre pertença e medos na cidade*. Coleção Cadernos do GREM, v. 11. Recife/João Pessoa: Bagaço/Edições do GREM.

Koury, M. (2018). *Sobre perdas, dor, morte e morrer na de cidade de João Pessoa-PB*. Coleção Cadernos do GREM, v. 13. Recife/João Pessoa: Bagaço/Edições do GREM.

Koury, M. (2019). Sobre Erving Goffman e a análise do fracasso em The Presentation of Self in Everyday Life. *Dilemas, 12*(3), 525–540.

Mead, G. (1934). *Mind, Self and Society*. Chicago: The University of Chicago Press.

Regt, A. D. (2017). Ofensiva civilizadora: do conceito sociológico ao apelo moral. *RBSE Revista Brasileira de Sociologia Da Emoção, 16*(47), 137–153.

Scheff, T. (2016). A vergonha no self e na sociedade. In M. Koury & R. Barbosa (Org.), *A vergonha no self e na sociedade* (pp. 63–109). Recife/João Pessoa: Bagaço/Edições do GREM.

Schütz, A. (1974). *El problema de la realidad*. Buenos Aires: Amorrortu.

Silva, L. M. (1997). Forma urbana e cotidiano na evolução de João Pessoa. *Saeculum, 3*, 161–186.

Simmel, G. (1910). How Is Society Possible? *American Journal of Sociology*, *16*(3), 372–391.

Simmel, G. (1908). *Soziologie: Untersuchungen über die Formen der Vergesellschaftung*. Berlin: Duncker & Humboldt.

CHAPTER 5

Urban Foodscapes and Media Horizons: A New Gastronomic Experience

Tito Vagni

INTRODUCTION

Food processes are treated here as one of the areas of greatest innovation for media theory, despite the coldness, particularly in the European context, which is recorded about food as a key communication issue. This is probably a legacy due to the classical sociological perspective, for which food has always been considered an appendix of society (Bourdieu 1987; Durkheim 1915; Elias 1994; Simmel 1997). Between food and society, there is a constant tension that tends to favour the centrality of social issues over food issues, considering food a problematic node of life in common and the mirror of a wider social situation. The media studies, especially those of Anglo Saxon origin, which were the first to systematically problematize the cultural question of food, seem to have moved away from this perspective, as demonstrated by the important work of Kathleen LeBesco and Peter Naccarato dedicated to the "food in popular culture" (2018, 1). This book, which adds to a long series of works of

T. Vagni (✉)
Centre D'Études Sur L'Actuel et Le Quotidien, Paris Descartes University, Paris, France

© The Author(s), under exclusive license to Springer Nature Switzerland AG 2021
A. Scribano et al. (eds.), *Cities, Capitalism and the Politics of Sensibilities*, https://doi.org/10.1007/978-3-030-58035-3_5

the same genre (Bradley 2016; Leer and Povlsen 2018; Phillipov 2017; Rousseau 2012), has the merit of focusing attention on a neuralgic theme of the present, proposing food as one of the last territories occupied by the cultural industry, and therefore as a macro genre of mass culture. Recognizing food and food practices as *topos* of our time is fundamental because in this way attention is given to one of the areas in which the mediatization of social and cultural processes produces the most pervasive and evident effects.

The perspective that I propose here tends to dwell on the "effects" of electronic and digital media on food and the gastronomic experience. What is intended to show is that in contact with the cultural industry, gastronomy has profoundly changed its connotations, taking on a new form, involving dishes, cooks and consumption practices. Food is taking on the form of the media and culture of this particular historical time: it can no longer be traced only to its material aspects, but must be taken into consideration as a communicative and cultural form that has gone beyond the edible dimension. To do so, an ecological perspective must be adopted (Benjamin 1969; McLuhan 1994; Postman 1979), which tries to read together the oscillations of the media system and those of the food system, considering them together and not as separate spheres that randomly come into contact.

Through a mediaological analysis of contemporary food phenomena, we will, therefore, try to show that we have fully entered into digital food culture (Lewis 2020; Lupton 2018), and that, above all, we are faced with indistinguishability between food and media, which has changed the status of food and, consequently, the gastronomic sensibilities of contemporary users/consumers and their sensory complex.

Metropolis and the Boundless Pleasure of Food

The metropolitan streets have once again become one of the main stages of the gastronomic experience: it is increasingly common to come across a cooking show or restaurants that overlook the boulevard and prepare their dishes live, to entertain passers-by completely, taking up the tradition of the old craft shops, which invaded the streets with their workshop, an amphibious place of production and consumption. The street expresses all the libidinal nature of desire (Lyotard 2015), the route that is built which is always linked to the circumstance; it offers repeated satisfying possibilities and, at the same time, foreshadows an endless consumption, attracting the eye of the passer-by who begins to live immersed in pure consumption. The stimuli that impose themselves on his attention are unexpected opportunities or dangers, which transform the apparent continuum of the road into small segments of desire, ready to free themselves towards different directions. The vision of the food-market tunes the passer-by to an otherworldly dimension and leads him into a ghostly world where nothing seems precluded. As in a dream, the outpouring of goods eradicates the passer-by from the earthly condition and makes all forms of consumption appear plausible: the showcase is the device that leads back to the power of the instant and the immersion in a dream world (Benjamin 1996), pushing towards a possible future, as does contemporary gastronomic communication, which multiplies the images of food to satisfy the public's desire to see and know before eating; it is a form of consumption that never exhausts its function and places the user in a constant desiring tension. The road—like the contemporary media—lays the concrete psychological foundations for a complete loss of the limit. The pleasure found in it generates an intoxication due to the fluidity of events that appear to be unstoppable. The road imposes itself on the eye as an illiberal space in which reasonableness in food consumption gives way to the emotional shock that alters spatial and temporal perception, allowing a man to access joy through experiences of rare intensity. These are sensible pleasures in which the bodily sphere becomes predominant. It is the body itself that crosses every limit of the ego, that becomes the motor of action and perception. Every social actor is less an agent than an act. Each person differs infinitely, depending on the *kairos*, the occasions and situations that arise (Maffesoli 1995).

The consequence of this physical and psychological training, which Walter Benjamin compared to immersion in a "reservoir of electric energy tank" (2006) pushes the metropolitan type to the continuous search for the shock. But the metropolitan dimension, its seamless glitter, does not seem sufficient to fully satisfy the needs that it produces, so it is requiring of dream worlds, places with high intensity of stimuli, which can provide citizens accustomed to their environment with new revitalizing stimuli. In the spasmodic search for an escape from the world, temples of consumption are created, such as the passages or the great universal exhibitions, which create proximity between the various industrial products, such as to produce a paralysis of the capacity of perception, real hypnosis. But if Georg Simmel (1991) read the experience of the universal exhibition as pure *amüsement*, determined by the effect of extraordinary incoherence of heterogeneous goods, packed into a single context, a few decades later television marks a fracture concerning that kind of experience. It does not leave the spectator's reverie free in the face of objects, but it directs it decisively, making the object disappear behind its advertising. The TV is not a traditional shop window: in it, size, object and advertising are an inseparable whole. Advertising has built the scaffolding around the goods on which the consumer's desire will rest. Hence the need to enhance the "showcase quality of the objects", their seductive appearance. The arrangement of which Simmel writes achieves a centrality in television that goes beyond that of the object. With the language of television, it is no longer the indistinct set of goods that makes up a world and develops reciprocal relations in this coexistence; there is no longer any need to create in the metropolis enclaves of consumption, such as the Universal Exhibitions, department stores or shopping malls, in which to find a place other than ordinary life. TV goes beyond the mechanism of the exhibition because it becomes the world itself: the consumer is constantly immersed in his imagination, in contact with his screen and illuminated by its lights. The communication mechanism is no longer that of the frustrated look that seduces (Schiwelbusch 2015), typical of the showcase: the viewer is present, he feels part of an expanded narrative, which includes every fragment of television. The object itself becomes secondary, what counts is to tune into the narrative flow, that is to absorb its motifs, figures, ethics, to feel part of a more seductive world. Those who are outside this great tale of consumption, and buy goods according to their usefulness and price, are sidelined.

Electronic and digital media have therefore transported the phantasmagorical power of metropolitan shop windows into homes, with the proliferation of screens that radiate the need for consumption in the private sphere, but unlike the experience mediated by technology, the desire that matures in the open space of the metropolis cannot be amended, it is tactile, shocking and leaves no escape. It is an invitation to immerse oneself in the instant, while the television showcases, which lights up an endless multitude of heterogeneous desires, constantly postponing consumption. The eventual nature of street food anchors consumption in the instant, therefore in the present: in the street, time becomes uniform, it becomes a space in which the canonical division of meals disappears in favour of a more instinctive and ancestral condition of life. The street exalts man's animality because it takes him away from conventions, and instead it is in satisfying one's desires that man puts aside every primitive form of programming linked to subsistence and merges with one's present. The contemporary streets with their continuous audio-tactile stimuli are spaces de-formed by seduction. Street food enters this vortex as the spectre of scarcity gives way to the omnipresence of gastronomy (Baudrillard 1998). Shops, bakeries, restaurants, kiosks, pastry shops, posters, advertisements, shop window diners: the hyperstimulating environment in which the passer-by is immersed deprives him of control: the consumption of food abandons all forms of reasonableness to become a simple topos of pleasure. For this reason, in recent years, there has been an exponential increase in street food activities, apparently due to the contingency of an adverse economic scenario—in which to prefer commercial activities that require less investment and offer low-cost consumption—but driven, instead, by a consumerist afflatus, a form of pure consumerism (Featherstone 2007) linked to the desire for an informal and total cuisine, always available and sought after, spectacular and satisfying, transparent and as extensive as possible to every possible consumer.

Such a return to the street as a flow of goods, information and desires was triggered by the fortunate collision between gastronomy and the media. An unprecedented convergence between metropolitan and information flows are now allowed by food delivery services, i.e. digital applications that allow you to receive all sorts of consumer goods, even food products, very quickly at home. The functioning of these applications is perfectly summarized by the Deliveroo tagline, one of the main European food delivery companies: "Your favourite restaurants, delivered fast to your door". There is no longer any need to leave home to eat a meal, the home is becoming a hub into which the whole world converges. Foodora's tagline, a Berlin-based online food delivery company, focuses on another aspect, that of the user's laziness and Foodora's desire to make food consumption comfortable: "We deliver, you enjoy!" They have little in common with the take-aways of yesteryear; take-away food was a way of consuming food often linked to a lack of attention to food or the short time available for cooking, therefore a form of emergency consumption. Food delivery services understand and support these needs, but they give rise to a much more complex phenomenon: the home and, more generally, any private place from which it is possible to place orders, can become at any time the operations centre where the outside world converges. This is the most interesting aspect of any delivery service, the possibility of

finding immediate satisfaction for every desire that arises from a physi-
ological need or a whim. It is a sort of "Google effect" (Auletta 2009)
applied to the field of consumption: if you have a desire, just turn to
one of the delivery apps to satisfy it. Delivery food services combined
with the potential of the web, transform the physical place where you
work or spend your free time into a large boulevard of pleasure: digital
shop windows seduce the user into a whirlpool of stimuli, which for the
first time can be satisfied almost instantly. The food delivery services do
nothing but make possible and instantaneous a consumption that was
previously destined to be constantly procrastinated, with a series of post-
ponements that kept the user's desires in constant tension without ever
being able to fully satisfy them. Today the technical conditions exist to
make one's room coincide with the metropolis, and to transform every
vision of food into a moment of consumption.

THE CONVERGENCE CULTURE
AND THE "TRANSGASTRONOMY"

As we have seen, the metropolis and contemporary media can combine
and generate increased consumer experiences, i.e. the media can function
both as an extension of the metropolitan dimension and as its evolution.
The media, in fact, according to the perspective that is being adopted,
are environments in which human experience takes shape (Benjamin
1969; McLuhan 1994; Meyrowits 1985; Moores 2012). The relationship between media and places has had a relevant evolution, due to the
diffusion of digital languages, network technologies and mobile devices.
Pierre Levy's idea of "anthropological space" (1997) as plastic spaces that
arise from the interaction between people, small bubbles that form at the
moment of an encounter and then disappear, is one of the first and most
interesting formulations on the dislocation of human relations from the
physical space of the metropolis to the net. Significant advancement of the
reflection on these themes has been made recently by Danah Boyd (2015)
who, studying the relationship between young people and communication practices in social networks, dwelt on the concept of networked
publics, that is the space created by network technologies and the imagined community that emerges as a result of the intersection of people,
technologies and habits. Danah Boyd understands the public at the same
time as places and relational communities because it gives technology a
constituent power, that is, the ability to question old relational modes by

creating new forms of living. Also, social networks, as happened for electronic media, generate the collapse of social situations, but this happens with completely different modalities: the focus of the public is the essential element for the understanding of social situations, but as happened in television, also in digital platforms different contexts are superimposed with different logics of functioning, connected randomly by the same reception activity. The idea of networked publics developed by Danah Boyd goes beyond the instrumental vision of networks to extrapolate a cultural form, just as Lee Ranie and Berry Wellman (2012) did, who with their research has outlined the long transition from a group company to a network company. To be networked means to have at one's disposal a refuge that guarantees a sense of belonging and support, a porous place that has no precise geographical location, but lives thanks to the performativity of its inhabitants. This does not mean that physical places have lost their value, as they become central in contemporary lifestyles because they acquire the role of "operational bases" from which to practice their networking with the outside world. The phenomenon described so far takes on an even more radical connotation in light of the enormous diffusion of the model of digital platforms. This type of environment can be defined as:

> programmable digital architecture designed to organize interactions between users - not just end-users but also corporate entities and public bodies. It is geared toward the systematic collection, algorithmic of user data. Single platforms cannot be seen apart from each other but evolve in the context of an online setting that is structured by its logic. (van Dijck et al. 2018, 4)

The authors allude to the particular "spatial" sense expressed by the architecture of online platforms, which are proposed as the space in which today a certain type of relationships and experiences "take place". Like the metropolis, the media, therefore, generate forms of living that follow the mechanisms of its functioning, in this sense they can be considered at the same time as technologies and cultural forms (Williams 2003). They are capable of projecting their influence on every sphere of human life, and therefore also on gastronomy, which today is affected by the production mechanisms typical of the "convergent culture" (Jenkins 2006), which has imposed a new gastronomic experience and a new sensibility. Each dish presents itself as formal unity, but in the contemporary media system, its value is no longer linked only to taste or appearance. The convergent culture in which we are immersed requires it to be fragmented and spread in the many contemporary channels of communication in very small portions so that the user-consumer has the opportunity to participate in its birth and forge a strong empathic bond with it. It is as if the dish incorporates its storytelling and its materialization in front of the consumer, and automatically evokes all the content previously enjoyed as a user. This particular social condition produced by the pervasiveness of digital media has made occasional or distracted consumption inappropriate: every form of food consumption is preceded by the possibility/duty to inform oneself about the final product and to take part in its definition to arrive with awareness at the moment of the performance; although, in this logic, the determining aspect is not the final result, the path is taken to reach it. Every single piece of consumption takes on its value, as happens in spectacular forms, so in addition to what you eat, what you believe you are eating becomes essential (Barthes 1972). Each creative process, therefore, has *in nuce* the idea of the contemporary presence of the dish on several overlapping levels, each of which corresponds to a specific form of consumption, but none, taken individually, is now able to fully satisfy the consumer. The user has therefore required of him a substantial activity of recomposition of all the elements scattered in traditional publishing, online, television or live shows, and then finds himself in front of the dish and consumes it completely. The effect sought by the food industries, but also by the cook and the user/consumer, is no longer that of formal perfection, but completeness (Maffesoli 1995), or the coexistence and coherence of a web of autonomous but interconnected fragments. The final result can, therefore, be considered achieved if the set of fragments is an organic and functioning whole, and if the client can devote himself in succession to each of them. In this sense, it is possible to consider the dishes that are consumed today as transmedial products, i.e. completely mediated objects, circulating on several communication platforms, which require the consumer to contribute, through different forms of consumption, to their recomposition, overcoming and expanding the mere act of eating.

Contemporary media, regardless of their differences and peculiarities, converge in the effect of pushing food towards its culturalization (Baudrillard 1998). Each medium does this according to its functions, applying a specific filter and consequently returning profoundly different images. In both cases, however, the image is not a falsification of the food, it is rather to be understood as a veil that creates erotic indistinguishability between the visual sign and its referent. The image of a dish constitutes its addition, a surplus that induces one to turn to it with greater attention. The photo acts on the plate like a showcase on the goods: it creates a phantasmagoria in which the goods acquire their dignity and life, regardless of the use that will be made of them. The shop window isolates the goods in a dream world (Codeluppi 2007) which provides dual access: one linked to the visual connection of the passer-by with the goods on display, and one of a more concrete act of consumption. In the same way, photography brings its user closer to the plate, but it can also be an autonomous object of consumption, which does not need a referent to seduce the observer. This means that the food product and all the elements that compose it have the value of enunciative visual signs, that is, they acquire expressive capacities. This is how the social process described by Jean Baudrillard (2006) takes shape, according to which, in a consumer society, a food product like any other object acquires the faculty to express itself, to communicate, regardless of its consumer. This does not only happen to the works of art created by the most important chefs such as Massimo Bottura[1] in which there is clear expressive intentionality: each object has a communicative power disseminated in the visual traces that compose it. The use of the word "trace" is not casual, the aim is to refer to an existing sign, which must be identified by the consumer through an effort of understanding. There is nothing immediate, extraordinarily evident in the image of a food, everything is hidden and must be sought through conjunction between the individual consumer and goods.

New Aesthetics of Food: The Centrality of the Procedure

The fusion between communication and gastronomy also changes the status of the dish. It is not addressed directly to the diner but undergoes the first test of the camera or photographic lens. The food is addressed to the camera that mediates its relationship with the public and like a probe, the plate falls into the bowels of the contemporary imagination. The telephoto lens gives birth to a new cuisine and new consumption. The dish

---

[1] Italian chef, owner of the restaurant Osteria Francescana in Modena, nominated in 2016 and 2018 as best restaurant in the competition "The World's 50 Best Restaurants".

is composed to attract the eye of the media and is always accompanied by a complex verbal explanation, which describes in detail its preparation, a glossa, which in social networks such as Facebook or Instagram is attached to the shared photo. But the fake dish is not the only thing that interests the public, the particular technological and cultural configuration produced by contemporary media makes the process, i.e. the stages leading to the outcome, take centre stage. Consumers with their armamentarium of knowledge and experience claim to access the dish more directly and consciously. The dish no longer speaks only through its taste, it acquires a polyphonic nature, a high linguistic complexity; the food goes beyond the edible dimension and becomes a stratification of multiple symbolic levels. Similarly, after viewing a representation of a dish in a specialized magazine, on television or digital platforms, it is talked about as if it had been eaten. Vision is a superficial form of consumption, but today it has become equally central and widespread to the point that taste seems to have been downgraded to an instrument of childish knowledge: it is characteristic of children to put the objects they eat in their mouths to get to know them in detail, while a gourmet needs only a glance to find on his plate the unmistakable signs of a style, an idea, a cooking philosophy. In the infinite circumstances in which a chef finds himself cooking, the dish is rarely eaten; the only place where this practice still has a characterizing value is in the restaurant. In television, in digital platforms, in live performances, what counts is the procedure: the backstage of the dish made to emerge from the television and explored in a capillary manner by digital environments. It is increasingly common that the public has never set foot in a restaurant of contemporary cuisine, but possesses a high level of knowledge about avant-garde cooking techniques, fashionable products and chefs in vogue. The walls of the kitchen are crumbled by the camera, and the kitchen becomes accessible to the general public, adapts to it to involve them and takes on the connotations of the medium that transformed it. The reason for this unprecedented interest in the process is not due to the desire to dominate the recipes to replicate them; the desire to contemplate the production process of the dish is a sign that gastronomy has absorbed the connotations of contemporary mediascapes. As McLuhan wrote, in fact, unlike photography, the audiovisual and in particular television, works according to "a continuous, exploratory action [that] does not give the moment or the isolated aspect, but the contour, the iconic profile and transparency" (1994, 201). Television, in particular reality TV, has accustomed the audience to simultaneously contemplate the limelight and the backstage, abolishing—or simulating the abolition—of any perceptual barrier and here the disappearance of any shadow or secret zone. The spectator has free access to the backstage and this shifts his attention from the outcome (the dish) to the procedure that is necessary to get there (execution). It is a mechanism typical of any spectacular form, as Roland Barthes (1972) explains, according to which events of this kind are a sum of isolated shows, none of which is a function: each moment imposes the total knowledge of a passion that arises on its own, without ever extending towards the crowning of a result.

Under this new attention to the process, the gastronomic experience undergoes many changes, starting from the rituals that take place in restaurants to the multi-channel communication that restaurants and chefs are forced to practice to be perfectly integrated into the participatory culture inaugurated by the contemporary media.

Despite the obsessive search for transparency, contemporary dishes are comparable to what the English sociologist Anthony Giddens (1990) called "expert systems": modern cooking techniques, globalized raw materials, the aesthetics of dishes are so far removed from the ordinary experience of everyone that consumption has become a profession of trust. Sitting at the table of a restaurant, a profane or prudent customer does not dominate the production process of the dishes he eats; instead, at one time, every bite was matched by daily experience. This condition should generate fear—in fact, many people refuse to eat what they do not know or recognize as familiar; instead, most people respond to obscure food innovations with unconditional enthusiasm. It happens because a symbolic pact is established with the cooks to whom the media system has conferred a prestige that they did not have in the past. As a result, in our time, dishes, especially haute cuisine, stop having a mental reference point: neither the purest innovation nor the oldest of flavours have a clear and definitive correspondence, this happens because of the changing nature of contemporary experience, which tends to burn in an instant what it serves, and because of its vocation for polyphony and complexity.

Transparent Kitchens and Multi-level Chefs

Transparency has become a dogma irreproachably respected by related audiences in the gastronomy sector as well. The distance between the public and private spheres has progressively narrowed to satisfy the (strategic) desire for sharing, and privacy has begun to be perceived as a limit, a withdrawal of life into its private dimension and, consequently, a renunciation of social relations, with the aim of immunizing oneself from the other. The contemporary sense of privacy in this area has returned to its original etymology, that of "deprivation": the cook, renouncing sharing through digital platforms in the name of his privacy, deprives himself of the possibility of establishing multi-dimensional relationships with clients. The chefs who spread through television circuits and digital networks show themselves with an insistence comparable to the merchandise on display in the shop window and, becoming informational merchandise, their media body is devoured by the public. The chef becomes edible, for an anthropophagic mechanism typical of mass culture. For cooks coming from the electric tradition this way of communicating is mere advertising, for the digital ones, on the contrary, it is an essential moment of their profession. When the camera lingers on gastronomy, restaurants are emptied and the star chef is born. By feeding himself to his audience, the chef completes the mission of saturating every desire, but when he is not visually consumed, he is destined to oblivion. The absence from the timeline of the public not only sanctions its lack of media coverage, but its disappearance *tout court*. Thanks to the redundancy of digital communication, every content advertised on social networks are transformed into an extension of the chef's personality, a symbolic extension that broadens his range of action. The chef who shuns his media reproduction to mark a distinction with his most exposed colleagues, to preserve his value, generates the opposite effect: his professional value is immediately impoverished because it is perceived as incomplete. The ghetto that is built around to preserve its mythical halo is the result of a miscalculation, which does not take into account the mechanisms for building popularity and the reconfigured picture of contemporary Italian gastronomy. After all, the cook has always been a communicator: the creation of a dish places him in a direct relationship with the diner. Communication that makes use of the many details of his restaurant (sign, furniture, tablecloth, cutlery, glasses) and goes as far as the food menu, often inaugurated by learned quotes or thoughts signed by the chef. Besides, it is increasingly common for the chef to enter the dining room at the end of the service to chat with his customers; a gesture with which you want to approach diners accustomed by the media to observe simultaneously the scene and the backstage on the screens. The restaurant traditionally imposes a strict separation between the dining room and the kitchen, so the diners' experience would remain incomplete if the opportunity to exchange a few impressions with the chef were lost. It is no coincidence, moreover, that many chefs have also tried to formalize their cuisine by writing books with which to share the knowledge learned from their experience.

For the consumer/spectator, the chef acquires importance equal to or greater than that of his dishes, as evidenced by the photos found on the Instagram profiles of the world's most important chefs, in which users post photos with their kitchen idols—as they do with sportsmen and actors—and no longer or not only while eating their dishes. This trend has led to a fusion between the chef's (public) work and (private) leisure time dimension, to build a single large significant space in continuous communication with its public, thanks to communication technologies. The paradox of this new phase of cooking is that those cooks who have no customers can have a future, but they have no chance to preserve themselves without an audience.

While television in its origins, inspired by cinema, tended to hide its intervention on the world, contemporary television has chosen to seek the truth effect through a form of "hyper mediation" (Bolter and Grusin 1998), which does not obscure the manufacturing process that makes it (Vagni 2017): the exhibition of its artificial aspects constitutes the scenic truth. The chef's image is based on these workings of contemporary television communication: *Masterchef*'s audience is placed in a lateral position that allows it to simultaneously contemplate the multiple appearances assumed by television personalities—and chefs—beyond their public dimension, establishing "parasocial interactions" with celebrities (Meyrowitz 1985), fuelled by continuous media exposure. The kitchen in this way acquires a seductive aura that imposes it as a new territory of fashion and consumption. The stars of the kitchen have begun to write books, to conduct television programmes, to advertise products, allowing the world of gastronomy a visibility and importance that it had never had before.

In the controlled distraction regime of contemporary society, chefs, restaurants and food producers stand as pillars of the collective imagination, helping to structure the individual ego of people.

Conclusion

The proposed path has shown how the kitchen has stopped being a simple canteen to become a cultural phenomenon, resulting in two distinctly different moments of food, which correspond to two different fields. Nutrition is connected to the biological reproduction of life, it is, therefore, a private fact that takes place mostly in the domestic dimension. With tele-cooking and digital food, food becomes a relational medium, becomes part of the public scene, emancipates itself from the role of food and becomes an extension of individual identity. We no longer speak of simple cooking, that is the art of preparing food to eat it, but of gastronomy, whose purpose differs from the immediate response to a primary need. It aims to entertain the diner with dishes that, when they appear, shock the spectator/consumer, depositing themselves in his memory and imagination as the shot from a gun creeps into the flesh, and continues to radiate pain until the moment of its extraction. It is a persistent message that produces indirect and much more lasting effects than the simple sense of satiety and enjoyment generated by the food.

In its contact with the modern media, gastronomy changes shape, assumes a strong cultural value and becomes a territory of interest for a mass audience that before its mediatization had never felt interested. As Joanne Finkelstein (2015) argues, the restaurant is less and less a canteen and more and more a stage onto which modern man stumbles in search of different forms of satisfaction. More generally, food, in its new media form, becomes a playful, recreational moment involving changes within the sphere of gastronomy.

It is as if, to quote Baudrillard (1988), we were living a "video phase" of food. For Baudrillard the video phase can be explained by the ecstasy that in the 1980s produced the Polaroid, that is the "ecstasy" of having almost at the same time the object and its image. Baudrillard says that it is instantaneous refraction without depth, and this, in my opinion, the limit of his reflection, the limit of a reflection according to which an image is a form of grafting, of grafting on itself, therefore unproductive. The perspective that we have tried to adopt instead tends to analyse the encounter of food with electronic and digital media as a new form of food experience, as food in its condition increased by the media.

For this reason, the aesthetics of food, its forms, techniques, flavours, restaurant architectures and their specializations are in continuous transition to support the change induced by the media system and the new sensibility it conveys.

REFERENCES

Auletta, K. (2009). *Googled: The End of the World as We Know It.* London: Penguin Press.

Baudrillard, J. (2006). *The System of Objects.* Brooklyn: Verso.

Baudrillard, J. (1998). *The Consumer Society: Myths and Structures.* London: Sage.

Baudrillard, J. (1988). *America.* London: Verso.

Barthes, R. (1972). *Mythologies.* New York: Noonday Press.

Benjamin, W. (2006). *The Writer of Modern Life: Essays on Charles Baudelaire.* Cambridge: Harvard University Press.

Benjamin, W. (1996). *Selected Writings, vol. I: 1913–1926.* Cambridge: Harvard University Press.

Benjamin, W. (1969). *The Work of Art in the Age of Mechanical Reproduction.* New York: Schocken Books.

Bolter, J. D., & Grusin, R. (1998). *Remediation: Understanding New Media.* Cambridge: MIT Press.

Boyd, D. (2015). *It's Complicated: The Social Lives of Networked Teens.* New Haven: Yale University Press.

Bourdieu, P. (1987). *Distinction. A Social Critique of the Judgement of Taste.* Cambridge: Harvard University Press.

Bradley, P. (2016). *Food, Media and Contemporary Culture. The Edible Image.* Basingstoke: Palgrave Macmillan.

Codeluppi, V. (2007). *La vetrinizzazione sociale. Il processo di spettacolarizzazione degli individui e della società.* Torino: Bollati Boringhieri.

Durkheim, E. (1915). *The Elementary Forms of the Religious Life.* London: Allen & Unwin.

Elias, N. (1994). *The Civilizing Process.* Hoboken: Wiley-Blackwell.

Featherstone, M. (2007). *Consumer Culture and Postmodernism.* London: Sage.

Finkelstein, J. (2015). *Fashioning Appetite: Restaurants and the Making of Modern Identity.* New York: Columbia University Press.

Giddens, A. (1990). *The Consequences of Modernity.* Stanford: Stanford University Press.

Jenkins, H. (2006). *Convergence Culture: Where Old and New Media Collide.* New York and London: New York University Press.

LeBesco, k, & Naccarato, P. (Eds.). (2018). *The Handbook of Food and Popular Culture.* London: Bloomsbury.

Leer, J., & Povlsen, K. K. (2018). *Food and Media: Practices, Distinctions and Heterotopias.* London: Routledge.

Levy, P. (1997). *Collective Intelligence: Mankind's Emerging World in Cyberspace.* Cambridge: Perseus Books.

Lewis, T. (2020). *Digital Food: From Paddock to Platform.* London: Bloomsbury.

Lyotard, J. F. (2015). *Libidinal Economy.* New York: Bloomsbury.

Lupton, D. (2018). Cooking, Eating, Uploading: Digital Food Cultures. In K. LeBesco & P. Naccarato (Eds.), *The Handbook of Food and Popular Culture* (pp. 66–79). London: Bloomsbury.

Maffesoli, M. (1995). *The Time of the Tribes: The Decline of Individualism in Mass Society*. London: Sage.

McLuhan, M. (1994). *Understanding Media*. Cambridge: The MIT Press.

Meyrowitz, J. (1985). *No Sense of Place*. Cambridge: Harvard University Press.

Moores, S. (2012). *Media, Place and Mobility*. London: Macmillan Education.

Philipov, M. (2017). *Media and Food Industries: The New Politic of Food*. Cham: Palgrave Macmillan.

Postman, N. (1979). *Teaching as a Conserving Activity*. New York: Delacorte Press.

Rainie, L., & Wellman, B. (2012). *Networked: The New Social Operating System*. Cambridge: The MIT Press.

Rousseau, S. (2012). *Food and Social Media: You Are What You Tweet*. Lanham: Altimira.

Schivelbusch, W. (2015). *Das verzehrende Leben der Dinge. Versuch über die Konsumtion*. München: Carl Hanser Verlag GmbH & Co.

Simmel, G. (1997). Sociology of the Meal. In D. Frisby & M. Featherstone (Eds.), *Simmel on Culture* (pp. 130–136). London: Sage.

Simmel, G. (1991). The Berlin Trade Exhibition. *Theory, Culture, and Society, 8*(3), 119–123.

Vagni, T. (2017). *Abitare la TV. Teorie, Immaginari, Reality Show*. Milano: Franco Angeli.

van Dijck, J., Waal, M., & Poell, T. (2018). *The Platform Society*. New York: Oxford University Press.

Williams, R. (2003). *Television: Technology and Cultural Form*. London: Routledge.

CHAPTER 6

Perry—Deep Mapping and Emotion in Place-Writing Practice

Charlie Mansfield, Derek Shepherd, and Philipp Wassler

The Phases of Place Inquiry

This chapter proposes a place-writing methodology, which uses deep mapping from archive material and literary sources alongside a set of literary methods for travel writers to elicit emotional responses to spatial practices as they are experienced in the field. From the authors' preparation for their fieldwork as travel writers, a synthesis of the journey and urban scenarios are positioned as elements of place inquiry. Literary narrative is proposed as a form of sensible, interrogative writing that responds to affect and shares authors' and readers' sensibilities. The planning phase for later literary travel writing is presented in detail as a model of place inquiry for other projects of emotional ethnography. This chapter shows

C. Mansfield (✉) · D. Shepherd
University of Plymouth, Plymouth, UK
e-mail: charlie.mansfield@plymouth.ac.uk

P. Wassler
Bournemouth University, Poole, UK

© The Author(s), under exclusive license to Springer Nature   97
Switzerland AG 2021
A. Scribano et al. (eds.), *Cities, Capitalism and the Politics of Sensibilities*,
https://doi.org/10.1007/978-3-030-58035-3_6

the preparation for the fieldwork in Cherbourg. Through this presentation, alongside discussion of the design process, it is hoped that a robust, reproducible and critically sound method of practice for this type of analytical travel writing will become evident. The design of the planning phase results in an organised array of available cultural knowledge plateaus in the imaginary of the researcher-writers; this available state of knowing is here called the hexis. This is developed below.

The fieldwork will entail a sea crossing from England in search of an agricultural and production process that has been erased from the city of Cherbourg but may remain in its hinterland, the Cotentin peninsula in Normandy, France. Perry production and distribution appear to have been lost from Cherbourg and its surrounding farmland; why has this mutation taken place? The second theme is in the symbolic realm, using close-reading from literary theory of a dramatized autobiography, which is set in Cherbourg in the early 1940s. Finally, ideas from the travel writing of the literary theorist, Roland Barthes (12 November 1915–26 March 1980), will form an articulation point for place inquiry. Barthes' life has recently been commemorated in Cherbourg with an emotive statue in the city where he was born. This sculpture, *Metamorphosis* (2014) by Christine Larivière, loads the urban space of the Esplanade de la Laïcité with new meaning; this will be a site of investigation, a plateau in this practice.

THE LITERARY TEXT, TIME AND EMOTION

Wolff identifies within the writing of W G Sebald a genre that she calls 'literary historiography' (Wolff 2014, 68); it is a layered hybrid discourse, she explains, which produces a '[n]ew form of transdiscursive knowledge, a specifically aesthetic knowledge, [that] emerges from this way of working through both material and text' (Wolff 2014, 68). For Sebald, this material consists of newspaper advertisements read during his journeys, historical and everyday events associated with the places he visits, the emotionally charged sojourns of other literary writers at these places and his own sensibilities as he finds overnight lodgings or chooses where to dine. Arguably, it is the literary, or literariness of his writing on place that provides additional space for his sensibilities to be encoded and to generate an *affective* social practice for the reproduction of emotional engagement with places in the towns he has visited. The activities in the places where he stays, are his actions driven by the historical events that have marked his body emotionally. In this passage from Sebald's travel vignette, 'A Little Excursion' in *Campo Santo* (Bell [trans.] 2005), all these elements are deployed with a narrative effectiveness to recount the story of a moment in history:

> In the evening I walked along the Cours Napoléon, and then sat for two hours in a small restaurant not far from the Gare Maritime with a view of the white cruise ship. Over coffee I studied the advertisements in a local paper and wondered whether to go to the cinema. I like to visit the cinema in foreign towns [...] At about ten, therefore, I was back in the hotel where I had taken a room late that morning. [...] Traffic was still driving down the streets, but suddenly everything fell silent, just for a few seconds, until [...]. (Sebald 2005, 15)

Benjamin notes that 'true literary activity cannot expect to take place in a literary context - in fact that is the usual expression of its failure to bear fruit. Significant literary effectiveness can only come about within a strict interchange of doing and writing' (Benjamin 2009, 46). In this interchange Benjamin proposes publicity bills, newspapers and the prompt language of opinion to discretely oil the turbine that generates literature. In the creation of these experiences during the time of heightened sensibilities during holidaymaking the processes of narrative knowledge offer a method of recording emotion for communication. The resulting mediated artefact of narrative knowledge then remains as an accessible object for sharing the experiential knowledge with other potential holidaymakers.

Small Stories as a Research Instrument

In 2020 Sylvie Patron brought together a collection of research on narrative to define the term, 'small stories' (Patron 2020, 5), and offer it as an analytical tool for other researchers using literary theory in the social field. In Patron's collection, the chapter by Annick Madec (Patron 2020, 267–283) unlocks very short observed and overheard scenes on public transport as a type of knowledge that is sensible to or manifests a sensibility to social structuration and, in her examples, also to the subtle indicators of social class, using a notion from Barbara Carnevali (Carnevali 2013, 30).

En paraphrasant la définition hégélienne du beau, on pourrait donc définir l'esthétique sociale comme le savoir qui a pour objet la manifestation sensible de la société. Ce savoir considère la société comme un phénomène esthétique: tout ce qui est social apparaît en effet sensiblement, donc esthétiquement. Mais en quoi consiste et comment s'exerce concrètement cette forme de connaissance? Et quel rapport institue-t-elle entre le savoir philosophique et les sciences sociales? (Carnevali 2013, 30)

This approach of assigning aesthetic value to captured scenes by articulating the mundane description with emotion can be seen in the travel writing of Annie Ernaux; notice her literary turn of the keyword, *comme*, 'like' which unlocks the device of simile:

In this scene a couple are waiting for a train which must take one of them: 'Le train que l'un des deux devait prendre allait arrive, comme la fin du monde' (Ernaux 2000, 107)' The verbs of movement are compressed here and shifted to an expectant imperfect tense generating tension and anticipation in true narrative sense in what otherwise would have been a documentary text. (Mansfield 2012, 57)

Literary devices then, including imagistic language and the shifting of tenses to the past, allow readers to feel the collective space of the railway station. As a method for the travel writer, this literariness, produces a strategic revaluation of an otherwise quotidian time and site, integrating it into a larger space to be enjoyed for its emotions.

A Practice-Led Methodology for Place Inquiry

The methodology for this place writing is practice-led. It makes use of, and tests the theory of the toureme (Mansfield 2015, 2018), and establishes a new planning phase for literary travel writers, the hexis. The theory of the toureme is developed from Blanchot's concept of the recounted story, *le récit* (Mansfield 2015). The desk preparation for data collection design for the perry project attempts to create the necessary conditions in the participant team for them to experience the toureme during the fieldwork in Cherbourg. Previous reading, which may be literary or from the participant's own personal cultural capital interests will be completed. This directed reading must have references to the places or socio-economic practices of this port city, in this way the literary reading is of the form proposed by Onfray (2010), expanded later. During the fieldwork the participants will separate and, while taking notes, search for the places from their reading, thus creating walking routes through the townscape that do not necessarily coincide with the tourism product. On the spot, the plateaus, they take notes of their emotional and memory responses with a view to sharing them at the end of the reconnaissance. At fixed times the participants gather so that their notes can be recounted to the rest of the research team, and recorded for later synthesis.

Places to Visit, Making the Holiday

A three-stage methodological template for the analysis phase of place inquiry in tourism development management is proposed. It must be remembered, that in this discipline, tourism studies, the concern is with the happiness, satisfaction and accomplishment of the visitors, often now referred to as holidaymakers. This approach to urban space is not that of urbanists who consider the city as a place where people live and work, but as one where they stay and play.

   i. Desk research to identify 6 parts for the hexis, being: (a) heritage sites, (b) cultural sites linked with an author and (c) food and ethnobotany sites, often using the visitor's hotel as a start and end point and restaurant or local food shop.
  ii. Conversion of desk research to the field planning *cahier des charges* (CDC). Using a formal, critical language to arrange the parts of the hexis topographically in the researcher's imaginary. This might also be mapped onto a town plan to estimate walking times and distances, and to choose particular streets that can later be found by the holidaymaking readers of the final synthesis.
 iii. Capturing of a place-making narrative for tourism planners and stakeholders, and city authorities in a form directly comprehensible to a public readership. These are notes made from recordings of the participant researchers recounting in the past tense their experiences brought back from the field. The template, then, is a meticulous plan for sorties from the hotel to walk out to sites from the planned reading; the three expedition plans are as follows, with an inquiry associated with each one to provide the dialectic or cross-reading for each component:

1. In search of pears, perry and the changing economics of local pear orchards and brewing around Cherbourg. How is this reflected in the labelling of pears and perry in Cherbourg? Where can perry still be found?
2. In search of the house of the heroine in the French biographical novel, and her journeys into Cherbourg centre. What does the walk up to the streets of the rue Lohen and rue Loubet feel like?
3. In search of Roland Barthes' birthplace in the suburbs, and the walking routes of his mother alone in Cherbourg and the new statue of her son. Where is the centre of the town for Henriette Binger?

GHOST MEMORIES OF HOME

In narrative research methodologies, for instance in recounting personal stories, Dunne proposes a synthetic process, that she calls restorying; 'The *restorying* or re-authoring process, in turn, involves constructing a revised narrative embedded with new personal meaning and emotion that results from the experience of this process' (Dunne 2016, 142). By working with co-authors in the field team, this restorying process can take place soon after data collection, by providing an interested audience for the experiences of the day or half-day to be recounted, and reworked with literary methods. In effect this step in the data collection becomes a performance which provides the opportunity to elicit the emotions that Dunne (2016) underlines in her methods work.

Bartlett's experiments with memory from the 1920s and 1930s, as explained in Wagoner et al. (2019, 16–18) furnish a ready-made method for retelling experiences from memory by case-participants which, after his work, shows how the reteller makes qualitative changes as the experience is retold. It suggests that memory is not a storage place but is instead, transformative, in that it integrates the reteller's own culture as it is mediated appropriately for the next group of listeners. The reteller is thus an active subject, which, for this research can be considered an enrichment of the recalled experience. In this research method, the retelling stage may be repeated after, say, the following day to allow this enrichment to develop further. In the context of this project, too, which is ostensibly seeking the lost art of perry-making, these two periods of organic change are echoed. The first is the fermentation of the fruit sugars, and the second, longer period, the malo-lactic fermentation which converts L($-$)-malic acid to L($+$)-lactic acid.

The key literary work that the researchers use in this research is *For Freedom: The Story of a French Spy* by Bradley Kimberly Brubaker (Brubaker 2005). Although aimed at the young adult market, it is a valuable document of memory writing since the author has created a biography of the wartime memories of Suzanne David, from long meetings and interviews with David many years later in America. Of particular resonance with this work on Cherbourg is the emotional map Brubaker's story of the young singer traces for the researcher as reader. The street where Suzanne, the girl, lives in the story is still easy to find on the map of Cherbourg. In the story, the occupying authorities have seized the space of her home, so that she no longer has rights to this territory (Sassen 2006). It is for the heroine and for the visitor-researcher a toureme, a space that marks the body emotionally and thus loads this street space with meaning, both for the occupier that was and the visitor that will occupy it. It is noted that it is often difficult to source a literary or cultural artefact associated with provincial towns. In this project on Cherbourg, only this and a more recent novel, entitled simply *Cherbourg*, were discovered from desk and archive research. It is worth considering newspapers from a specific date, or works from the visual arts, too.

Theory of the Planning Hexis and the 6-Part Diathesis

In Hervé Breton's consideration of how the writing subject creates narrative knowledge from lived experience (Breton 2019, 78–79) he draws upon Aristotle's concept of *hexis* to show how writers historicise elements of their knowledge to constitute these elements as available resources. In developing the methodology for this research, the process of historicising is achieved by use of the past tenses to recount the field experiences. The preparation of a hexis, then, is time-consuming but essential as to create an armature for the researcher's imaginary. This process is fully explored for this project below. *Hexis* is an arrangement or disposition. In fact, the French word, *disponible*, provides a useful tension for an English reader; *disponible* translates as available, in simple terms, but the subject, the travel writer, holds an arrangement of collected knowings, using and deploying them in combination, sometimes to recount story, sometimes to report history (Breton 2019, 78–79), thus showing their disposition of emotions and sensibilities to their readers. In the methodology for this fieldwork, emotion experienced in place is sought out to act as a catalyst for the literary writing of the delivered outcome. Like an exquisite minia-ture, Thomas Mann paints a hexis of emotions in this scene from *Death in Venice* (1912). One of the characters travels by vaporetto through the port. Without spoiling the story, here is sufficient quotation to illustrate how sensual experiences of the urban tourist space are held arranged, and *disponible*, by the character, by the narrator, and thus, by the readers. It communicates the emotional disposition of the character:

> The atmosphere of the city, this slightly mouldy smell of sea and swamp from which he had been so anxious to escape - he breathed it in now in deep, tenderly painful draughts. Was it possible that he had not known, had not considered how deeply his feelings were involved in all these things? (Mann 1996, 231)

Mann, as a travel writer, articulates emotions dialogically with tourist spots that can still be found today: the Rialto, the Piazzetta extension of St Mark's Square, and finally, the text reads, he 'entered the station torn by this acute inner conflict' (Mann 1996, 231). This disposition or hexis of emotions for Mann's character, mapped along his character's inquiring movement across the city, is the key to the method that will be applied for the inquiry into seeking out traces of the semiotician, Barthes, who was born here in Cherbourg, of the drama of the biographical novel, and of the ethnobotany associated with perry production and consumption in this region of France.

BARTHES AND THE CENTRE OF THE WRITTEN CITY

Where is the centre of a city? City centres are a paradox for old sea ports. Apart from Venice, the sea is usually inaccessible to tourists once they have disembarked from their ferry. In tourism studies, the holiday-makers' hotel often becomes their centre, since this is where they first arrive to unencumber themselves of their luggage and travelling clothes, establishing a sanctuary for the duration of their stay. While for the day visitor, the centre may be the railway station, or the ferry terminal itself. In Roland Barthes' own example of travel writing (Barthes 1970, 44) he explores a city of which the centre is a void (Mansfield 2004, 155). In his exploration, then, Barthes turns instead to the railway station, *la gare*.

The station is a centre, he explains, but an empty one, devoid of spirit (Barthes 1970, 52–53). However, the careful reader of his city travel book is alerted to a metaphor which links the pleasure that Barthes the writer experiences at the point of departure, not the urban point of departure, *la gare*, but the point of starting to write, when all the elements are at his disposal for composition, and he is disposed to write:

> 'Peut-être va-t-il à la gare parce qu'elle est le lieu de départ. Comme désir, la gare est le point dans la grande ville où se trouve le renouvellement du voyage et, pour Barthes, il y a un lien fort entre un lieu nouveau et son travail de l'écriture : 'visiter un lieu pour la première fois, c'est de la sorte commencer à l'écrire'. (Barthes 1970, 51; Mansfield 2004, 156)

What did Cherbourg railway station represent for Henriette Binger in 1915? Was it her point of departure and arrival connecting her to her husband, who was often away at sea, or to her mother, Noémie in other cities? Was 107 rue de la Bucaille not home but a temporary resting place for the duration of her visit? One hundred years later the city council unveils a statue to her son in an attempt to create a new cultural centre for their city hidden away behind the old theatre in a non-place that has been a building site. The route proposed then for the travel writer-researcher would be to walk first from the hotel in the port area, possible Hotel Ambassadeur, to rue Bucaille. This is a walk of 16 minutes, 1.2 kilometres. The return journey would head back into town to find the statue on the Esplanade de la Laïcité, then continue on to the railway station. The return route is 22 minutes, 1.7 kilometres.

PLACES OF DRAMA FROM THE LIVED BIOGRAPHY

In his 2007 book *Théorie du voyage: Poétique de la géographie* French contemporary philosopher Michel Onfray offers his outlook on 'growing one's desire' for travel. Accordingly, 'travel begins in the library' (Onfray 2010, 23), where one 'realizes the first travel, undoubtedly the most magical and surely the most mysterious' (Onfray 2010, 24). More than anything, Onfray suggests literature and poetry over guidebooks and maps as preliminary readings, as these involve the five senses to create anticipation and pleasure.

In this case, the authors make use of Kimberly Brubaker Bradley's 2005 novel *For Freedom—The Story of a French Spy* to '*grow their desire*' for future travel to the northern French City of Cherbourg—where most of the story takes place. The novel retells the true story of Suzanne, which was interviewed for the book by the author; Suzanne is a thirteen-year-old French girl facing the horrors of World War Two in Cherbourg. From the beginning of the war up to its very end, Suzanne lives through bombings, Nazi occupation first of her town and later of her very own house from which the family is forced to move. Refusing to give into her fears, the heroine keeps to her passion of singing and dreaming of a future in opera. One day, her strength of character is noticed by her local doctor, and she is eventually secretly enrolled in the French Resistance as a spy and message carrier throughout Cherbourg. Fighting through her fears and conflicts with her family, she is finally arrested by the occupying forces after delivering messages for many months; but the liberation of France saves her life and earns her the respect of her family as a true French hero.

Suzanne's function as a spy makes her a particularly complex character, and through her story readers relive a major social movement, the resistance to authority, through her own emotions. The social sciences have a long history of putting emotions in the centre stage of collective actions, protests and movements (e.g. Flam and King, 2005; Goodwin et al. 2001). Our heroine is largely driven by love; particularly in her decision to enrol as a spy. Love for her family and friends, love for her career as a singer and love for her country. Bourdieu points out that love as a driver for social actions is often marked by confusion, such as tensions between duty and transformations, the politically correct and the incorrectness of emotions. Scribano (2017) shows that love can produce collective actions as an 'interstitial practice'; collective practices and relations which deny traditional normative contents of a certain cultural context. It could thus be assumed that Suzanne, through her interstitial emotion of love and the conflicting social decisions this implies, is changing the urban space of Cherbourg for the reader. This is considered as the second walking route is planned for this fieldwork; the route will use the heroine's plateaus of drama that are still extant in the city today. The researcher will thus see the streets through her eyes, and seek out traces that may have been left from her interstitial practices in otherwise mundane urban space.

Onfray states that a deep reading of the text can allow reader-tourists to 'hear colours, smell perfumes, touch sounds, hear temperatures, see noises' (Onfray 2010, 28)—imagining places through a true coming together of a five-sense experience. *For Freedom—The Story of a French Spy* allows the researchers to grow their desire for reliving Cherbourg through the eyes of the young spy—and the various faces of love she experiences. Some of the key locations in the city are given around which to plot the field route:

There is the Place Napoleon, described as '*the big square near the Gare Maritime, the station where trains could pull up right to the harbour to load and unload the ships. The Church of La Trinité formed part of the square and from the benches around the edge, we could watch the ships in the harbour, the waves curling, and the birds wheeling overhead. People strolled back and forward across the square*' (Brubaker 2005, 4). It is the wind blowing in from the English Channel across the square's cobblestones (Brubaker 2005, 3), which brings a fresh spring breeze to the benches which line the sunny seaside quay (Brubaker 2005, 4). The novel also allows readers to imagine Place Napoleon as the spiritual heart of Cherbourg, a place where locals stroll and mingle in cafés, where the local fish and vegetable market is held on Saturdays, and local merchants sell fresh butter and seafood in the salty sea air of sunny spring days. It is here that Suzanne first experiences the devastating bombings, with blood staining the cobblestones and a lonely bench from which she was first confronted with the horrors of World War II (Brubaker 2005, 22). As the novel progresses, it is precisely the square where this bombing took place which offers a stage for all the suffering of Cherbourg and its people: the cobblestones still glittering in the sun, but scrubbed clean of the blood of the first victims; the lonely bench still there, but now surrounded by never-repaired bomb craters; the Saturday market finally gone, as German soldiers tell Suzanne and her mother to '*Go home, madame*' (Brubaker 2005, 42) when they try to buy groceries. It is also here, as is implied by the narrator, that much later American and British ships will dock to liberate France and where Suzanne will eventually meet her future husband; an American soldier with whom she would spend the rest of her life in the United States (Brubaker 2005, 180). The sea breeze, the smell of fish and salt, the cobbled street glittering in the sun, the noises of a busy Saturday market, the empty and long winters of occupation, the sufferings of the departed and the final liberation on a sunny day on Place Napoleon; the beginning of our journey in the library in Suzanne's company.

Then there is the house of the heroine, where Suzanne lives with her brothers and parents. Situated in Rue Lohen and parallel to Rue Loubet (Brubaker 2005, 38), the house was part of the only two streets which were taken over by and subsequently housed enemy soldiers in the early stages of the occupation. On a shady street on top of a hill, this is where the daily life of Cherbourg plays out. Suzanne lives in a big house with a beautiful hall and dining room, decorated by a sea-mural painted by her mother (Brubaker 2005, 84). A quiet street, where only the noise of the big hallway clock can be heard—but it is disrupted by invading soldiers breaking open the front door (Brubaker 2005, 32). Much of the personal lives of the novel's characters play out in this area. Further from the sea and shaded by big trees, Suzanne used to walk this hilly neighbourhood to see her school friend, Yvette, go down the hill to the seaside Saturday market with her mother, and—at the far end of the street—visit Dr Leclerc's office, where she will eventually be enrolled into the French Resistance Movement as a spy. It is also here that on long spring and summer days, the air sometimes smells like salt although it is far from the sea (Brubaker 2005, 70); it is here that the grass grew taller and the streets dustier as the war raged on (Brubaker 2005, 96) and it is on these streets that Dr Leclerc was paraded after being discovered to be a member of the Resistance (Brubaker 2005, 173). It is also on these shady and hilly streets where spring leaves fall and increasingly cover the abandoned taxi of one of Suzanne's black neighbours; making her realise that something has happened to him, too. This is a Cherbourg which smells of countryside, is quiet and peaceful, neighbourly and family-oriented; but this is also the Cherbourg which ultimately suffers most, where daily life and human dignity are brutally suspended by an invading force. It is here in the shady hills that all four seasons of Cherbourg truly play out: long summer days; green spring evenings; falling leaves in the autumn; and bleak, cold winter nights. It is here that the traveller can hear the footsteps of Suzanne and Dr Leclerc while walking the alleys; but also, the marching boots of soldiers on patrol; ready to disrupt the life of any passer-by at gunpoint to check identification papers, to questioning them and to set up roadblocks.

   In addition to these key locations, there are other places in Cherbourg where the heroine's tale leads the reader. The convent school where Suzanne initially stays, '*high among the hills of Cherbourg*' and farther from the beach than her own home (Brubaker 2005, 1); the gloomy second-floor apartment facing the graveyard, where the family is forced to move after their house is occupied by troops where '*the walls were yellowed, and every inch of the floor was filthy; a smell of old grease hung in the air*' (Brubaker 2005, 44); the crowed café by the theatre, where

Suzanne delivers a message to another spy and as real coffee is not available during war times, '*vile, burnt-tasting, stagnant liquid*' (Brubaker 2005, 115) is served instead; aunt Suzanne's house several miles out of Cherbourg, where '*grassy fields smelled fragrant and rich in the summer sunshine*'; and the opera house in the city, where our heroine has her first on-stage performances and is forced to hurry home before the evening curfew (Brubaker 2005, 92).

Suzanne's Cherbourg is a city of cobblestones, squares, cafés, markets, ringing church bells and French *joie-de-vivre*; a city which looks outwards to the sea, but also inland to Paris as a role model—fiercely proud to be French and yet open to the world; a city of salty sea air, grassy fields, shady hills and fresh summer breezes; but also of stormy winters and bleak, long autumn days. It is a city where Suzanne is allowed to dream of her future career as an opera singer, on the grand stage in Paris, but also of a normality which has been taken away from her by the war. This is the Cherbourg not only of Suzanne, but also of the reader growing one's desire to visit. In fact, Onfray would say that it is growing the reader's desire to come to the destination again, rather than to visit it for the first time; as we have followed Suzanne through her very own Cherbourg, reading about her journey, her life and her dreams; breathing the sea air, anxiously hiding from occupying soldiers in the small alleyways; and seeing the ships depart on the horizon. 'Dreaming of a place, in this frame of mind, allows us more to find it *again*, rather than to find it' (Onfray 2010, 30), emphasis added.

PERRY AND THE PEAR IN NORMANDY

Archive research by the travel writer reveals early mentions of perry, as a wine-like drink made from pears. This historical documentation lends an aspect of authenticity to local food products and to the ethnography of the communities who processed crops in this way; 'these practices sometimes testify the organisation of a group or of the entire society' (Bérard and Marchenay 2006) so that these practices become a cultural product to be shared and enjoyed. For holidaymakers, who are reading literary travel writing, providing this link with past records and writings helps to show how local ethnobotany can be enjoyed in its traditional setting, often, too, as this section will show, helping them to understand local land use. An early mention does exist in Gerard's herbal from the late sixteenth century showing that the practice of perry-making was already known at that time, and further, that he noted that it had some positive affects as a drink, but that the question of secondary, malo-lactic fermentation, mentioned earlier in this chapter was still an issue:

> Wine made of the juice of peares called in English, Perry, is soluble, purgeth those that are not accustomed to drinke thereof, especially when it is new; not withstanding it is as wholesome a drink being taken in small quantitie as wine; it comforteth and warmth the stomache, and causeth good digestion. [*sic.* for all spellings]. (Gerard 1597)

The malo-lactic fermentation, then, for the travel writer can become a dialogic element. It can provide a cross-reading between two of the plateaus in the hexis that are visited by the travel writer when interviewing in the field. In that way, the technical knowledge can produce 'dialogic interaction between characters in a text' (Roberts 2016, 65), for example, when dining or when speaking with staff in a local produce shop. To understand how perry-pear trees were grown in Normandy, the historical and cultural region of France, recent scholarship provides an entrée into archive material, for example Tracy (1989) is certain that the region's meadow orchard system, in French *le pré-verger*, dates from the medieval period. By interpreting the travel writings of Gurney (1848), an English traveller in this area. Gurney mentions pear orchards in the Pays de Bray, which has been a natural border between Normandy and Picardy since 911 'this valley of much beauty and well-wooded both as forests and hedgerow timber, with a great deal of pasture, and both arable land covered with apple and pear trees for the making of cider and perry; the effect of this is highly picturesque' (Gurney 1848, 255). More recently, Bérard and Marchenay (2006) note that the production of cider, perry, pommeau and calvados has traditionally been based on and largely still is on the meadow orchard system. This system of cultivating trees over a long period yields from the same land a mixture of complementary products, including pears and perry, with milk and dairy products, particularly cheese and butter (Clout 2003). Bérard and Marchenay (2006, 112) go as far as to assert that 'The Norman meadow orchard corresponds to a historical and current reality which is simultaneously interesting to farming, the environment, the local economy the cultural heritage and biodiversity'.

An example of a 4% ABV premium perry, le Poiré Domfront AOC & AOP was developed in the 1990 s to create a branded product for pear growers mainly around Barenton. Barenton is 150 kilometres south of the city of study, Cherbourg, so the researcher-writers will have to find commercial and traditional links between this hinterland and the sea port on the northern tip of the Cotentin peninsula. The perry, Poiré Domfront, was awarded the protection of AOC, *l'appellation d'origine contrôlée*, status in 2002 and AOP status in 2006; AOP is the EU equivalent of AOC. The growing area is in the Domfrontais, which lies on the edge of the Massif Armoricain with its deep soils and maritime climate. The 100,000 pear trees of this area were under threat but now that they have been incorporated into a commercially viable system they could survive; the AOC requires that 40% of the pears pressed must be from the *Plant de blanc* variety. These trees need to be 50 years old to come into full productivity, which is a challenge for capitalisation of new projects. A technical account of perry production can be found in Arthey and Ashurst (1996). This, along with the names of pear varieties, and examples of the older, manual equipment for picking and processing will provide the researchers in the field with dialogic materials to create links between places to eat and the cultural ethnobotany of the peninsula. It is clear from preliminary web searches that a range of perry in on sale in Cherbourg.

Literary travel writing, rich with cross readings from history to locally available food can offer leadership, like an imprimatur that visitors follow, not by using the imperative command to visit a particular spot, but by creating a dialogic reading at that place. Roland Barthes (1972) remarks on the process that happens when a catalyst text places a well-known figure in an accessible place. In his text Barthes recounts his moment in the style of one of Patron's (2020) *Small Stories* of how he finds himself in the same restaurant as a well-known author, an imprimatur, prefixing the moment with a literary, imagistic word, gloom. In his autobiography, Barthes communicates that emotion of excitement when he spies Nobel laureate and travel writer, André Gide (1869–1951) eating a pear in the Lutétia brasserie:

> Imagine wanting to copy not the works but the practices of any contemporary [writer] —his way of strolling through the world, a notebook in his pocket and a phrase in his head (the way I imagined Gide traveling from Russia to the Congo, reading his classics and writing his notebooks in the dining car, waiting for the meals to be served; the way I actually saw him, one day in 1939, in the gloom of the Brasserie Lutétia, eating a pear and reading a book)! (Barthes 1977, 76–77)

CONCLUSION

Hexis as a preparatory framework for the literary travel writer planning inquiry into a new urban space is developed here, taking Cherbourg, as a case study. It can be seen that by establishing six points of reference from archive work, and from initial literary reading, after Onfray (2010), that potential for creating toureme moments (Mansfield 2015) in the research participants is feasible, and that the same process could be reused for other towns in tourism development. The points are referred to as plateaus in the development of this research. The plateaus also offer places of articulation in urban space where the researchers' emotional responses are stimulated by the additional reading associated with their existing personal cultural capital. The affect of these plateaus may be further enhanced by the literary travel writer endeavouring to create dialogic cross-readings between initially disparate elements from the hexis, for example between a local food product and a moment from history in a resident's life or work. This method may be applied in place inquiry to detect and to value cultural heritage, both from the tangible built environment of the streets and from the intangible cultural heritage, the ICH, lived through the emotions of the visiting travel writer in contact with the residents and their day-to-day interactions.

REFERENCES

Arthey, D., & Ashurst, P. (1996). *Fruit Processing*. London: Blackie.
Barthes, R. (1970). *L'empire des signes*. Geneva: Skira.
Barthes, R. (1972). *Mythologies*. New York: Noonday Press.
Barthes, R. (1977). *RB by RB*. Berkeley: University of California Press.
Bell, A. (2005) (trans.). *W G Sebald's Campo Santo*. London: Penguin.
Benjamin, W. (2009). *One Way Street and Other Writings*. London: Penguin.
Bérard, L., & Marchenay, P. (2006). Local Products and Geographical Indications: Taking Account of Local Knowledge and Biodiversity. *International Social Science Journal, 58*(187), 109–116.
Breton, H. (2019). Les savoirs narratifs en contexte de validation des acquis de l'expérience : perspectives épistémologiques. In M. Lani-Bayle (Ed.), *Mettre l'expérience en mots. Les savoirs narratifs* (pp. 75–85). Lyon: Chronique Sociale.
Brubaker, B. (2005). *For Freedom: The Story of a French Spy*. New York: Bantam.
Carnevali, B. (2013). L'esthétique sociale entre philosophie et sciences sociales. *Tracés Revue de Sciences Humaines., 13,* 29–48.

Clout, H. (2003). The Pays de Bray: A Vale of Dairies in Northern France. *Agricultural History Review, 51*(2), 190–208.

Dunne, P. (2016). Restoried Script Performance. In S. Pendzik, R. Emunah, & D. Read Johnson D. (Ed.), *The Self in Performance. Autobiographical, Self-Revelatory, and Autoethnographic Forms of Therapeutic Theatre* (pp. 141–154). New York: Palgrave.

Ernaux, A. (2000). *La Vie extérieure*. Paris: Gallimard.

Flam, H., & King, D. (2005). *Emotions and Social Movements*. London: Routledge.

Gerard, J. (1597). *The Herbal or General Historie of Plantes*. London: John Norton.

Goodwin, J., Jasper, J., & Polletta, F. (2001). *Passionate Politics. Emotions and Social Movements*. Chicago: University of Chicago Press.

Gurney, D. (1848). *The Record of the House of Gurney*. London: Nichols.

Mann, T. (1996). *Death in Venice*. London: Minerva.

Mansfield, C. (2018, June). Cultural Capital in Place-Making. *Journal of Hospitality & Tourism*, 1–17.

Mansfield, C. (2015). *Researching Literary Tourism*. Plymouth: Shadows Media.

Mansfield, C. (2012). *Traversing Paris: French Travel Writing Practices in the Late Twentieth Century; an Analysis of the Work of Annie Ernaux, François Maspero and Jean Rolin*. Saarbrucken: Akademikerverlag.

Mansfield, C. (2004). Lire L'empire des signes de Barthes comme écriture de voyage. In Y. Kaniike, S. Kadowaki, & Y. Kobayashi (Eds.), *Bulletin Barthes—Résonances des sens* (pp. 151–157). Tokyo: University of Tokyo Centre for Philosophy.

Onfray, M. (2010). *Filosofia del viaggio*. Milano: Ponte alle Grazie.

Patron, S. (2020). *Small Stories—Une nouveau paradigm pour les recherches sur le récit*. Paris: Hermann.

Roberts, Z. (2016). *River Tourism: The Pedagogy and Practice of Place Writing*. Plymouth: TKT.

Sassen, S. (2006). *Territory, Authority, Rights: From Medieval to Global Assemblages*. Princeton: Princeton University Press.

Sebald, W. (2005). *Campo Santo*. London: Penguin.

Scribano, A. (2017). Amor y acción colectiva: una mirada desde las prácticas intersticiales en la Argentina. *Aposta, Revista de Ciencias Sociales, 74*, 241–280.

Tracy, M. (1989). *Government and Agriculture in Western Europe, 1880–1988* (3rd ed.). London: Harvester-Wheatsheaf.

Wagoner, B., Brescó, I., & Awad, S. (2019). *Theories of Constructive Remembering*. New York: Springer.

Wolff, L. (2014). *W G Sebald's Hybrid Poetics—Literature as Historiography*. Berlin: De Gruyter.

PART II

Cities Today: Situated Analyzes and Sensibilities

CHAPTER 7

(In)Sensibilities to the Vigilance of Others in the City

Lucía Carmina Jasso López

INTRODUCTION

In most contemporary cities, public and private surveillance technologies[1] have been deployed to watch what others do or do not do. It is a phenomenon of the city on a global scale (Ramírez and Valenzuela 2017), one which has become "a key dimension in the modern world" (Bauman and Lyon 2013, 4).

Behind this urban unfolding, there is a public discourse that refers to these technologies being emplaced in order to reduce crime, and what is expected is that they are perceptible to the populations who transit public space with the purpose of dissuading them from any incivility or criminal activity, attributing to these devices a symbolic power. However, over time the presence of these surveillance technologies to which society has become accustomed and even desensibilized has been normalized.

[1]Video surveillance cameras and drones are mainly considered.

L. C. Jasso López (✉)
Institute of Social Research, National Autonomous
University of Mexico, Mexico City, Mexico
e-mail: carmina.jasso@sociales.unam.mx

© The Author(s), under exclusive license to Springer Nature Switzerland AG 2021
A. Scribano et al. (eds.), *Cities, Capitalism and the Politics of Sensibilities*,
https://doi.org/10.1007/978-3-030-58035-3_7

117

This article aims to analyse the (in)sensibility to surveillance of others in the city. In principle, it focuses on the study of the social effects of surveillance technologies in contemporary societies and cities, and the implications of watching others as the potential violation of fundamental prerogatives such as the right to privacy, to mobility, to the protection of personal data and to not be discriminated against.

The research is located in Mexico City where I have carried out field-work to study the planning and organization of surveillance technologies that converge in public space, and I have also conducted interviews with inhabitants of this city regarding their perceptions and sensibilities. However, in addition to studying the phenomenon at the local level, these social practices are also taken up on a global scale.

The analysis is circumscribed within the framework of a politics of sensibilities[2] to study the social practices that normalize the presence of surveillance technologies in the city, as well as those that perceive and assume them as a latent threat in their daily lives and in response to which they have generated new horizons for action.

POLITICS OF SENSIBILITIES AND SURVEILLANCE

Surveillance technologies with different social purposes and different technological scopes have been installed and are operating in practically all cities. The diversity of possibilities of these technologies is so wide that it is complex, at least to outline it in a few pages, in addition to permanently contributing to new forms and characteristics through technological innovation. However, in general, they all have the same objective: to watch the others.

Watching is associated with observing, and with the sight which is one of the five human senses. Sight is the motor of surveillance and is central to social life because, as Barreto Durán points out: "the eyes are my main connection with the world, with them I am constantly evaluating and questioning my surroundings" (2009, 7). Through the sense of sight, it is possible to look at objects, examine behaviours, understand the world,

---

[2] It is understood that "the body as the first relationship with the world structures our wanderings and experiences, where sensations and emotions express the differential ways of feeling in the world, as the right ways of feeling, giving place to social sensibilities" (Scribano et al. 2012, 8).

among many other possibilities that, connected with the other senses, enhance our existence through sensibilities.

However, we do not observe objectively or neutrally, our glances are charged with subjectivities because there is an established order in which "shared symbols and accepted conventions give order to our lives, a refuge where we can rest easy, knowing what is right, how our environment has been determined and what we must see as real" (Barreto Durán 2009, 8); so, the possibilities of looking are multiple, and in a broad sense:

> We never look at just one thing; we always look at the relationship between things and ourselves. Our vision is in continuous activity, in continuous movement, continuously learning the things that are in a circle whose centre is itself, constituting what is present for us as we are. (Berger 1972, 1)

The glance is dynamic and changes over time and in the face of various circumstances and contexts, but it is always related to our existence as individuals who are part of a society, accompanied by wisdom, knowledge, prejudices and social symbols. Thus, "there are a number of ways to see the world, to explore and understand it" (Barreto Durán 2009, 8). In summary, we could say that there is a force that homogenizes, but at the same time it coexists with another that advances in the opposite direction towards diversity, free will and discordance.

In our daily life in the city, "heterogeneous ways of seeing, saying, feeling and doing are promoted", but also other ways that "condition them, showing the structural mechanisms that make it a particular socio-spatial and classist geometry" (Cervio 2015, 21). Urban design, the showcases and spectacular advertisements that present us with products, the lights and all that visual arsenal that nourishes the cities, are there influencing the views of society, potentially unifying sensations and, at the same time, providing information that can be discerned by each individual.

In this context, surveillance carried out through the sense of sight is impregnated with all this social baggage. Those who watch with the support of surveillance technologies are people who watch with prior prejudice, knowledge and beliefs. This includes those who watch from home, companies or businesses with a few cameras, and government institutions or police corporations that have hundreds or thousands of cameras in the city. In all cases, the people behind the surveillance technologies, receive and process these images according to their own prior knowledge and prejudice. Even the images that are selected and analysed by artificial intelligence will eventually become part of the human glance and judgement for their interpretation.

Thus, even those who have received training and are trained to watch and find certain patterns of behaviour, cannot avoid their own subjectivities because "what we know or what we believe affects the way we see things" (Berger 1972, 1). When watching, and especially in the effort to do it "efficiently", we will bet on the observation of certain types of people that according to their physical and social characteristics correspond to a certain ethnic, age, religious, ideological group, etc., "potentially" characterized—previously—as risky. This could be considered, to a large extent, as discriminatory by directing surveillance more intensely towards certain types of people than others.

In public video surveillance, watchers play a fundamental role, because they are the ones who, permanently—as humanly possible—are observing the images of the surveillance technologies deployed in the city and interpreting whether or not there is any abnormality, some data or image that corresponds to any incivility or crime. To enter that job, each of them participated in a training course in which they explained what they should observe, and what they should report as an emergency or incident, but of course their prejudices and socially shared symbols are added to their training allowing them to discern between one image and another.

It is evident that the watchers, when observing, do so with the received indications and with the social baggage and previous knowledge. But it is also clear that "our perception or appreciation of an image also depends on our own way of seeing" (Berger 1972, 2), and even when there are indications about what to look at, each one will see what they choose to see, even in the same image there will be those who appreciate a normal situation and where someone else perceives an unusual or suspicious situation.

Thus, the sensations that "arise as a result and as an antecedent of the perceptions that give rise to the emotions" (Scribano et al. 2012, 8), are there permanently influencing what we see and how we see it, and this is enhanced through surveillance technologies that magnify the quantity and quality of the images that reach human eyes.

SURVEILLANCE IN CONTEMPORARY CITIES

In contemporary cities, cameras and drones are watching what is happening, collecting images from different places in the territory, and have the ability to track events in real-time or remotely.

The cameras "can reach a wide spectrum by making possible the recording (and reproduction) of the activities of any person who is in the observed place" (Cordero 2015, 361). And even when surveillance is directed at a specific property or person or group, it will also record the activities of those who pass through it, violating their right to privacy.

But, "drones are changing the possibilities of our way of seeing, looking and observing" (Scribano 2017, 65). They are able to move quickly from one side to the other and obtain images of precise situations, they introduce a "vertical glance" (Arteaga 2016) to watch certain spaces such as borders, airports, roads or social manifestations, marches, confrontations or protests, at the moment in which these occur. All this serves to reduce the risk to those who monitor, and increases surveillance capabilities.

At the time of COVID-19, these technologies showed the potential of surveillance, especially in Asian cities, but also—keeping the proportions—in Latin American cities where even when surveillance technologies do not have the scope—both numerical and in capacity—as in Asian cities, have increasingly shown more possibilities.

In the media, we have witnessed how the health contingency has "accelerated the use of Artificial Intelligence (AI) systems and surveillance technologies in China" (Vega 2020). It is largely a process that has been brewing for years in the cities of this country whose "artificial intelligence technologies and has set up the world's most sophisticated surveillance state [...] tracking citizens' daily movements" (Feldstein 2019).

Starting from the contingency, there are cameras with computerized vision and infrared sensors capable of detecting the temperatures of people in public spaces, as well as having the ability to identify if people are using their masks properly (Vega 2020).

It is no secret to anyone that in China there has been a huge deployment of surveillance technologies for years, and that various activities of daily life are observed through different technologies with facial recognition, artificial intelligence, among other means that generate huge databases and the possibility of conceiving intelligence from its analysis.

It is no secret either that Chinese governments and companies have exported these technologies to various parts of the world. In Latin America, there is evidence that governments—from different orders—have received advice for the implementation of their surveillance systems and have even accepted donations from Chinese companies and governments (Jasso 2020).

Thus, it is known that there are cameras and drones capable of carrying out "dystopian uses" orienting surveillance to social control in cities. In this regard, Chokshi presents some of these uses:

> In one, a politician requests footage of his enemies kissing in public, along with the identities of all involved. In another, a life insurance company offers rates based on how fast people run while exercising. And in another, a sheriff receives a daily list of people who appeared to be intoxicated in public, based on changes to their gait, speech or other patterns. (Chokshi 2019, 1)

To these amazing every day uses of surveillance is added the fact that through drones and cameras more and more can be known about us. For example, the technology that, with the support of the cameras in the electronic advertisements on the streets, "recognizes our reactions and adapts to them" in order to have "a greater impact" on people's preferences. These technologies have been used in Tokyo, Japan, allowing people to be discriminated according to their preferences and manipulated to consume, but for governments—particularly authoritarian ones—they can serve to "regulate social behaviour without anyone being able to protest" (Medina 2017).

Any place can be conducive to watching and observing. Facial recognition cameras have been placed in the public toilets in Beijing, China,[3] the purpose of which is to deliver toilet paper to people who have not previously been in a certain period of time, and thus avoid wasting paper and using it responsibly. However, in terms of human rights, it is a latent violation of privacy, in addition to the right to the protection of personal data when compiling information from millions of faces.

---

[3] The first machines were installed in 2016 in the restrooms of the Olympic Park, "an area where up to 20 devices are counted and which, according to workers at the venue, has generated a saving of 2100 yuan per month (about 285 euros) per restroom" (Arana 2017).

In Latin America there is also evidence of these dystopian uses. In Mexico, in some gated communities in the Metropolitan Area of Monterrey, Nuevo León,[4] surveillance cameras have been equipped with artificial intelligence that allows them to detect certain types of clothing or behaviour associated with youth groups.[5]

As Guzik (2016, 3) notes, there are a "large amount of surveillance capabilities", and with these dystopian uses surveillance technologies have unveiled the control capabilities they have over society, as well intervention to generate data and intelligence in crisis situations and the management of cities. This is relevant, because the analysis of databases implies the "material surveillance of massive amounts of information about people and societies" (Scribano 2017, 65).

But these surveillance technologies, like all affordable technologies, are not neutral and there is the possibility of making different uses of them. Thus, it is important to emphasize that "technology in itself does not have to lead us to create dystopian cities, it is only a tool. It is how it is used and for what purposes what constitutes the difference" (Medina 2017).

SENSIBILITY TO THE VIGILANCE OF OTHERS

In Foucault's (1975) terms, vigilance is power. The fact that someone can be observed and cannot know who is observing them, generates "power mechanisms". Above all, when there is no possibility of reciprocity and you cannot see who is watching, and—in the best of scenarios—you can only see the device that is located somewhere.

According to Berger (1972), there is a "reciprocal nature of vision" in which we can see something or someone, reciprocally they could also see us. However, in surveillance technologies, this reciprocity is broken because the glance is done remotely, and with difficulty, someone watched by the camera or drone will not be able to see who is watching him, at the most he will be able to see the device, but not who is really watching.

---

[4] Commented upon by Leily Hassaine at the Round Table: "Urbanizaciones y barrios cerrados", on August 27, 2018 at Instituto de Investigaciones Sociales of the Universidad Nacional Autónoma de México.

[5] The use of facial recognition software can identify the gender of passers-by with an accuracy of 85–90%, ethnic origin and approximate age (Fitzpatrick 2010).

In cities, most surveillance technologies are visible to passers-by on public roads (Bauman and Lyon 2013), precisely because they have a symbolic function in which they discourage certain social conducts or behaviours. In this sense, the "vigilant architecture" is displayed as "the technology of power in order to repress individuals, manufacture subjected and exercised bodies and impose silence" (Cortés 2010, 17).

The goal of these surveillance technologies is that their presence inhibits or dissuades social control. They are placed and managed hoping that populations are sensible to their presence and thus behave according to the established rules because they have the feeling that they are being observed. This agrees with human nature and the sense of sight, because "soon after being able to see, we are aware that we can also be seen" (Berger 1972, 1). In short, it is surveillance that constantly coerces by being permanently present in the cities, manifesting itself as Foucault refers, in the form of "the physics of power" in which:

> control over the body is carried out in accordance with the laws of optics and mechanics, in accordance with a whole set of spaces, lines, screens, beams, degrees, and without resorting, in principle at least, to excess, to force, to violence. A power that is apparently so much less bodily as it is more wisely physical. (Foucault 1975, 108)

Surveillance technologies in cities, especially public ones, are placed in the urban area in a way that they are visible to everyone who transits through there. These are everywhere and it is about "privatized public spaces kept under constant surveillance" (Harvey 2008, 32). In some cases, even advertisements referring to the presence of these devices are placed, either as a way to warn about the vulnerability of the right to privacy or to increase the symbolic, bodily and emotional effects on society. But whatever the case, they are made visible to maximize people's perception and sensibility.

The visibility of surveillance can go beyond the symbolic and go to unsuspected extremes. In Medellín, Colombia, through the loudspeakers on the posts with surveillance cameras, citizens are warned that they are discovered or are about to commit an offence.[6] That is, they show that

---

[6] That was the proposal of the Agreement Project 185 of 2019, which was filed with the Council of Medellín, Colombia (Restrepo 2019).

people are being observed and that could be evidenced and subject to a sanction.

In China, giant screens are displayed on the main streets of Xian, projecting images captured by cameras in the city. Therefore, watchers ensure that everyone who is there is aware of and is sensible to the presence of the surveillance devices and the possibility of disclosure of their image.

In this logic, the State "has the possibility and uses image and sound capture means, it is not illogical to think that this will have an impact on the behaviour of the individual in spaces open to the public" (Cordero 2015, 370). At least, this impact is what is expected to control society.

In the particular case of drones, it is noted that: "the propensity of the modern State to place, on one side, its ability to observe from a certain height, as well as to place itself symbolically above society" (Arteaga 2016, 269). They exercise hierarchical vigilance, not only because of their physical position above us, but also symbolic, as they can disappear from one moment to the next.

Thus, surveillance "affects the direct exercise of citizens' rights that are exercised in public places. The fact of knowing that you are permanently observed and registered represses and restricts your full exercise" (Cordero 2015, 370) of the right to free transit, to privacy, to the protection of personal data and not to be discriminated against.

To this sense of surveillance in cities, we must add the unavoidable fact that the trend of surveillance technologies is incremental. Even though there are more and more voices criticizing the effectiveness of cameras and drones, and questioning the potential violation of fundamental prerogatives, the numbers of cameras in the urban structure are actually increasing.[7]

It seems that society has begun to internalize the presence of surveillance technologies and "one look is enough. A look that watches, and that each one, feeling it weighing on himself, ends up internalizing it to the point of watching himself; each one will exercise this vigilance on and

---

[7] In Mexico City, 8088 public surveillance cameras were installed in 2008. In the first months of 2020, they totaled just over 15,000, but in August 2019, the Head of Government announced that the installation of 58,000 cameras inside the neighbourhoods with high crime rates would start (*La Razón* 2019). To these are added the tens of thousands of cameras that the victimization surveys identify as having been installed in homes and businesses in the city.

against himself" (Foucault 1980, 18). It is largely a new social contract in which we give up part of our rights in exchange for vigilance that watches over me and others and maintains social order.

In the interviews conducted in Mexico City,[8] there is evidence that society is sensible to the presence of surveillance devices and the permanent glance that is exercised.

An interviewee reported that, while we are being sensible to this surveillance, it has a regulatory function in society and serves "so that we are better people". As a specific case, she pointed out that images are shown in the media and on social networks in which people are seen abandoning pets, but these videos manage to sensibilize society, because "knowing that they are being observed by the cameras, they no longer abandon dogs on the street". This occurs either because they are sensibilized to images of abandonment and internalize the consequences, or because they are afraid of social sanction, but from the point of view of the interviewee, society is sensible to surveillance and also modifies its behaviour.

In several interviews, men and women reported behaviour modification in the presence of surveillance technologies, in such a way that when they know that they are being recorded—even when they get used to it—they behave differently because they have knowledge that they are being observed. In this regard, an interviewee shares:

> In the cameras of the shopping centres you start to behave differently if you notice that there is a camera right in front of you. Because of course, you know that someone is going to see that recording, for me it is that someone is going to have my image, for some reason we have the instinct to behave under normal standards and [you have to] demonstrate that you are a normal person, even if you don't have the intention to carry out criminal activity, but it is like an instinct to demonstrate that you are an ordinary person who will not draw attention.

---

[8] They were carried out anonymously—no socio-economic data was recorded—with inhabitants of Mexico City during March 2018–March 2019 as part of the field work of the Project: "Prevención del crimen y tecnología. Los efectos de la videovigilancia. Análisis de la incidencia delictiva y de las percepciones ciudadanas para la elaboración de políticas públicas".

But what happens with the thousands of public cameras that are permanently monitoring in Mexico City?[9] The probability that our daily activities are monitored is high and in this sense, "it can inhibit your normal activities" or "if you know that there is some kind of observation in you, you may change some behaviours" as two interviewees pointed out. And although we are aware of the location of the cameras either by the signs that point to them or by the diffusion of the places where they are placed,[10] it is difficult for us to be fully aware of when and when we are not under the glance of surveillance technologies. Furthermore, considering that, in the colonies, both households and companies and businesses have added hundreds of thousands of cameras (Jasso 2020), how can we assess whether they are effectively watching us or not? Under what circumstances are we sensible to this surveillance that is everywhere?

In response to this question, an interviewee stated that "unconsciously, you feel watched", and there are those who even express the social panic of being watched and persecuted permanently. But they warn that this effect increases when there is the certainty of a sanction for inappropriate behaviour, in such a way that: "your attitudes change when there is a sanction involved. The fact that there are cameras must have a follow-up, a result, a consequence or something [...] it is more the fear of sanction".

In summary, I agree with Bauman and Lyon (2013, 4) who affirm that "in many countries, people are very aware of the way in which surveillance affects their lives". This holds even in circumstances where there is an absence of certainty about in which place or moment they are being observed. I particularly agree that surveillance is "a unidirectional process in which the glance of the watchers prevails over the watched" (Arteaga 2018, 9), thus the watched are not necessarily certain of when they are observed, and precisely in this uncertainty lies the power of surveillance because although the dream of the Panopticon, which allows one to

---

[9] "C5 operates and monitors more than 15 thousand surveillance cameras that exist in Mexico City (Closed Circuit Television, CCTV), in order to prevent and immediately alert the authorities of security and capital emergencies about any situation of risk". See: https://www.c5.cdmx.gob.mx/dependencia/acerca-de/video-monitore.

[10] In Mexico City a database was published in which "the locations of the posts of the Command, Control, Computing, Communications and Citizen Contact Center (C5) of Mexico City with security cameras, panic buttons, speaker, pole type and georeferencing can be consulted". See: https://datos.cdmx.gob.mx/explore/dataset/ubicacion-acceso-gratuito-internet-wifi-c5/table/.

"see with a glance everything that is done in it" (Bentham 1971, 37) is impossible, the sensation of surveillance permanently affects society.

INSENSIBILITY TO THE VIGILANCE OF OTHERS

In the architectural design of cities "the problem of the total visibility of bodies, individuals, things, under a centralized view, had been one of the most constant basic principles" (Foucault 1980, 10). To a large extent, it became an aspiration to be able to observe others and a necessity to maintain order, thereby avoiding crimes and incivilities.

With surveillance technologies, the ability to observe was magnified. These devices have the ability to systematically watch for long periods of time, as well as to record enormous amounts of information in images. They can perform much more "effective" surveillance than is possible with human eyes.

Thus, the trend towards hierarchically structured cities, with the distribution of bodies in space and densely watched, is aspirationally one of the objectives of contemporary societies, and in the effort to achieve them permanent vigilance is accepted and assimilated (Jasso 2021).

Faced with this technological deployment, a kind of new social contract was generated in which society gives up[11] all or part of its liberties and rights, such as privacy, free transit, not being discriminated against, in exchange for surveillance of itself and the others that, in turn, allows us to live in an orderly and controlled environment. In this context, drones and "surveillance cameras have become omnipresent and their presence is already understood as something normal "normal" that few of us come to question" (Cortés 2010, 33).

Much of society tends to the normalization of surveillance technologies, and "citizens dedicate themselves to their affairs almost without noticing the surveillance cameras that point from the top to the streets of all major cities" (Garland 2001, 31). In consequence we arrive at a situation in which "what scares is not the arrival of a surveillance society, but rather that we live in it without it worrying us" (Bauman cited by Ramonet 2016). Although a society in the midst of a social panic about

---

[11] Consciously demanding the presence of more surveillance technologies in the public spaces of the city, directly financing it with its own resources to protect its physical integrity and watching its heritage or requesting it from governments. But this also entails an unconscious agreement when normalizing the presence of this surveillance.

surveillance is not convenient, neither is one that normalizes and does not question the implications of surveillance.

Why does the normalization of surveillance technologies occur in contemporary societies? There are several answers, but in order to contribute to the debate in these studies, I will briefly state some of them.

One answer is associated with the "imperceptibility of surveillance"; even though most cameras and drones are exposed to the eyes of passers-by just to make them sensible, there are also other schemes where "architecture and technology come together to achieve social control through the imperceptibility of surveillance" (Cortés 2010, 47). Especially when the aim is to surprise potential attackers, the devices are hidden as a strategy from homes or businesses, and even more so when it comes to national security intelligence operations.

On the other hand, the watchers are anonymous and the watched face the uncertainty of not knowing how, when and where they are being observed (Jasso 2021). It is not even possible to know if all the devices are working,[12] and if they are also being observed at that precise moment by someone. Thus, it is known that there is a possibility of not being seen.

In this context, it is clear that surveillance is not, nor can it be, absolute. Even with the most powerful technologies, it is not possible to watch everything, much less in cities that are in constant movement and territorial expansion. There will always be something that escapes the glance of these surveillance technologies—both public and private—there will always be some object that in the structure or design of the city prevents the partial or total view of something that wants to be observed, from a tree, a pole, a building or a billboard.

Furthermore, from a different angle, the images about the same event could be so different that they manage to generate debates among those who observe them. Leaving a key person or perhaps a vehicle out of sight can make a real difference in investigating a crime. At the same time, it shows the impossibility of total surveillance and the implications for decision-making.

In addition, the possibilities for change and movement in the city are of such magnitude that it is not surprising that people assume that they are not necessarily watched in their daily activities. Furthermore, when it is known that although cameras and drones can record a large number of

[12] The Government of Mexico City disclosed that in the first months of 2019, of the total of 15,310 cameras in the city, 500 were not working, representing 3.3%.

images, they are useless if there is no one behind them to analyse what is happening (Jasso 2021). Humanly speaking, it is impossible that the thousands of cameras installed in cities are being permanently watched, and even assuming that a person was hired to observe each of the thousands of cameras that are in the city, there would be moments of fatigue or distraction that would impede observation entirely.[13]

Finally, I dare to propose that the normalization of surveillance technologies, and the insensibility to their presence, occurs because they are considered necessary to maintain order, and society prefers it to avoiding chaos in cities. In contemporary cities, there is a strong demand for surveillance technologies and consequently, as Whitaker (quoted in Cordero 2015, 360) argues "the contemporary panopticon is surprisingly different [...] The prisoners of Bentham dreamed of escaping; the Orwell dissidents in 1984 ardently wanted to flee to a better place, but they could not, for there simply was no such place. On the contrary, our panopticon is accepted, and above all demanded". That is a new reality.

Also, it should be considered that in this process of normalization it could happen that people "get used to despising the public eye and become insensible to shame" (Bentham 1971, 42). In this way, it is not surprising that people even look at the cameras and smile and act as if no one were watching them,[14] but it should be noted that what is risky is normalization to such a degree that it reflects insensibility as a society.

Before the occurrence of high impact events, such as a crime, an interviewee in Mexico City reported:

> [...] I watched a video on where a guy comes out of the trunk and it is believed that it was because he was being kidnapped. He falls to the ground, and want to remove the bandages. The incredible thing is that a car recorded all this, but nobody stopped it [...] many people have watched the video, it was on the news, but when talking to the authorities there was no lawsuit, no investigation folder, not even culprits, it is not known who is the person that flew out of the trunk.

---

[13] The United States Department of Justice has said that watching those images is "boring and fascinating", and that the attention fades after about 20 minutes (Chokshi 2019).

[14] In Mexico City, there was a circulation of "videos and photographs from security cameras of the moment when thieves, without fear of being recorded, look at the camera at all times" (Colín 2019) while committing the offences.

In another interview, we reviewed the case in which "the murderer records everything that is happening and then publishes it on social networks. As if he had made sense of his crime and spreading it was part of his goal". With these types of events, the level of insensibility to images is revealed where "in society, the fact of recording is more for morbid curiosity than for doing justice".

With these type of cases, the underlying reflection is that, although the witnessing and recording of an event through a cell phone manipulated by a person can become insensible, the more the glance through the video surveillance systems that operate *en masse* in the city, not only because they could escape the eyes of the watchers or the scrutiny of artificial intelligence and facial recognition, but because behind the decisions of which cases to attend, there are also social actors who prioritize what is priority, as well as what is possible and suitable for them to do.

It would be considered that "the fact that criminals smile at the cameras is an unusual attitude", however, it is also a consequence of the fact that there is no effect on criminal behaviour. Thus, it happens that the cameras "inhibit us because we do not commit criminal acts, but when you are already doing something that you know has no consequences, that they are not going to punish you, then you take it as a joke".

The existence of a sanction when a crime is committed is not always the rule, not even when the cameras are present, and this is the reason why those who commit crimes act with total unconcern even in front of the cameras. The case recalled in an interview stands out:

> you can see in the assaults on the foreign trucks that all have cameras and the assailants get on, take off their headscarves and smile, they literally smile, they say: "look at what I do with your video" because there is no fear of the consequence, then there is no use in recording.

It is clear that in society the standardization of surveillance technologies has permeated to such a degree that they become insensible to its presence. In some cases, even extreme situations are recorded in which crimes or incivilities are committed in the presence of the camera.

CONCLUSIONS

Studies on surveillance technologies in cities are relevant because they represent a wide range of possibilities for urban coexistence and also have diverse social effects. But above all they are fundamental, because in most cities, particularly Latin American ones, they are constantly expanding, even more so after the context of COVID-19 that has revealed the potential of these technologies.

It is important to study which effects surveillance has on individuals and society, what does it represent socially that someone else can observe us without us being able to look in reciprocity and without us knowing what happens to the images that are compiled from us every day. In short, how it affects our sensibilities.

Thereon, one of the main conclusions is that the effects of surveillance in society are not homogeneous. While some are permanently violated because they are sensible to the possible observation by others, there are those who manage to normalize this surveillance and even be insensible to its presence.

On the one hand, it is unavoidable that surveillance technologies potentially violate people's rights by violating their privacy, the protection of personal data and the right to mobility. These devices are capable of making people feel persecuted and observed, particularly when urban design insists on manifesting the presence of surveillance devices and generates sensibilities in people that consequently force them to modify their behaviour.

However, there are those who normalize the presence of cameras and drones. It is a form of "normalized sensibilities" (Scribano and De Sena 2019) that is partly due to a process of rationality in which the impossibility of total surveillance is known, as well as the absence of information and the latent "imperceptibility of surveillance" (Cortés 2010), which is further accentuated when the devices are hidden for national security reasons, or for some other reason that warrants it.

But the process of normalization and insensibility also occurs because people accept this surveillance in a new kind of social contract, in which prerogatives are given in exchange for control in the city and more security. In this way, it is observed that as they demand more vigilance, and even in some cases finance it with their own resources, the criticism and questioning of the vigilance of others diminishes.

At the extreme are those who are totally insensible to the surveillance of others and to the images of crimes and violence recorded by these technologies. The fascination with the image is lost and even when scenes that should be important and shocking to our senses are shown, we normalize them and even make them invisible.

Surveillance in cities is a fact, and it is likely that it will increase in time both numerically and in its capacities. In this sense, what is socially pertinent is that the surveillance exercised by others be limited and controlled in order to avoid dystopian uses that further violate the social rights and sensibilities of those who inhabit the cities.

REFERENCES

Arana, I. (2017, March 22). Tecnología de reconocimiento facial en los baños públicos de China contra los ladrones de papel higiénico. *El Mundo.* https://www.elmundo.es/f5/comparte/2017/03/22/58d128 f6468aeb98558b45c0.html. Accessed 3 May 2020.

Arteaga, N. (2016). Política de la verticalidad: drones, territorio y población en América Latina. *Región y sociedad, 28*(65), 263–292.

Arteaga, N. (2018). *Videovigilancia en México. Protesta política, conflicto y orden social.* México: FLACSO.

Barreto Durán, J. (2009). *Cómo veo lo que veo.* Proyecto de Grado, Universidad de los Andes, Bogotá.

Bauman, Z., & Lyon, D. (2013). *Vigilancia líquida.* Buenos Aires: Paidós.

Bentham, J. (1971). *El Panóptico.* Madrid: Las Ediciones de La Piqueta.

Berger, J. (1972). *Modos de ver.* London: British Broadcasting Corporation (BBC) and Penguin Books.

Cervio, A. (2015). Experiencias en la ciudad desde las tramas de los sentidos. Lecturas sobre la vista, el oído y el olfato. En R. Sánchez Aguirre (Comp.), *Sentidos y Sensibilidades: Exploraciones Sociológicas sobre Cuerpos/Emociones* (pp. 17–48). Buenos Aires: Estudios Sociológicos Editora.

Chokshi, N. (2019, June 13). How Surveillance Cameras Could Be Weaponized with A.I. *The New York Times.* https://www.nytimes.com/2019/06/13/us/aclu-surveillance-artificial-intelligence.html. Accessed 29 April 2020.

Colín, B. (2019, March 6). Graban asaltos a casas y negocios de la Condesa; los ladrones ni se inmutan. *Crónica.* https://www.cronica.com.mx/notas/2019/1112299.html. Accessed 15 April 2020.

Cordero, L. (2015). Videovigilancia e intervención administrativa: las cuestiones de legitimidad. *Revista de Derecho Público, 70,* 359–376.

Cortés, J. M. G. (2010). *La Ciudad Cautiva: Orden y vigilancia en el Espacio Urbano.* Madrid: Akal.

Feldstein, S. (2019, April 22). How Artificial Intelligence Systems Could Threaten Democracy. *The Conversation.* http://theconversation.com/how-artificial-intelligence-systems-could-threaten-democracy-109698. Accessed 5 May 2020.

Fitzpatrick, M. (2010). Advertising Billboards Use Facial Recognition to Target Shoppers. *The Guardian*. https://www.theguardian.com/media/pda/2010/sep/27/advertising-billboards-facial-recognition-japan. Accessed 3 May 2020.

Foucault, M. (1975). *Vigilar y castigar. Nacimiento de la prisión*. Madrid: Siglo XXI.

Foucault, M. (1980). El Ojo del Poder. Entrevista con Michael Foucault. En J. Bentham, *El Panóptico* [Trad. de Julia Varela y Fernando Álvarez Uría]. Madrid: Las ediciones de La Piqueta.

Garland, D. (2001). *La Cultura del Control: Crimen y Orden Social en la Sociedad Contemporánea*. Barcelona: Gedisa.

Guzik, K. (2016). *Making Things Stick: Surveillance Technologies and México's War in Crime*. Oakland: University of California Press.

Harvey, D. (2008). El derecho a la ciudad. *New Left Review, 53*(4), 23–39.

Jasso, C. (2020). Seguridad ciudadana y tecnología: Uso, planeación y regulación de la videovigilancia en América Latina. *DÍKÉ. Revista de Investigación en Derecho, Criminología y Consultoría Jurídica*.

Jasso, C. (2021). *La Ciudad Videovigilada. Entre la prevención del crimen y el control social*. México: Instituto de Investigaciones Sociales de la Universidad Nacional Autónoma de México (in press).

La Razón. (2019, August 5). Cámaras vecinales enlazadas al C5 llegan a zonas peligrosas. https://www.razon.com.mx/ciudad/sheinbaum-anuncia-ins talacion-de-camaras-en-colonias-de-la-cdmx/. Accessed 3 May 2020.

Medina, S. (2017, May 25). La distopía de las ciudades inteligentes. *Nexos, La brújula. El blog de la metrópoli*. https://labrujula.nexos.com.mx/?p=1302. Accessed 2 April 2020.

Ramírez, J., & Valenzuela, P. (2017). *Videovigilancia en el espacio público: el monitoreo de la ciudad como dispositivo de control poblacional*. Memoria para optar por el Grado de Licenciado en Ciencias Jurídicas y Sociales, Universidad de Chile, Santiago, Chile.

Ramonet, I. (2016). *El Imperio de la Vigilancia*. Madrid: Clave Intelectual.

Restrepo, V. (2019, May 6). ¿Cámaras con altavoces para sancionar gente en Medellín? *El Colombiano*. https://www.elcolombiano.com/antioquia/cam aras-de-seguridad-con-parlantes-para-sancionar-a-la-gente-en-medellin-pro pone-el-concejo-BD10646744. Accessed 12 May 2020.

Scribano, A. (2017). Drones: una manera de ver. *Boletín Científico Sapiens Research, 7*(2), 65–77.

Scribano, A., Cena, R., & Peano, A. (2012). Políticas de los cuerpos y emociones en los sujetos involucrados en acciones colectivas en la ciudad de Villa María, 2001–2008. *Papeles del CEIC, 77*. http://www.identidadcolectiva.es/pdf/77.pdf.

Scribano, A., & De Sena, A. (2019). Los programas sociales como mecanismos de "represión desapercibida" en Argentina (2007–2019). Un análisis desde las políticas de las sensibilidades. *Polis, 18*(53). http://doi.org/10.32735/s0718-6568/2019-n53-1383.

Vega, J. (2020, April 2). Covid-19: ¿un Caballo de Troya? *Reforma*. https://www.reforma.com/covid-19-un-caballo-de-troya-2020-04-02/op177353. Accessed 15 April 2020.

CHAPTER 8

"We Were Never Informal Ones": Aymara Qamiris and Independent Work in the Cities of Peruvian-Bolivian High Andean Plateau

Edwin Catacora Vidangos

INTRODUCTION

The main body of studies produced by the sociology of labour[1] privileged the analysis of the industrial, unionized worker with rights,[2] granting this social subject the central role in lines of research formulated by

---

[1] Studies on the world of labour appear in nineteenth century, in an international scene of increasing industrialization, technological development and modernization of production, but also of sharpening of social, political and economic conflicts. Such was the context of Marx's initial work, *Capital*, which focused on the capital–labour relationship. In pursuit of scientific rigor, the Marxist approach was divided into "determinism vs. voluntarism, science vs. revolution, materialism vs. idealism, the old Marx vs. the young". See Burawoy (1990, 775).

[2] Labour rights and social rights, such as retirement, job stability, social security and benefits, among others.

E. Catacora Vidangos (✉)
Universidad Nacional del Altiplano, Puno, Peru
e-mail: e.catacora@unap.edu.pe

© The Author(s), under exclusive license to Springer Nature
Switzerland AG 2021
A. Scribano et al. (eds.), *Cities, Capitalism and the Politics of Sensibilities*,
https://doi.org/10.1007/978-3-030-58035-3_8

137

both the structural perspective[3] and by political economy. Traces of this leading role are also found in Latin American sociology, in the theory[4] of formal and salaried work (Ghiotto 2015). Nevertheless, when analysing the heterogeneity[5] of labour and the structural precariousness of current capitalism, approaches focused on the notion of the "working class" seem to be insufficient if we consider that the senses of labour vary according to subjects, groups and classes, and respond to different national and cultural contexts. Given this situation, it is necessary for sociology of labour scholars to propose alternatives within the structural perspective that enable the study and the comprehension of the changes produced by global capitalism in the world of labour, at both economic and social levels.

In Latin America, such changes are the outcome of neoliberal policies whose implementation led to privatization and closure of public companies, massive dismissals and the risk of a general anomie in Latin American populations scared of becoming not a market society but "a society turned into a market" (Castell 2010). In this context, there are certain forms of labour articulation in the Aymara society of the Peruvian-Bolivian high Andean plateau (*altiplano*)[6]—a region with low rates of formal and salaried work[7]—whose study requires a cultural type of analysis, more flexible when addressing the importance of the confluence of market and labour in Aymara social life: its cultural aspects appear as the impulse of independent work and the basis for the social reproduction of Aymara spaces, practices, sensibilities and habitus.

Although a sector of the academy and press have popularized a negative image of Aymara commercial activities by associating them with informality and illegality, I consider it evident that such activities respond culturally to alternative forms of non-salaried work—arising from the

---

[3] Deterministic Marxism based on economy.

[4] I highlight Enrique de la Garza (Mexico), Ricardo Antunes (Brazil), Julio Neffa (Argentina) and, in Spain, Juan Castillo, whose work are influenced by the theory of French regulation.

[5] Caused by the entry of the female contingent into the capitalist system, intense subproletarianization, increase of non-salaried part-time work and precarious work through subcontracting and outsourcing.

[6] The high Andean plateau (also known as *el altiplano*) is the common name of the Collao Plateau, a region around Titicaca Lake, shared by Peru and Bolivia.

[7] The informality index reaches 73% in Peru, and 85% in Bolivia.

weak presence of the State and the scarce generation of formal employment—which, nevertheless, have maintained the reciprocity of peasant communal work. Following this path, I analyse the independent work carried out by the Aymara traders of the Peruvian-Bolivian[8] high Andean plateau, especially by the *qamiris*,[9] using for this purpose the data obtained in the ethnography that I have undertaken, at different intervals, during the last decade, in the altiplanic cities of Puno and Juliaca (Peru), and El Alto and La Paz (Bolivia).

THE PATHS OF LABOUR: A CRITICAL REVIEW

The International Labour Organization (ILO) influenced the sociology of labour in Latin America by proposing the research of non-salaried and self-employment work twice: in 1970, ILO introduced the term informality "to explain the structure and dynamics of labor market in developing countries" (Poblete 2018); in 2002, this term is redefined as "unregistered business and workers who do not practice labor laws" (De la Garza 2017). Both approaches show little clarity to explain the heterogeneity of both regional and global informality (Quijano 2000; Tassi et al. 2013; Poblete 2018), a limitation seemingly accentuated at present. Indeed, De la Garza (2017) considers it insufficient to analyse classical informality (self-employment and non-salaried workers), as he observes the rising of a "new informality", promoted paradoxically by the formal enterprises that eliminate the collective contract, union organization, job stability and social security. By doing so, this new informality acquires characteristics of precarious informality. In this context, it is necessary, in my point of view, to test a conceptual and methodological turning point that enables an adequate analysis of Aymara independent work. Then, I offer a proposal for this turning point considering the following points:

[8] Peru and Bolivia are the countries with the highest informality rate in Latin America. According to S. Levy (Interamerican Development Bank), labour informality reaches 80–85% in Bolivia, 70–75% in Peru, 60% in Mexico and 20–25% in Chile. See https://www.youtube.com/watch?v=nWkLhOSfYAg.

[9] Wealthy Aymara traders. After emigrating from rural peasant communities, they now live in the main cities of the *altiplano* and enjoy admired success in the region. See Llamque and Villca (2011).

a. Conceptually, it must be remembered that labour in the contemporary world is ductile: it is not restricted to the dependency relationship between worker and employment; it can rather flow, becoming outsourced work, intermittent work, subcontracted work or other forms of the so-called informal work. In face of this, I highlight Brown's definition of labour:

> labor means any physical or mental activity that transforms materials into a more subtle form, *provides or distributes goods or services to others*, and extends the human knowledge and wisdom [...], a definition of labor, therefore, includes references to both to the activity as to the purpose for which the activity is carried out [...], the world of labor is actively constructed by the interpretive acts of the agents involved in it. (Ghiotto 2015, 274. Our italics)

To conceive labour as a "distribution of goods" enables a better treatment of Aymara commercial activity, contextualized by job precariousness and weakening rights in both the public and the private sectors. Therefore, I use the concept cited as the basis of what I call "independent work" in this study, taking Aymara commerce as a case study.

b. Also, conceptually, it is necessary for the sociology of labour to generate theoretical alternatives to overcome the path followed by informality theorists.[10] These theoretical alternatives should enable us to think about the complex cultural background of labour in Latin American societies, such as the Aymaras. To do this, four facts must be assessed: (i) the distant and difficult relationship between State and civil society in Latin American countries[11]; (ii) the predominant, popular economy on the Peruvian-Bolivian high

---

[10] The discussion on informality or informal work has generated four approaches. Keith and ILO's dualistic approach differentiates a formal sector, subjected to law, from an informal one, outcome of the former's inability to assimilate it. De Soto's legalistic approach points to the legal order as obstacle in the required formalization of the informal sector. The structuralist approach proposes that in the face of high competitiveness, the actors follow flexible strategies to survive, outsourcing informal companies. The voluntary approach considers informality as an actor's own choice. See Galicia (2018).

[11] "Taxally speaking, there were 'liberated' markets where informal and illegal products were sold, mixed with those of legal origin, places where SUNAT [National Superintendence of Customs and Taxes Administration] could not enter, that is, the State. In addition to the thousands of formal small and medium-sized companies detected in

Table 8.1 Urban and rural population in Peru

Year	Urban area %	Rural area %
1940	35.4	64.6
1961	47.4	52.6
1972	59.5	40.5
1981	65.2	34.8
1992	70.1	29.9
2007	75.9	24.0
2015	77.0	23.0
2017	79.3	19.4

Source: Own elaboration based on Population Census (Peru-INEI). http://censo2017.inei.gob.pe/

Andean plateau, influenced by agricultural and livestock production, practiced outside the formal economic circuit; (iii) said predominance is socioculturally nourished by the continuous internal migrations from the countryside to the city (since 1940, in the Aymara case), and the consequent urban–rural demographic transformation (see Tables 8.1 and 8.2); (iv) this migratory process had a decisive influence on the labour market because, among other reasons, it poses—for both the private company and the State—the challenge of absorbing a large migrant labour force. For this reason, in both countries, and in the high Andean plateau, demographic change

Table 8.2 Urban and rural population in Bolivia

Year	Urban area %	Rural area %
1950	26.2	73.8
1976	47.4	58.7
1992	57.5	42.5
2001	62.4	37.6
2012	67.5	32.5
2018	69.5	30.6

Source: Own elaboration based on Population Census (Bolivia-INE) https://www.ine.gob.bo/index.php/salud/censos/

the database, it was necessary to add many other informal enterprises that do not exist statistically and whose quantification becomes very difficult" (Durand 2007, 50).

was followed by economic, cultural and even political changes. It goes without saying that by prioritizing external factors (political economy or legality) in understanding these facts, informality theorists have overlooked its internal factors (cultural and social ones), thus limiting both their analysis and results.

  c. From the above I consider, at a theoretical-methodological level, that some labour relationships analysts have repeatedly overlooked its cultural aspect, thus relegating its valuable epistemological utility and reducing possibilities for analysis. From my point of view, this is due, in part, to the fact that the main body of studies on the world of labour carried out from the structural perspective have privileged Eurocentric categories of labour that colonize their means of explanation. This scenario demands revaluing cultural aspects in the analysis of the economy and labour in Latin American societies, such as Aymara. For this reason, I find Bourdieu's theoretical contribution appropriate to appreciate the cultural aspects objectified on an ethic and a habitus in the actions of Peruvian-Bolivian Aymara traders.

It is well known that Bourdieu's theoretical work describes a conceptual transition between the notions of agency and structure, i.e. a "sociology of mediation" (Ortiz 1983). In this framework, the notion of ethos, introduced by Weber,[12] is used by Bourdieu to conceive the category of habitus[13] (Martínez 2007). Habitus constitutes a theoretical-methodological tool to think about the mediation between external social

---

[12] The methodology developed by Weber allows us to analyze ideas as aptitude creators of certain practical behaviors, considering their material conditions; in this sense, the ethos is an internalizer of actions, producer of permanent states and principle of new operations.

[13] See A. Martínez, Pierre Bourdieu, p. 41: "It is in Weber's texts that we find the sociological uses of the concept of ethics, unifying principle of behaviors that allows us to conceive them as a system, even if they are not unified in the form of a conscious project: it is what Bourdieu explained to us in La société traditionnelle and Travail et travailleurs en Algérie. The link made in Bourdieu's texts between the concept of ethos and the phenomenological analysis of the consciousness of time, allows us to better understand the particularities of the colonized world as a peasant world and as a world subjected to colonization, and therefore to a compulsive change of the economic system, among others".

conditioning and subjectivity.[14] For social subjects, habitus constitutes an open system of dispositions—apprehended and incorporated unconsciously—permanently confronted and affected by new experiences, which guides decision-making and guides social reproduction; it is a lasting system, though not immutable (Bourdieu 1992). Habitus is objectified as a regulating cultural principle and generator of practices and identity, a principle that in the Aymara case is historically associated with the high Andean plateau culture, as well as with its agriculture and livestock economy. My aim is to understand, based in these three points, how the Aymara independent work practices respond to a habitus whose culturally structured dispositions allow the *qamiris* to objectify modes of labour which integrate Andean experiences and behaviours. Following this habitus, Aymara traders enter an adverse order in social, economic and cultural terms, adapting themselves to the global free market economy through the practice of their own ethics. In order to emphasize the analysis of the cultural aspect of labour, I take the habitus as an analytic category of independent work in the Aymara qamiris, using the ethnographic data that I have on this case.

QAMIRIS AND AYMARA TRADE
IN THE PERUVIAN-BOLIVIAN HIGH ANDEAN PLATEAU

From Migration to Commercial Success in Urban Spaces

The *qamiris* have grounded their economic success on commercial activity in the altiplanic cities of Juliaca and Puno (Peru) and El Alto and La Paz (Bolivia), in the Collao Plateau, Andean region surrounding Lake Titicaca, a region with which they are historically and culturally identified, given the pre-Incan origin of the Aymaras. Their cultural roots can be seen in the strong commercial dynamics unfolded in this area,[15] inherited from the mobility that Aymara society developed centuries ago through the "caravan trade along the Andes" (Golte and León 2014; Llamque and

---

[14] Social realities are objectified and internalized. They refer to objective rules and institutions, external to the agents; they function both as a limiting condition and as a support point for action. In turn, they refer to subjective worlds, constituted by forms of sensibility, perception, representation and knowledge.

[15] Some important nodes of the commercial network around TItikaka Lake are Desaguadero, Yunguyo, Tinicachi, Moho, Tilali, Ninantaya and Cojata.

Villca 2011). This dynamic has prevailed despite the territorial division of the national states of Peru and Bolivia, keeping cross border flows intact. Rural migration[16] to the city during the second half of the twentieth century constitutes a first historical milestone of Aymara independent work, followed by the social change generated by the agrarian reforms applied by the governments of Bolivia (in 1953) and Peru (in 1969).

In this context, Aymara traders began to import and sell transistor radios in the 1960s and televisions in the 1970s; from then on, they sold cars and computers. In this period, the cities of Iquique (Chile) and Oruro (Bolivia)[17] were integrated into the altiplanic commercial circuit. Although qamiris had been widely known at this point, during the 1980s and 1990s, the success of the *qamiris* took shape, almost simultaneously with the implementation of neoliberalism[18]: the *qamiris* hegemonized commercial activity in this region by buying merchandise through both smuggling and open import[19] at the binational border, selling wholesale and retail in popular neighbourhoods and emerging urban markets. The import of low-cost merchandise was consolidated, covering various items from household appliances to transnational clothing brands, fostering the maturity of the Aymara popular economy. The successful *qamiris* gained greater visibility in the 2000s, selling "last generation products up to vehicles", institutionalizing social and commercial networks (composed by both Aymara and mestizo people), in a frequently hostile arena (Tassi et al. 2013). Excluded from the benefits of bank credit, the *qamiris* practised the collective fund: the sum of individual capital of associated *qamiris* allowed them to pay for investments or larger commercial ventures; among them, the funding of recent trips to China— a main import nexus—to directly acquire naval containers of merchandise without intermediaries, and sell it in the high Andean plateau in highly

---

[16] Mostly from Aymara rural communities in the provinces of Camacho, Manco Kapac, Los Andes and Ingavi, in the department of La Paz (Bolivia); and Chucuito, El Collao, Huancané, Moho and Yunguyo, in the department of Puno (Peru). In Yunguyo, I highlight the districts of Unicachi, Ollaraya and Tinicachi.

[17] The altiplanic commercial circuit begins in the naval port of Iquique and continues in Oruro, the city from where merchandise is distributed to Juliaca, Puno, El Alto and La Paz.

[18] 1985 in Bolivia, and 1990 in Peru.

[19] For Bolivian and Peruvian traders, it is occasionally worthwhile to cross the binational boundary to buy merchandise at a lesser cost.

commercial seasons, such as Christmas. The history of the *qamiris* shows how they have boosted the altiplanic economics following traditional and modern paths.

In Peru, Aymara migration to the capital city of Lima led to the formation of traders' associations and, after that, of *qamiri* investment associations. I present two cases:

a. The Unicachi Group is an Aymara real estate company from Unicachi district in Yunguyo (Puno). Initially, the Unicachinos sold charqui (dried cattle meat) and worked as dock workers in Callao,[20] beginning to acquire stalls in the Lima markets (Suxo 2008). In 1996, the Unicachi District Association bought a 3450 m^2 property in the commercial area of Caquetá, in the limeño district of San Martín de Porras, in which it started a new popular market, repeating this real estate trade system in various districts of Lima. Of the total of 29 initial shareholders, 80% came from Unicachi, like most of the 51 shareholders around 2008.

b. The Gamarra Shopping Centre, in the Lima district of La Victoria, is the largest textile production and trade zone in Peru. The migrants from Ollaraya district in Yunguyo initially worked as street traders around the "La Parada" interprovincial bus terminal in La Victoria, living precariously in the nearby neighbourhoods of Cerro San Cosme, Balconcillo and Matute, among others (Mamani 2010). Since 1976, the Ollarallinos have formed textile production and trade associations that later became part of the Gamarra Shopping Centre, started by the textile mills owned by Arab migrants.

The commercial success of the *qamiris*, in both the high Andean plateau and the main cities of Peru and Bolivia, carries with it the imperative desire for progress and the discovery of opportunities for social fulfilment. In this process, the Aymara cultural practices are incorporated into a habitus on which they have reproduced their social world, a point that I analyse hereunder.

[20] The most important sea port of Lima, and Peru.

Aymara Ethics in Independent Work

Although some mestizos usually despise Aymara commercial success, this one responds to both an austere life and a habitus that influences independent work, as witnessed by Antonio Velásquez Oscco,[21] Aymara Unicachino (Alejo 2017) who migrated to Lima in the 1960s, where he lived "working day and night, saving what he could and sleeping on the streets, at first" (Vargas Llosa 2011). Instead of submitting to anomie, Aymara migrants followed an economic and labour route guided by an Aymara ethic in order to progress, despite the experience of marginality, exclusion and discrimination (because of their language, clothing and working ways) that they lived during their urban insertion. Thus, Aymara traders increased their well-being through actions aimed at achieving material wealth and capital accumulation, emerging as the new urban sector in the altiplanic social life, receiving different names: Chola bourgeoisie, wealthy popular class, Proto-bourgeoisie, *qamiris* or successful traders (Rea 2016; Toranzo 2013; Tassi et al. 2013; Llamque and Villca 2011).

The *qamiris* practice independent work based on an Aymara ethic that is culturally grounded on reciprocity, the basis of Andean agricultural and livestock community labour, oriented to both the redistribution of their products and resources. The purpose of labour for the Aymara society is not the remuneration or the activity itself, rather it merges in its practice the Andean industry[22] with capitalist individualism, that is, the collective with the individual, the traditional with the modern, so that "the Aymaras manage to articulate two rationalities presented as opposites: community rationality (affective and traditional) and instrumental rationality" (Rea 2016). The Aymara ethic fosters the emergence of a habitus centred on the idea of progress (Catacora 2013), articulating Andean cultural heritage and western capitalism, as well as austerity, industry and

---

[21] The novelist Mario Vargas Llosa reserves the identity of this character with the pseudonym "Tiburcio".

[22] In the Andes, industry is related to a very difficult world that requires intense effort, especially collective effort. The pressure to meet this demand leads to people being incorporated from childhood into agricultural and livestock economic work. See Catacora (2013).

saving. This would explain why the commercial success of the *qamiris*—descendants of shepherds and farmers—lies in the social reproduction[23] of the Aymara habitus, the economic and social mechanism on which the *qamiris* support their practice of independent work.

THE STRATEGIES OF THE AYMARA POPULAR ECONOMY IN URBAN SPACES

Independent work is a concept that allows me to link the heterogeneity of Aymara economic activities with the notion of popular economy,[24] the use of which enables the analysis of its material and immaterial dimensions (Duclos 2017), considering the dialogic relationship of its economic, social, symbolic and cultural aspects. This clearly shows, firstly, that the Aymara economy has maintained its historical and cultural dynamics in the Peruvian-Bolivian high Andean plateau; and, secondly, that the Aymara economy has adapted to various socioeconomic and political processes, showing itself at present as independent work. On the other hand, it is important to observe the essential cultural role that social capital[25] has played in the Aymara popular economy and, consequently, in the independent work of the *qamiris*. In this way, the popular economy developed by the Aymaras in the city has fostered, in the *qamiris*, a social and economic rise to a "new middle-class". Hereunder, I analyse the three types of strategy[26] with which the Aymara popular economy dialogues.

---

[23] It is the recognition of a structuring structure in material and symbolic reproduction, objectified through a "system of permanent and transferable dispositions, structured structures, organizers of practices and representations" (Bourdieu 1992).

[24] It is a Chilean academic category. Here I distance myself from the notion of informal economy (also named traditional economy or marginal economy), which defines as such the activities outside the legality carried out by a homogeneous mass, activities related to poverty and self-exploitation. See Quijano (2000) and Tassi et al. (2013).

[25] Social capital "is made up of the potential resources associated with a lasting network of more or less institutionalized relationships". It is not separated from both economic and cultural capitals (Bourdieu 2001, 148–150).

[26] Bourdieu (2011, 53) understands the strategy as the "principle of practice from the agents", as processes of permanence and inheritance of a social world.

Social Strategies

They are observed through the different modes that the social capital assumes among the Aymaras in the city: (a) peasantry networks and kinship networks, needed for the generation of both business and enterprises; (b) both provincial and district associations, places for the socialization of migrants and the use of the Aymara language; (c) social networks, useful for commercial positioning in urban markets; (d) social honour, a "world of mouth" guarantee in business deals. These modes of social capital promote a constant exchange of economic aid, generating and strengthening networks of social cohesion used by the *qamiris* in the practice of independent work.

Cultural Strategies

Culturally, the Aymara independent work ethic is grounded on the practice of reciprocity in both the social and economic spaces of the city, expressed through the *Pasanako* and the *Aynupa* in the Bolivian Aymaras:

> *Pasanako* is a basic funding system used in the Andean region that is grounded on commitment within a group, whose members make financial contributions to be used by turns [...]. *Aynupa* [is] a mixed form of collective and individual property, proper to the Aymara world. In the context of popular trade, despite the fact that there is a family commercial capital, it is divided into different capitals in order to avoid vertical hierarchies. (Tassi et al. 2013)

Among Peruvian Aymaras, reciprocity is practiced through the *ayni* and the *minka* (Catacora 2013). In Andean peasant communities, the *ayni* is the mutual provision of labour aid among the members of an *ayllu*[27]; the *minka* is the collective participation in labour and enjoyment of the community's goods: farm and pasture lands, mountains, rivers and streams, lakes, trees, shrubs, roads and sacred places. According to Apaza (2009), Aymara people[28] often practice reciprocity along with honesty, loyalty, austerity and an entrepreneurial spirit. In the city, the Aymaras

---

[27] *Ayllu* is a pre-Hispanic association: its members are united by spiritual, territorial, economic and kinship ties.

[28] It refers to the case of Puneños who migrated to Huancayo, from Juliaca, Asillo, Lampa and Ichu.

practice the *pasanako*, the *aynkupa*, the *ayni* and the *minka* in the social cohesion networks, which become their social capital. These strategies are reserved to Aymara relatives and countrymen, a protectionist practice to keep this resource within the migrant community. Therefore, besides the independent work, the social reproduction of these strategies is especially observed at Patron saint festivities.

Symbolic Strategies

The Patron saint festivities in honour of the Virgen de la Candelaria (Puno) and the Señor del Gran Poder (El Alto and La Paz), as well as the Carnival entrance (Juliaca), are the largest in the cities of the Peruvian-Bolivian high Andean plateau.[29] For urban Aymara networks, the feast promotes both the deployment of social capital and the practice of reciprocity, by being a means for the reproduction of the Aymara popular economy strategies. Dance also objectifies this social reproduction, La Morenada being the most popular collective dance in this region. The *qamiris* express their economic and symbolic power at the feast and at the dance, as they centralize the social, economic, religious and cultural aspects of Aymara independent work.

Indeed, the *qamiris* extend their spiritual kinship networks at feasts and dances by contacting potential coparents, godparents or godchildren in order to make commercial and credit deals with them, based on trust and honour. The social reproduction of Aymara networks also occurs in social reception,[30] a central moment during the feast in which the *qamiris* strengthen their networks of friendship and co-parenthood, making alliances for future businesses. Following Bourdieu (2011), I could argue that both the party and dance are a symbolic investment for *qamiris*: while both social and cultural strategies of Aymara work establish and sustain social relations (social investment), the Patron saint feast preserves and increases recognition (symbolic investment).

---

[29] Other religious spaces are the fair of *alacitas* and the cult of the *ekeko*, divinity of abundance.

[30] The *qamiris* offer the social reception in their own buildings called "cholets", a neologism resulting from the fusion of the words "cholo" and "chalet". "Cholo" is a racial-cultural term, historically associated with a derogatory meaning towards the Andean indigenous people in the cities; "Chalet" refers to a luxurious home.

In order to obtain the largest symbolic recognition, for the *qamiris* it is of utmost importance to get to be a Pasante, the highest and most important ritual post in the festivities of Candelaria Virgin, the Lord of the Great Power,[31] and every patron saint feast in the Peruvian-Bolivian altiplanic region. The Pasante is the feast protagonist: he plans, organizes and meets every production cost and religious activity, including minor events such as the offerings, folkloric exhibitions or performances of musical ensembles. He participates in parades and exhibitions, escorted by lavish dance groups (fraternities) and musical bands hired for the occasion. The Pasante fulfils a programme of activities throughout the year, exceeding the two weeks of the holy dates. Its main ritual partner is the major Alferado, Preste or Pasante, and its minor support couples are the minor alferados, prestes or pasantes. The Pasante is a rotating and annual ritual post that wealthy Aymaras fulfil through the *ayni* and the deployment of the social capital required to fund the feast. Therefore, the feast and dance are spaces for both social reproduction and symbolic recognition; its importance is lyrically illustrated in the song titled *Pasante soy*, by the Bolivian folk orchestra Los Kjarkas:

> I am Pasante this year / for you, for you, I dance Morenada /
> if being Pasante comes first / I am the Preste even if it costs me money /
> for my Bolivia, out of devotion, I am Pasante / I dance in front, always elegant, I am Pasante /
> with my compadres, with my fraternal ones, for our nation / long live Bolivia, the Morenada, I am Pasante.[32]

---

[31] "The *qamiris* invest nearly US$90,000.00 on the Great Power feast, and in this, even some Pasantes lost US$8000.00 in deals and contracts, although some of them recovered their money by making business alliances in order to import automobiles" (Toranzo 2013).

[32]

> Pasante soy por este año / por ti, por ti, bailo Morenada /
> si ser Pasante es lo primero / yo soy el Preste aunque me cueste dinero /
> por mi Bolivia, por devoción, Pasante soy / bailo adelante, siempre elegante, Pasante soy /
> con mis compadres, con mis fraternos, por nuestra nación / viva Bolivia, la Morenada, Pasante soy.

In the context of the feast, the *qamiris* strengthen both their social and commercial networks, and reproduce their recognition through the reciprocity of the *ayni* or *apxata*.[33] The practice of the *apxata* is objectified in future businesses, economic alliances and loyalty among *qamiris*; because of this, it is institutionalized in the annual Patron saint feasts (but also in festive micro-spaces such as weddings, birthdays, baptisms, ritual haircuts or business inaugurations). The Aymaras participate in the great Patron festivities, integrating fraternities of dancing groups, different in prestige and the quantity of "fraternal ones". When they parade in troupes through the main streets and squares of the cities, the *qamiris* fraternities wear expensive costumes, gold ornaments and bodyguards. Some Aymara and mestizos criticize the *qamiris* pageantry, regretting that the feast has been losing its "religious faith [for being] indecent and exaggerated" (Tassi 2010). Thus, these popular feasts turn into a space for social reproduction, through which the *qamiris* show both their economic and symbolic power, fostered by independent work and the deployment of the social, cultural and symbolic strategies of the Aymara popular economy.

EVERYDAY LIFE AND CULTURE IN THE INDEPENDENT AYMARA TRADE

The Aymara strategies observed in the deployment of their independent work can be appreciated in the weekly markets and fairs[34] of Puno, Juliaca, El Alto and La Paz, commercial points where a great diversity of merchandise is offered, from livestock to new automobiles. Every Thursday and Sunday, the "16 de julio" fair in El Alto[35] "brings together more than 10,000 stalls and mobilizes around US$2 million" (Yampara 2007); and, according to Deutsche Welle, US$20 million per week in 2018. Cultural manifestations also influence consumption and economic reproduction in markets and fairs: merchandise and services are offered

---

[33] In Aymara and Quechua: action of donating to later receive, a reciprocal and permanent supply of goods between members of a family or community, observed, for example, in the festive donation of beer, one that will be returned in similar conditions of quantity and quality at a future feast.

[34] Also known as *qhatus* or peasantry fairs.

[35] Initially, El Alto was a small commercial point located at the crossroads of Oruro, Copacabana, Laja and Viacha. In 1950, eleven thousand people inhabited El Alto; by 2012, it had expanded to nearly one million people.

for the Andean ritual of *pago a la tierra*,[36] the Patron saint feasts made the organization of dance groups; *alacitas* and *ekekos* are also offered. An approximate calculation counts 19 associations of clothing traders in Puno, each one made up of a number of 100–120 members and an average of 2000 workers; in Juliaca, the figures are similar. This growing economic success is materially perceived in the "cholets", the lavish buildings that the *qamiris* have had built as a family home and a celebratory place for Patron saint feasts; in the high Andean plateau cities, the "cholets" are a sign of opulence (their value can reach one or two million dollars), visible to the outsider for its innovative design in which some people recognize the emergence of a neo-Andean architecture. Half a century after its appearance, fairs and markets have become spaces that enable and boost independent work in the urban-popular sectors, as can be seen in the testimony of Mrs. Julia, a trader at the Saturday fair in Puno:

> Seven years ago, I ventured into this type of business, for lack of work because other jobs paid me very little [...] at 6:00 am, I am already setting up my tent offering my clothes, people come early to choose the clothes [...] On Mondays, I take clothes to Juliaca, I have my little selling stall there. [...] In rainy season, it is impossible to sell, business is pretty slow. When there are Patron saint feasts it is the same [...]. I bring [merchandise] from Tacna, Juliaca. We do not have the support of the local government at all[37]. (Julia)

The relationship between globalization and the popular sectors can be observed in the "16 de Julio" fair in El Alto, the Saturday fair in Puno and the Sunday fair in Juliaca, mainly in the commercial trade of imported clothing[38] and electronic devices; sneakers and garments of transnational brands such as Nike, Adidas, Reebok, Calvin Klein or Tommy Hilfiger

---

[36] Payment to the earth, an Andean agrarian ritual.

[37] "Desde hace siete años me incursioné en este tipo de negocio, por falta de trabajo porque otros trabajos me pagaban muy poco [...] a las 6:00 am, ya estoy armando mi carpa sacando mis ropas, la gente viene temprano para escoger las ropas [...] Los lunes llevo a Juliaca tengo mi puestito. [...] en tiempos de lluvia no se puede vender, es bajo el negocio. Cuando hay fiestas igual [...]. Yo traigo de Tacna, Juliaca. Nosotros no tenemos el apoyo de parte del gobierno local".

[38] Clothing mainly imported from the U.S.A., packed in Mexico in *pacas* (bales), and then distributed globally.

are the most commercialized by the *qamiris*, a reflection of their socioeconomic rise in Peru and Bolivia (Tassi 2011; Uccelli and Garcia 2016).
Regarding self-identification, the testimony of Aymara traders expresses
their self-recognition as independent workers, rejecting the epithet of
"informality":

> We really feel marginalized and even discriminated against by the author-
> ities. We were never informal ones, because we are registered in Public
> Registries as a formal traders association and we pay our municipal taxes
> when they come to us to cash them[39]. (Ruperto)

> Some people call us informal ones, sometimes I shout at them and tell
> them that I do work, I am not stealing, but we are associated and therefore
> we are not afraid, also our president went to the municipality to talk to
> the mayor[40]. (María)

Now, does independent work represent a means of survival or an alternative form of economy? The answer seems complex, given that along with
the current economic success of the *qamiris*, a large sector of independent
traders still wears a face of misery.

CONCLUSIONS

In this article, I have tried to show how in societies with low rates of both
formal and salaried employment, culture can boost practices and alternative modes of independent work, capable of promoting economic success.
In Latin America, the rise of the Aymara *qamiris* as an urban-popular
subject in the main cities of the Peruvian-Bolivian high Andean plateau
(Juliaca, Puno, El Alto and La Paz), is culturally based on a habitus that
articulates the global market to an Aymara ethics, by adapting to the
neoliberal economic model.

In order to understand the *qamiris* and the Aymara independent work,
I have privileged the analysis of their cultural aspects and the way in

---

[39] "Realmente nos sentimos marginados y hasta discriminados por las autoridades.
Nosotros nunca fuimos informales, porque estamos inscritos en registros públicos como
una asociación formal y pagamos nuestros tributos municipales que vienen a cobrarnos".

[40] "Varios nos dicen informales, a veces les grito y les digo yo trabajo no estoy robando,
pero estamos asociados y por lo tanto no tenemos miedo, además nuestro presidente fue
al municipio a conversar con el alcalde".

which Andean culture articulates the free market economy to an Aymara habitus. The popular economy practised by the *qamiris* has created jobs for a large urban-popular sector—historically excluded from the official economy—that has managed to leave poverty behind. Within popular economy, the independent work of Aymara traders combines social strategies (social capital and networks), cultural strategies (Andean reciprocity) and symbolic strategies (Patron saint festivities and the ritual post of the Pasante). All these strategies—simultaneously traditional and modern— are linked to the globalization process and consolidate a social space where Andean ethics, social capitalization, popular economy and social reproduction come together, supporting the labour of Aymara traders.

In Aymara society, social relations constitute the central column of the organization of labour. Its understanding requires an adequate analysis of its cultural aspects. Informality as a neo-colonial category fails to address the heterogeneity of the independent work practised by the Aymaras, since it prioritizes the quantification of the formal, salaried worker with rights, according to the labour conditions conceived by the classical perspective on labour.

The independent work of Aymara traders shows certain principles of social reproduction grounded on collective work: reciprocity, Aymara ethics, industry, kinship networks and the desire to progress. In this sense, the Patron saint festivities constitute a space for social reproduction in which the *qamiris* express the economic and symbolic power fostered by the deployment of the strategies of the Aymara popular economy. Finally, it is necessary to emphasize that cultural aspects associated with independent work, Aymara habitus and social capital have strengthened the Aymara popular economy, leading it to experiences of progress and commercial success by adapting to the global market and contemporary capitalism.

References

Alejo, G. (2017, July 28). La conquista del migrante aimara en el Perú. *Diario Los Andes*, p. 7.

Apaza, M. (2009). *Migración, inserción y trayectoria de puneños en la ciudad de Huancayo.* http://tesis.pucp.edu.pe/repositorio/handle/20.500.12404/94. Accessed 3 March 2019.

Bourdieu, P. (1992). *El sentido práctico.* Madrid: Taurus.

Bourdieu, P. (2001). *Las estructuras sociales de la economía*. Buenos Aires: Manantial.

Bourdieu, P. (2011). *Las estrategias de la reproducción social*. Buenos Aires: Siglo Veintiuno.

Burawoy, M. (1990). Marxism as Science: Historical Challenges and Theoretical Growth. *American Sociological Review, 55*(6), 775–793. https://doi.org/10.2307/2095745.

Castell, R. (2010). *El ascenso de las incertidumbres: trabajo, protecciones, estatutos del individuo*. Buenos Aires: Fondo de Cultura Económica.

Catacora, E. (2013). Ética andina: migraciones, trabajo y reconfiguración de los habitus en el Perú contemporáneo. *Revista Sures, 2*, 59–81.

De La Garza, E. (2017). Crítica del concepto de informalidad y la propuesta del trabajo no clásico. *Trabajo, 9*(13), 51–70.

Duclos, M. (2017). La (re)socialización desde abajo. Socialidades alternativas y nuevas economías populares en el caso de los mercados de pulgas informales de París, Francia. *Antipoda. Revista de Antropología y Arqueología, 29*, 199–215. https://doi.org/10.7440/antipoda29.2017.09.

Durand, F. (2007). *El Perú fracturado: formalidad, informalidad y economía delictiva*. Lima: Fondo Editorial del Congreso del Perú.

Galicia, S. (2018). Informalidad laboral: debate monopolizado. *Revista Quehacer, 1 - Segunda época*. http://revistaquehacer.pe/n1#informalidad-laboral-deb ate-monopolizado. Accessed 15 May 2020.

Ghiotto, L. (2015). ¿Qué es el trabajo para la Sociología del Trabajo? Una discusión conceptual. *Bajo el Volcán, 15*(22), 267–294.

Golte, J., & León, D. (2014). *Alasitas: Discursos, Prácticas y Símbolos de un "liberalismo aymara altiplánico" entre la población de origen migrante en Lima.* Lima: IEP; CBC; Universidad Nacional de Juliaca.

Llamque, R., & Villca, W. (2011). *Qamiris aymaras: desplazamiento e inclusión de élites andinas en la ciudad de Oruro.* La Paz: Fundación PIEB.

Mamani, S. (2010). *Ollaraya. Historia social y política de un pueblo de frontera: Monografía del Distrito de Ollaraya, Yunguyo, Puno, Perú, 1964–2007.* Lima: Press Color.

Martínez, A. (2007). *Pierre Bourdieu: Razones y Lecciones de una Práctica Sociológica.* Buenos Aires: Manantial.

Ortiz, R. (1983). *Pierre Bourdieu: Sociología.* São Paulo: Ática.

Poblete, L. (2018). Informality, Precarious Work and New Approaches to Complex Realities. *Work, Employment and Society, 32*(5), 967–970. https://doi.org/10.1177/0950017018759907.

Quijano, A. (2000). *Globalización, colonialidad del poder y democracia.* http://economiassolidarias.unmsm.edu.pe/sites/default/files/Anibal%20Quijano2.pdf. Accessed 15 May 2020.

Rea, C. (2016). Complementando racionalidades: la nueva pequeña burguesía aymara en Bolivia. *Revista Mexicana de Sociología, 78*(3), 375–407.

Suxo, M. (2008). *La voz de una Nación: los aymaras de Lima Metropolitana. Caso Unicachi.* Lima: Editorial San Marcos.

Tassi, N. (2010). *Cuando el baile mueve montañas: religión y economía cholomestizas en La Paz.* La Paz: Fundación PRAIA.

Tassi, N. (2011, June 17). El Gran Poder de un modelo económico exitoso. *Periódico Digital PIEB.* http://www.pieb.com.bo/sipieb_notas.php? idn=5869. Accessed 17 June 2018.

Tassi, N., Medeiros, C., Rodríguez Carmona, A., & Ferrufino, G. (2013). *"Hacer plata sin plata". El desborde de los comerciantes populares en Bolivia.* La Paz: Fundación PIEB.

Toranzo, C. (2013, September 17). Burguesías cholas y Burguesías cunumis. *Diario Página Siete,* p. 3.

Uccelli, F., & Garcia, M. (2016). *Solo zapatillas de marca: jóvenes limeños y los límites de la inclusión desde el mercado.* Lima: Instituto de Estudios Peruanos.

Vargas Llosa, M. (2011, December 31). El orden espontáneo. *El País.* https://elpais.com/diario/2011/12/31/opinion/1325286011_850215. html. Accessed 18 May 2020.

Yampara, S. (2007). *La cosmovisión y lógica en la dinámica socioeconómica del* qhathu/*feria 16 de Julio.* La Paz: Fundación PIEB, UPEA, CEBIAE, Centro de Promoción de la Mujer Gregorio Apaza; Red HABITAT; Wayna Tambo; CISTEM.

CHAPTER 9

Exploring the Politics of Sensibilities That Promote Marriage and Reproduction Among Young Chinese Adults Residing in Urban Areas

Xiangnan Chai

In China, intergenerational conflicts are emerging regarding marriage and reproduction. Confucianism emphasizes the value of "Xiao" (filial piety), which centres marriage and reproduction in China's patrilineal family system and patriarchal culture. This value system helps explain why getting married and giving birth to children were once considered to be sociocultural responsibilities that almost everyone was obliged to fulfil. However, in the present day, more and more young Chinese, especially those residing in urban areas, are beginning to delay or even abstain from marriage and reproduction. Compared to their parents, these younger generations are more likely to have access to, accept, and engage with individualistic Western cultures. They may be more likely to focus on

X. Chai (✉)
Department of Sociology, School of Social and Behavioral Sciences, Nanjing University, Nanjing, China

© The Author(s), under exclusive license to Springer Nature   157
Switzerland AG 2021
A. Scribano et al. (eds.), *Cities, Capitalism and the Politics of Sensibilities*,
https://doi.org/10.1007/978-3-030-58035-3_9

their own interests and personal development rather than prioritizing the collective, even if doing so means failing to meet their parents' expectations. Another possible reason for this is that young adults are confronted with significant financial pressure due to China's increasing cost of living, especially in the metropolises, where real estate prices are extremely high. As a result of these forces, young people tend to enter into marriage and start their own families at older ages than their parents did (Gaetano 2014; Guo and Gu 2014; Wong 2003). Such a situation may have created conflicts between the generations.

Politics of sensibilities that aim to promote marriage and reproduction thus have become prevalent in urban areas of China. The divide in economic development between urban and rural China has been well documented and explored. In short, complex sociohistorical factors have caused urban China to develop economically at a much faster rate than the country's rural areas (Chan and Wei 2019). The intergenerational conflicts discussed above are therefore more significant in urban areas. Moreover, people living in rural areas are more likely to be influenced by traditional cultural values such as filial piety, whereas young adults living in cities tend to embrace more individualistic values. As a result, promoting marriage and reproduction seems more urgent to the older generations and the government in urban China than in rural areas. China's ageing population and persistently low fertility rate raise concerns that the country's urban areas will face labour shortages in the future. On this matter, promoting filial obligations is therefore of great importance to help maintain the country's socioeconomic development, as well as social stability and harmony. It should also be noted that continuity is a core motive for Chinese families and clans to promote the traditional Xiao culture, wherein young people are obliged to establish their own families to show respect to their parents, grandparents, and ancestors. Practising the Xiao value as a family ethic is a moral standard that young people are expected to meet in order to be acknowledged by society (Sun 2017). These socioeconomic and ideological systems are an important context for the current research exploring the politics of sensibilities that endorse marriage and reproduction among young adults in urban China.

A Brief Introduction to China's Rapid Urbanization After 1978

Rapid urbanization has driven China's fast socioeconomic development over the past four decades. The starting point came in 1978 when the central government decided to carry out the Economic Reform and Opening Up Policy. At the core of this policy was the doctrine that the Chinese Communist Party (CCP) and the Chinese government should prioritize economic development over class struggle, to improve the population's wellbeing and quality of life (Tisdell 2008). According to China's official statistics, the urbanization rate, which is defined as the percentage of the population living in urban areas, increased from 10.64% in 1949 to 17.92% in 1978. The number has rapidly and consistently increased, reaching 60.60% in 2019 (National Bureau of Statistics of China 2019a). The government's 2019 annual report stated, "Solid progress was made in the pursuit of new urbanization, and close to 14 million people originally from rural areas gained permanent urban residency" (The State Council of the People's Republic of China 2019). Data from the World Bank Group (2014) also showed that China experienced rapid urbanization, at the rate of about 10% per decade, after 1978.

This trend is far from ending. The primary cause may be that the CCP has continued to prioritize urbanization and urban construction, and these goals are reflected in the central government's national policies. According to the government's annual report (2019), the central government will make efforts to encourage further urbanization while also improving the city-dwellers' quality of life. As proposed in the annual report: "New urbanization should be people-centred in every respect: We need to be better at conducting flexible governance and providing thoughtfully designed services to make our cities more livable and give them a more inclusive and welcoming feel" (The State Council of the People's Republic of China 2019). Consequently, China's urbanization rate is predicted to keep increasing, reaching about 75% in 2050 (World Bank Group 2014).

Previous studies have revealed two pertinent characteristics concerning the mobility of young Chinese between urban and rural China. First, young Chinese are much more willing to reside in urban areas, and they generally do not consider rural life to be attractive. Cities offer young people more educational, social, economic, entertainment, and medical resources than rural areas do. Therefore, many of these individuals, especially those who are floating labours from rural areas, are more willing to work in urban areas (Mohabir et al. 2017). Second, young adults prefer large cities over small ones because the former is perceived to have a better work environment and more social mobility opportunities (Chen et al. 2018). Many young Chinese choose to live in first-tier or second-tier cities, also known as metropolises or megapolises (Mohabir et al. 2017). In Mainland China, these include Beijing, Shanghai, Guangzhou, Shenzhen, Nanjing, Hangzhou, Tianjin, Wuhan, Chongqing, Chengdu, and other cities with millions of residents.

Two Demographic Transitions Facing Urban China: The Aging Population and Decreasing Fertility

The Chinese government has invested heavily in developing cities and many young adults choose to reside in urban areas. Even in such a context, urban China's population growth faces two challenges associated with demographic transitions that are China's ageing population and falling fertility. Due to these two demographic shifts, marriage and reproduction have become more urgent needs at both the macro- and micro-societal levels. Understanding these transitions can help scholars in exploring the politics of sensibilities that endorse and stimulate marriage and reproduction in urban spaces.

Ageing Population

Researchers have identified the ageing population as a severe social challenge threatening China's fast economic development. The increasing age of the population also increases social expenditures on caregiving and medical care (张鹏飞、苏畅 2017). In China, the number of older adults aged 65+ had reached by 175.99 million in 2019, and the share over the entire population was 12.57% in that year (National Bureau of Statistics of China 2019b). Also, the old dependency ratio, which is defined as the percentage of older adults aged 65+ per 100 working-age adults, has risen to about 17.8% in 2019 from less than 10% in the 1980s (National Bureau of Statistics of China 2019b). However, some researchers dispute the findings of urban China's increasing dependency ratio. For example, 唐钧 (2012) pointed out that the proportion of older adults residing in big cities, such as Beijing, Shanghai, and Guangzhou, is not as high as some researchers believe. This is because a huge number of young and middle-aged adults who migrate from rural areas, towns, or small cities reside in these large cities for education or jobs, but they are not registered in the Hukou system and, thus, are not counted as urban residents. Younger adults with rural Hukou choosing to pursue urban lives can also partially explain why rural areas are confronted with an even grimmer situation with populations ageing faster (Cheng et al. 2019; Wu et al. 2019). Nevertheless, big cities in China are experiencing population ageing, as is indicated by the faster growth rate of the older adult population compared to the average growth rate of the general population and the consistent increase in the number of older adults (Cheng et al. 2019).

Declining Fertility

China has had a low fertility rate for about four decades. China's total fertility rate (TFR) was 5.5 in 1970, and the figure has stably decreased to 2.6 in 1980, 2.3 in 1990, 1.7 in 2000, and 1.6 in 2010 (Raymo et al. 2015). According to Jiang and colleagues (2019), China's TRF has stayed below the replacement level since the 1990s. The One-Child Policy (1978–2016) has significantly impacted China's population structure. It decreased China's fertility to a low level, which contributed to younger cohorts comprising a smaller share of the total population. Furthermore, as I mentioned before, China's strict family planning programme is not the only reason for the decrease in its fertility. Financial pressure on young generations, especially those residing in big cities, may also have led them to postpone marriage and reproduction. The prevalence of individualistic Western cultures also has a certain impact on young adults residing in urban areas.

The ageing population and the low fertility rate may have led to serious socioeconomic and cultural consequences. First, China's working-age population is shrinking, which may cause negative economic effects and thus affect the government's ability to maintain long-term economic development (Banister et al. 2012). Given that importing foreign labourers has weak public support in China, improving fertility would be the best method to address this problem in the current sociopolitical environment. Second, the ageing population and falling fertility rate have sparked intergenerational conflicts regarding marriage and reproduction. Chinese adults born in the 1950s or 1960s typically want their children to establish their own families and give birth to children at an early age. This is mainly due to the Xiao culture, which emphasizes that adult children should respect their parents and ensure the continuity of their families and clans (Chan 2004; Mao and Chi 2011; Sun 2017; Wang et al. 2009). Another source of tension is the abolition of the One-Child Policy in 2016. The government now encourages people with urban Hukou (户口) of childbearing age to have two children, a doctrine called the Two-Child Policy (Zeng and Hesketh 2016). However, although their parents show strong interest in the Two-Child Policy, young cohorts are likely to refuse to comply. While it seems imperative to improve fertility among young adults residing in urban areas, marriage has become a less important priority for them. Young people tend to postpone or decline marriage and having their first child, and this is where the politics of sensibilities come into play. Such a dramatic change in behaviour and values demands a deeper analysis of the reasons for, and consequences of, this shift.

MARRIAGE AND REPRODUCTION: AN INDIVIDUAL CONCERN OR A FAMILY AFFAIR?

In traditional Chinese society, marriage is an important affair for a family or a clan. Confucianism, a fundamental ideology in Chinese people's daily lives, underscores the importance of marriage and reproduction. In traditional societies, marriage is undertaken for the sake of the patriarchal clan's continuity, and it is directly related to reproductive behaviours. Mencius writes, "There are three things that can be considered as unfilial, and the most severe is having no child ('不孝有三, 无后为大')." Furthermore, traditional social mores hold up the production of male offspring as the sufficient and necessary condition to ensure the clan's continuity. The socioeconomic and cultural reforms (or revolutions) of the nineteenth and twentieth centuries may have undermined this institutionalized idea. Nonetheless, the culture of Xiao, which emphasizes the importance of marriage and reproduction, has remained a leading principle in people's lives (Sun 2017). Having children has become a standard measure of a Chinese individual's filial piety, and thus, it remains a maxim for many people (Kwan 2000).

To contextualize the topic of marriage and reproduction in China, it is important to introduce how Confucianism defines Xiao, and how this moral value and social more guides individuals' daily behaviours and life events.

Confucianism and Xiao

Confucianism has a central role in Chinese culture. In brief,[1] Confucianism was one of the main systems of philosophical thought in the Spring and Autumn Period (770–476 B.C.) and the Warring States Period (475–221 B.C.). Since Dong Zhongshu (179–104 B.C.), it has become an institutionalized ideology that heavily affects the government's policy-making and guides individuals' daily lives, thoughts, and behaviours (强中华 2013). In the present day, Confucianism is still one of the leading ideologies in Chinese culture, and it plays a central part in maintaining the social operation of Chinese society (翟学伟 2019).

"Ren" and Xiao are two core ideas of Confucianism. Ren (仁) is a core idea put forward by Confucius (551–479 B.C.), and further developed by Mencius (372–289 B.C.) and subsequent Confucianists. Ren is often translated as benevolence. It is the "heart of Confucianism" (Wang 2012, 463). It is impossible to express the concept of Ren in a few sentences, but Wang (2012, 463) summarized it as follows: "Openness and sincerity of heart became the central meaning of ren in Confucian teachings and the root of Confucian moral cultivation." Xiao is another central component of Confucianism. 翟学伟 (2019) proposed that Xiao can be regarded as "an actionable manifestation" of benevolence (Ren). Specifically, Ren is an ontological concept of metaphysics; on the other hand, Xiao links Confucian thought with people's daily actions and behaviours, manifesting the idea of Ren. In Confucianism, Xiao emphasizes individuals' respect for their parents, grandparents, and ancestors. To practice the principle of Xiao, people are expected to marry and produce children to complete their filial duties and obligations, thereby maintaining the continuity of their families and clans (Jiang et al. 2019; Wang et al. 2009).

Practising the value of Xiao has important meaning not only to individuals, but also to the society in which they live. 翟学伟 (2019) investigated how the value of Xiao works to maintain the running of Chinese society, where the family-clan is the basic social unit. He explained that Confucianism emphasizes the notion of "repay the gift of life and return to the origin ('报本返始')," which has important theoretical implications for the

---

[1] For more studies on Confucianism: in *The Religion of China: Confucianism and Taoism*, Max Weber explored how Confucianism shapes Chinese individuals' personalities, and Cheng (成伯清 2018) identified the enlightenment tasks of Confucianism in the modern era.

idea of Xiao within the larger framework of "Heaven and Men ('天人认知')." 翟学伟 (2019, 128) wrote: "The reciprocal parent-child relation and its emotional roles are operated within this framework. At its core, the parent-child relationship is unequal and this inequality is what causes the guilty conscience and the forever gratitude towards one's parents. Filial piety encourages the Chinese to focus their entire social life on things like family continuity, social harmony, ethical behaviours, local networks, authority supremacy, etc., to promote social bonds in society."

China has a long history of centralism—that is, the central government reinforces the importance of an orderly family-clan system in maintaining a stable, harmonious society (Chow 2009). Managing the country by encouraging people to practice Xiao has been a strategy used by the central government for many dynasties (Chan 2004; Holzman 1998). Even in present-day socialist China, filial piety is a key vector for caregiving to older adults, especially in rural areas, where families have access to fewer financial and medical resources compared to their urban counterparts (Chow 1991).

Xiao plays an essential role in the daily lives of Chinese people. A folk adage says, "Among a hundred good virtues, filial piety is the first ('百善孝为先')" (Sun 2017). In the context of China's patriarchal clan system, the practice of Xiao highlights the importance of filial obligations, which are seen as a form of respect to parents and the clan to which an individual belongs. Giving birth to children is an essential symbol of the continuity of a family and clan. In this vein, whether an individual is a Xiao'zi (孝子, filial male children) or Xiao'nv (孝女, filial female children)—that is, an adult child who effectively practices the mores of Xiao—is an essential variable in moral appraisal in Chinese society. To practice Xiao, adult children often provide their parents with emotional and/or financial support and caregiving (Cheng and Chan 2006; Mao and Chi 2011). However, China's One-Child Policy may have undermined its patrilineal norms, as children without siblings are confronted with more onerous moral responsibilities to end singlehood and become parents, so as to ensure their own parents' happiness (Deutsch 2006).

From a historical perspective, Xiao has played an evolving role in the lives of Chinese people since 1949, the founding year of the People's Republic of China. During Mao's era (1949–1976), Confucianism was harshly criticized by the mainstream ideology—that is, Communism. In the current post-Mao era (1978 to the present day), rapid modernization and urbanization may have undermined filial piety, or Xiao, as a principal sociocultural value for the Chinese. For example, cultural feedback from children to parents has become a significant social phenomenon in today's China due to the country's socioeconomic development over the past few decades (成伯清 2015; 周晓虹 2000, 2017). Cultural feedback refers to the idea that the younger generation understands new knowledge (e.g. new technology) better than their parents; therefore, they are not just receivers of knowledge from their parents, but also givers. As Zhou (周晓虹 2015) pointed out, young cohorts can perform Xiao by respecting their parents, but it is hard for them to obey their parents' requirements. In other words, members of the younger generation—especially those living in urban China—can negotiate their duties and obligations to their parents in a way that previously would not have been possible. This suggests that traditional Xiao values have weakened during China's rapid social transition. Furthermore, beyond the individual level, Cheung and Kwan's research (2009) on the impact of modernization indicates that filial piety is more likely to be negatively affected in urban areas that are more advanced and more financially well-off. To conclude, Xiao has waxed and waned in its influence on the lives of Chinese people, and this influence has been shaped by complex socioeconomic, cultural, and political factors. Nonetheless, there are many ways to maintain the practice of Xiao. For example, moral education plays a role in helping urban Chinese residents resist the erosion of filial piety (Cheung and Kwan 2009). In this vein, Xiao still has a significant role in guiding Chinese people's daily lives.

Individualism Amongst Young Chinese Cohorts Living in Urban Areas

Young Chinese today are more willing to pursue "personal freedom and hedonistic values" (Yang and Neal 2006, 113). These young Chinese have strong desires to invest in their personal development rather than entering into marriage at an early age. These individualistic pursuits have affected young cohorts' interest in marriage and reproduction, which is reflected in the decline in marriage and fertility rates. Moreover, there is a certain proportion of young Chinese who choose to live alone (Yeung and Cheung 2015; Yeung et al. 2016). They may wish to pursue independence by enjoying their own living spaces, as do their counterparts residing in the Western countries and regions (Klinenberg 2012; Santos et al. 2017). Although the patriarchal system still exists in Chinese society, and marriage has been seen as one of the most essential milestones in life, the marriage rate has decreased sharply, especially in metropolises. Notably, the proportional increase in educational attainment among women may also contribute to their decrease in marriage. Qian and Qian (2014) found that highly educated women living in urban China have a lower likelihood of marriage than their counterparts, including those well-educated men and lower-educated women. Postponing or forgoing marriage among well-educated women, especially those in their 30s, is mainly due to the conflict between ambition in career development and traditional gender roles for women in marriage. Regarding fertility behaviour, research shows that especially young Chinese cohorts have a relatively low desire to have children, as reflected by the consistent decline in fertility rates in urban China (Zhao, Xu and Yuan 2017).

POLITICS OF SENSIBILITIES TO PROMOTE MARRIAGE AND REPRODUCTION IN URBAN SPACES

Politics of sensibilities are defined as "the set of cognitive-affective social practices tending to the production, management and reproduction of horizons of action, disposition and cognition" (Scribano 2017, 244). The politics of sensibilities or politics of emotions aim to regulate people's perceptions and daily behaviours and "make bearable the conditions under which social order is produced and reproduced" (Scribano 2019, 13). In the context of China, existing research has shown that promoting marriage and reproduction has important socioeconomic and cultural implications for the Chinese people. The Confucian concept of Xiao, an important moral value, exerts great influence in Chinese society, confronting young cohorts with pressure to complete their filial obligations. There are a few typical politics of sensibilities in urban spaces that endorse and embody the traditional Confucianist Xiao. These underscore marriage and reproduction, and can be seen in manifestations like dating shows, matchmaking corners in parks, and traditional education on "feminine virtue."

Dating TV Shows

Dating shows are an example of the politics of sensibilities that promote marriage and reproduction in urban China. There have been a few well-known dating shows, such as *If You Are the One* (《非诚勿扰》), *China's*

New Matchmaking (《中国新相亲》), and *New Matchmaking Assembly* (《新相亲大会》).

If You Are the One is the most successful dating show in Mainland China, and "it is the most popular yet controversial one among the many" (Li 2015, 519). It has created a new template for promoting marriage as a goal via TV shows. The show establishes a romantic field in which male and female guests can exchange personal data, such as educational attainment, job and position, income levels, interests, and family background. The core part of the show is that male guests share criteria and expectations for their potential partners, as well as their plans for marriage and family. Many male guests invoke their parents in their introductions by stating that they wish to be a filial son by finding a nice wife, getting married, and having their own children. In the first round, for each male guest, each of the twenty-four female guests (aka "24 women vs. 1 man," *see* Li 2015, 520) can indicate her decision about whether to continue by leaving a light on or turning it off. The male guest then has the option to "pick" two female guests who leave their lights on and whom he wishes to advance to the next round. If a female guest agrees to progress together with the male guest after exchanging personal information, they do so with the guidance of two "emotion supervisors" hired by the show.

Dating shows in China leverage strong politics of sensibilities to promote heterosexual marriage and reproduction. The prevalence of dating TV indicates that marriage and reproduction are essential not only to individuals and their parents and families, but also to Chinese society and the development of the country. This is consistent with the Confucian value of Xiao. These dating shows offer the male and female guests the opportunities to present their individual lives, interests, social achievements, and more, with the effect of impressing not only each other but also the audience. This emphasis on the guests' unique personalities gives the shows a sense of modernity and individualism that appeal to young audiences and viewers. However, as Li (2015, 531) wrote, Chinese women in such shows are depicted as "subordinates and dependents who need material support from men, and encouraged to become sexual subjects by internalizing the male gaze." Essentially, these shows also propagate the importance of individuals' filial responsibilities, grounded in the Confucian value of Xiao, which emphasizes heterosexual marriage. Indeed, Xiao emphasizes these responsibilities to the point of excluding those who have little interest in marriage or reproduction, and sexual minorities are ruthlessly marginalized in this discourse. Ultimately, these dating TV shows embody and reproduce the politics of sensibilities based on heterosexuality and gender that endorse traditional family values, even though the individualistic culture coexists in China's rapid urbanization and modernization process.

Matchmaking Corners in Parks

Another type of politics of sensibilities in urban China can be found in matchmaking corners or gatherings in parks. Like dating shows, matchmaking corners exist to promote marriage. In urban areas of China, many parks are used for matchmaking or blind date gatherings. Often, Chinese parents, rather than their adult children, are the main force behind the creation and organization of these matchmaking corners. Previous research described such collective activity as "Bai'Fa'Xiang'Qin (白发相亲)" which refers to "parents who wish to marry off their unmarried children" (Wong 2016, 373). They spontaneously gather in parks, normally during the weekends, in hopes of speeding their children's progress towards this life event (Sun 2012). Parents come with detailed information about their children written on a board, including heights, weights, age, job/position, annual income, family assets, and more. These parents exchange their children's information in order to help those children find marital partners. Matchmaking has deep roots in Chinese culture, as in traditional China, free love was prohibited and matchmakers played an important role in establishing relations between two families (Wong 2016).

Parents directly participate in their children's marriages, suggesting that marriage is never an individual's choice in China, even in urban areas where young people are affected by individualistic foreign cultures and generally have become more independent compared to previous generations at the same age. Nevertheless, many young people cannot refuse their parents' desire for them to be "successful" in the marriage market.

Therefore, it is not difficult to understand why matchmaking gatherings in parks may have a low success rate. Adult children who grow up in urban areas are economically independent and more culturally individualistic than their parents' generation. They view this method of finding marital partners as awkward, and they often do not participate enthusiastically. However, despite their limited effectiveness, matchmaking corners in parks are an important method for Chinese parents to meet peers who face similar "problems" in achieving their goal of marrying their children off.

Matchmaking gatherings in parks in urban areas can be regarded as spontaneous actions by anxious Chinese parents who worry about their adult children's marriage prospects and the continuity of their families. Such actions have deep roots in Chinese culture and illustrate the persistent importance of Xiao. However, young cohorts who are affected by both individualistic cultural characteristics and financial and life pressures may refuse to participate in blind dates like these, which is reflected in the low success rate of matchmaking. Nonetheless, matchmaking in parks is a type of politics of sensibilities that attempts to promote marriage and reproduction among young Chinese. In the context of China's rapid urbanization and modernization, matchmaking in parks is an emotional ballast for those parents who adhere to traditional moral values and have strong desires for grandchildren.

Traditional Education on "Feminine Virtue"

In many cities in present-day China, there has been a rise in traditional education on "feminine virtue" (女德教育). Here, "feminine virtue" does not refer to social or moral norms in the modern era, but rather to Confucian norms regulating what women should and should not do in a feudal patriarchal society. For example, "San'Cong'Si'De (三从四德)," which refers to the three obedient behavioural principles and four feminine virtues in Confucian ethics, rules women's behaviours in daily interactions. These outdated and obsolete feminine virtues were reflected in social mores and official regulations targeting women, who were expected to be submissive to their fathers and husbands. Women were required to be obedient, and giving birth to children (sons) was their main reproductive task; ultimately, the goal of this was to help their husbands practice the value of Xiao. Some researchers call these so-called "feminine virtues" "cultural dregs," mainly because they stereotype women and highlight women's subordinate positions to men in family and social lives (莫兰 2019; 潘允康 2014; 司马童 2018; 吴之如 2017; 肖歌 2018).

Although such traditional education has been harshly criticized, many Chinese parents send their daughters to programmes specifically focused on teaching "feminine virtue." Some influential celebrities even endorse these educational programmes. Feminine virtue education has been promoted in the name of traditional culture, but it is, in fact, regressive and cultivates a return to older norms. Essentially, it can be seen as a type of politics of sensibilities that aims to create gendered social norms by educating women of younger generations.

THE ROLE OF MATERIALISM AND CONSUMERISM IN PROMOTING MARRIAGE AND REPRODUCTION

The politics of sensibilities discussed above indicate that filial piety still plays an essential role in guiding marital and reproductive behaviours among Chinese people residing in urban areas. In particular, the capital features an enjoyable dating and marriage market targeting young Chinese at marriageable ages. Materialism and consumerism have exerted considerable influence in these people's daily lives, including their participation in this market.

Materialism may reduce people's marriage and childbearing desires (Li et al. 2015). Materialistic people would perceive that establishing intimate relations and families need much financial investment. However, materialism is widely accepted by Chinese (Yang and Stening 2012), ranging from children, adolescents to adults (Li et al. 2015). From this viewpoint, materialism may have a negative influence on young people's attitudes towards marriage and reproduction and thus offset the endorsement of those traditional family values and sensibilities on a societal level.

There was a consumption revolution in Mainland China after its economic reform since the 1980s. Nowadays, consumerism plays a significant role in intimate relations. Researchers have found that men's economic prospects may benefit them in the marriage market by increasing the chances on marriage due to the fact that consumption costs are essential to marriage among today's Chinese (Mu and Xie 2014; Yu and Xie 2015). Therefore, there seems a tendency for young adults living in cities to base intimate relations on consumption. In such a context, how about those men who perform poorly on economic prospects? Will the likelihood of them getting married and fathering children be negatively affected by the prevalence of consumerism? Will such a rise of consumerism create severer gender-based stereotypes? More studies are needed in this regard.

COUNTERACTING FORCES AGAINST THOSE POLITICS OF SENSIBILITIES

Although there are many politics of sensibilities endorsing filial obligations in the context of the Confucian Xiao culture, it is important to acknowledge counteracting forces in urban China that resist these politics.

First and foremost, the skewed sex ratio of young Chinese cohorts means that many Chinese men may not be able to find marital partners. The most recent research showed that in 2018, the sex ratios for all age groups of Chinese aged below 25 are above 110 men per 100 women (Textor 2020). Additionally, as of 2018, the sex ratio at birth is 114 men per 100 women (Textor 2020). These empirical findings are based on official statistics. Many factors, such as the One-Child Policy, preference for sons, and the abuse of gender screening technology, have caused these skewed ratios. Because they outnumber women so significantly, many Chinese men may find it difficult to find marital partners. The imbalanced gender ratio among future marriageable Chinese may increase the number of single men in the long run (Tucker and Van Hook 2013).

The improvement of women's socioeconomic position in urban China is another main force dismantling the traditional politics surrounding marriage and reproduction. Young Chinese women today have higher educational attainment than their parents' generation. A certain proportion of them are very economically independent, and they are focusing on personal development rather than obeying their parents' requirements to get married and give birth to children at an early age. Existing research indicates that, in recent years, the marriage rate among women in Mainland China has decreased while the divorce rate among them has increased (Chang 2020; Raymo et al. 2015). Similarly, data show that women of working age have a low marriage rate in some other East Asian countries, such as the Republic of Korea and Japan (Raymo et al. 2015). These so-called "leftover" women represent a demographic transition that has left young women with values and ambitions that are substantially different from their mothers' more traditional views on marriage and family values (Gaetano 2014). With this shift has come to a stigma around women who focus on their own careers and have control of their lives. Overall, these new politics of sensibilities surrounding women's lives may discourage marriage and reproduction.

While sexual minority Chinese as a collective culture has largely been ignored in the mainstream discourse, an increasingly individualistic social atmosphere may include more tolerance for sexual minorities. Dating shows, matchmaking gatherings in parks, educational programmes focusing on "feminine virtue," and the market strategies stimulating consumerism in marriage and reproduction are all based on a paradigm of heterosexual intimacy. From this viewpoint, sexual minority Chinese would not be heavily affected by these politics of sensibilities, although they are still confronted with great pressure from parents and peers to engage in heterosexual partnerships.

CONCLUSION

In this chapter, I have explored three types of politics of sensibilities that endorse and promote filial obligations, including marriage and reproduction, among young Chinese in urban China. The research was motivated by two demographic challenges facing urban China: the ageing population and low fertility rate. Since 1978, China has experienced rapid economic development, as is shown by its increasing urbanization rate. Meanwhile, the ratio of older adults in urban China has increased over time, and marriage and fertility rates have decreased. Reasons include the strict enforcement of the One Child Policy, high levels of financial and other types of pressure on young Chinese as they make life decisions, and improvement in women's educational attainment and socioeconomic position. The urban lifestyle and the influence of individualistic Western cultures have somewhat diminished young Chinese people's esteem for the Confucian value of Xiao, which highlights filial responsibility for the continuity of an individual's family and clan. Within this complex web of social, political, and economic forces, many types of politics of sensibilities promoting marriage and reproduction have emerged in urban China. These include dating TV shows, matchmaking gatherings in parks, and traditional education on "feminine virtue" targeting young urban women. These politics of sensibilities may have affected marriage and reproductive behaviours among young Chinese. Consumerism and materialism also play an important role in promoting marriage and reproduction in urban China. However, some counteracting forces also exist, including the imbalanced sex ratio among young people at marriageable ages, improvement in women's social position, and the potential resistance from sexual minorities in China.

This research has important cultural and social implications in the context of China's fast urbanization, ongoing demographic transitions, and the erosion of China's Confucian values and traditional family values. Future research may explore (1) other types of politics of sensibilities or emotions related to these issues, (2) whether and how these politics of sensibilities are enacted from a longitudinal perspective, (3) how materialism and consumerism actually function in encouraging or discouraging marriage and reproduction among young Chinese, and (4) the role of offsetting forces.

REFERENCES

IN CHINESE

成伯清. (2015). "代际差异, 感受结构与社会变迁——从文化反哺说起"。河北学刊, 第3期, 96–100页。

成伯清. (2018). "自我与启蒙: 儒家精神的现代转化"。学海, 第5期, 44–50页。

莫兰. (2019). "'女德' 流延之路已越走越窄"。中国妇女报, 年4月23号。

潘允康. (2014). "荒谬的 '女德' 是女性文化的倒退"。天津日报, 年12月03号 (013)。

司马童. (2018). "名为'女德班'实为'坑'女班"。中国教育报, 年 (002)。

强中华. (2013). "儒学的艰难历程——从荀子到董仲舒"。学术论坛, 第1期, 11–15页。

唐钧. (2012). "还原一线城市老龄化真相"。中国社会保障, 第10期, 30页。

吴之如. (2017). "'女德班' 必须被叫停"。中国文化报, 年 (003)。

肖歌. (2018). "'女德'. 文化糟粕, 腐朽本质"。中国教育报, 年(002)。

翟学伟. (2019). ""孝" 之道的社会学探索"。社会, 第39期, 127–161页。

张鹏飞、苏畅. (2017). "人口老龄化、社会保障支出与财政负担"。财政研究, 第12期, 33–44页。

周晓虹. (2000). "文化反哺: 变迁社会中的亲子传承"。社会学研究, 第2期, 51–66页。

周晓虹. (2015). "代际关系的一个重要迹象: '孝'易'顺'难"。北京日报, 年0914号。

周晓虹. (2017). "文化反哺: 生发动因与社会意义"。青年探索, 第5期, 78–87页。

IN ENGLISH

Banister, J., Bloom, D. E., & Rosenberg, L. (1998). Population Aging and Economic Growth in China. *The Chinese economy* (pp. 114–149). London: Palgrave Macmillan.

Chan, A. (2019). *Filial Piety in Chinese Thought and History*. London and New York: Routledge.

Chan, K. W., & Wei, Y. (2012). Two Systems in One Country: The Origin, Functions, and Mechanisms of the Rural-Urban Dual System in China. *Eurasian Geography and Economics, 60*(4), 422–454.

Chang, S. (2020). *Chinese Women, Marriage and Gender: Exploring the Idea of Women and Marriage Over Time in the Context of China* (Major Papers, 109). https://scholar.uwindsor.ca/major-papers/109. Accessed 30 May 2020.

Chen, H., Wang, X., Chen, G., & Li, Z. (2015). Upward Social Mobility in China: Do Cities and Neighbourhoods Matter? *Habitat International, 82*, 94–103.

Cheng, S. T., & Chan, A. C. (2015). Filial Piety and Psychological Well-Being in Well Older Chinese. *The Journals of Gerontology Series B: Psychological Sciences and Social Sciences, 61*(5), 262–269.

Cheng, Y., Gao, S., Li, S., Zhang, Y., & Rosenberg, M. (2019). Understanding the Spatial Disparities and Vulnerability of Population Aging in China. *Asia & The Pacific Policy Studies, 6*(1), 73–89.

Cheung, C. K., & Kwan, A. Y. H. (2017). The Erosion of Filial Piety by Modernisation in Chinese Cities. *Ageing & Society, 29*(2), 179–198.

Chow, N. (2014). Does Filial Piety Exist Under Chinese Communism? *Journal of Aging & Social Policy, 3*(1–2), 209–225.

Chow, N. (2019a). Filial Piety in Asian Chinese Communities. In K. T. Sung & B. J. Kim (Eds.), *Respect for the Elderly: Implications for Human Service Providers* (pp. 319–323). Lanham, MD: University Press of America.

Deutsch, F. M. (2019b). Filial Piety, Patrilineality, and China's One-Child Policy. *Journal of Family Issues, 27*(3), 366–389.

Gaetano, A. (2015). "Leftover Women": Postponing Marriage and Renegotiating Womanhood in Urban China. *Journal of Research in Gender Studies, 4*(2), 124–149.

Guo, Z., & Gu, B. (2014). China's Low Fertility: Evidence from the 2010 Census. In I. Attané & B. Gu (Eds.), *Analysing China's Population. INED Population Studies* (Vol. 3, pp. 15–35). Dordrecht: Springer.

Holzman, D. (2017). The Place of Filial Piety in Ancient China. *Journal of the American Oriental Society, 118*(2), 185–199.

Jiang, Q., Yang, S., Li, S., & Feldman, M. W. (2019). The Decline in China's Fertility Level: A Decomposition Analysis. *Journal of Biosocial Science, 51*(6), 785–798.

Klinenberg, E. (2012). *Going Solo: The Extraordinary Rise and Surprising Appeal of Living Alone.* New York: The Penguin Press.

Kwan, K. L. K. (2017). Counseling Chinese Peoples: Perspectives of Filial Piety. *Asian Journal of Counseling, 7*(1), 23–41.

Li, L. (2020). If You Are the One: Dating Shows and Feminist Politics in Contemporary China. *International Journal of Cultural Studies, 18*(5), 519–535.

Li, N. P., Lim, A. J., Tsai, M. H., & Jiaqing, O. (2019). Too Materialistic to Get Married and Have Children? *PLoS ONE, 10*(5), e0126543. https://doi.org/10.1371/journal.pone.0126543.

Mao, W., & Chi, I. (2008). Filial Piety of Children as Perceived by Aging Parents in China. *International Journal of Social Welfare, 20*, S99–S108.

Mohabir, N., Jiang, Y., & Ma, R. (2013). Chinese Floating Migrants: Rural-Urban Migrant Labourers' Intentions to Stay or Return. *Habitat International, 60*, 101–110.

Mu, Z., & Xie, Y. (2009). Marital Age Homogamy in China: A Reversal of Trend in the Reform Era? *Social Science Research, 44*, 141–157.

National Bureau of Statistics of China. (2019a). 城市化/*Urbanization.*http://data.stats.gov.cn/search.htm?s=城市化. Accessed 15 May 2020.

National Bureau of Statistics of China. (2019b). *Age Composition and Dependency Ratio of Population.* http://data.stats.gov.cn/english/easyquery.htm?cn=C01. Accessed 14 May 2020.

Qian, Y., & Qian, Z. (2014). The Gender Divide in Urban China: Singlehood and Assortative Mating by Age and Education. *Demographic Research, 31*(45), 1337–1364.

Raymo, J. M., Park, H., Xie, Y., & Yeung, W. J. J. (2016). Marriage and Family in East Asia: Continuity and Change. *Annual Review of Sociology, 41*, 471–492.

Santos, H. C., Varnum, M. E., & Grossmann, I. (2014). Global Increases in Individualism. *Psychological Science, 28*(9), 1228–1239.

Scribano, A. (2019). *Normalization, Enjoyment and Bodies/Emotions: Argentine Sensibilities.* New York: Nova Science Publishers.

Scribano, A. (2019). Introduction: Politics of Sensibilities, Society 4.0 and Digital Labour. In A. Scribano & P. Lisdero (Eds.), *Digital Labour, Society and the Politics of Sensibilities* (pp. 1–19). London: Palgrave Macmillan.

Sun, P. D. (2012). Parental Matchmaking for Children's Marriage: An Analysis of the Marital Spouse Selection Behaviours in the Parental Matchmaking Corner in Shanghai. *South China Population, 27*(110), 30–36.

Sun, Y. (2015). Among a Hundred Good Virtues, Filial Piety Is the First: Contemporary Moral Discourses on Filial Piety in Urban China. *Anthropological Quarterly, 90*(3), 771–799.

Textor, C. (2020). *China: Sex Ratio.* Statista. https://www.statista.com/statistics/282119/china-sex-ratio-by-age-group/#statisticContainer. Accessed 26 May 2020.

The State Council of the People's Republic of China. (2019). *Full Text: Report on the Work of the Government.* http://english.www.gov.cn/premier/speeches/2019/03/16/content_281476565265580.htm. Accessed 12 May 2020.

Tisdell, C. A. (2008). *Thirty Years of Economic Reform and Openness in China: Retrospect and Prospect* (No. 1742-2016-140737).

Tucker, C., & Van Hook, J. (2017). Surplus Chinese Men: Demographic Determinants of the Sex Ratio at Marriageable Ages in China. *Population and Development Review, 39*(2), 209–229.

Wang, D., Laidlaw, K., Power, M. J., & Shen, J. (2004). Older people's Belief of Filial Piety in China: Expectation and Non-expectation. *Clinical Gerontologist, 33*(1), 21–38.

Wang, H. (2015). "Ren" and "Gantong": Openness of Heart and the Root of Confucianism. *Philosophy East and West, 64*(2), 503–528.

Wong, O. M. (2018). Postponement or Abandonment of Marriage? Evidence from Hong Kong. *Journal of Comparative Family Studies, 34*(4), 531–554.

Wong, W. (2013). Past matchmaking Norms and Their Influence on Contemporary Marriage Markets in China. *Journal of the Anthropological Society of Oxford, 8*(3), 371–383.

World Bank Group. (2014). *Urban China: Toward Efficient, Inclusive, and Sustainable Urbanization* [PDF File]. https://www.worldbank.org/content/dam/Worldbank/document/EAP/China/WEB-Urban-China.pdf. Accessed 25 May 2020.

Wu, Y., Song, Y., & Yu, T. (2019). Spatial Differences in China's Population Aging and Influencing Factors: The Perspectives of Spatial Dependence and Spatial Heterogeneity. *Sustainability, 11*(21), 5959.

Yang, R., & Neal, A. G. (2000). The Impact of Globalization on Family Relations in China. *International Journal of Sociology of the Family, 32*(1), 113–126.

Yang, S., & Stening, B. W. (2017). Cultural and Ideological Roots of Materialism in China. *Social Indicators Research, 108*(3), 441–452.

Yeung, W. J. J., & Cheung, A. K. L. (2019). Living Alone: One-Person Households in Asia. *Demographic Research, 32*, 1099–1112.

Yeung, W. J. J., Feng, Q., Wang, Z., & Zeng, Y. (2016). *Living Alone in China: Projection of One-Person Household: 2010 to 2050* [PDF File]. Population Association of America Annual Meeting. Washington, DC. https://paa.confex.com/paa/2016/mediafile/ExtendedAbstract/Paper8169/PAA%202016%20submission%20OPH.pdf. Accessed 22 May 2020.

Yu, J., & Xie, Y. (2018). Changes in the Determinants of Marriage Entry in Post-reform Urban China. *Demography, 52*(6), 1869–1892.

Zeng, Y., & Hesketh, T. (2017). The Effects of China's Universal Two-Child Policy. *The Lancet, 388*(10054), 1930–1938.

Zhao, Z., Xu, Q., & Yuan, X. (2017). Far below Replacement Fertility in Urban China. *Journal of Biosocial Science, 49*(S1), S4–S19.

CHAPTER 10

City and Sensibilities: The Dynamics of Racializing Segregation

Ana Lucía Cervio

INTRODUCTION

City life in the twenty-first has entailed a (growingly) fragile balance between the assimilation, respect, and negotiation of differences. So far, this century has also witnessed tensions, conflicts, and disputes between various groups in numerous cities. Global economic restructuring has involved heavy transnational flows of people, among other processes, resulting in a dramatic reorganization of urban signs, resources, and time, that affect in various ways the daily lives of city dwellers (Congress 2017; Nicholls and Uitermark 2016; De Graauw and Vermeulen 2016; Iglesias-Pascual 2019).

The paths of people from different regions of the world, with diverse cultural identities, interests, and knowledge, and who occupy unequal socioeconomic positions, cross in urban space, where they brush past each other, and encounter the "old" dwellers. Among the former we find, for example, the population fleeing from the Syrian civil war, and men

A. L. Cervio (✉)
National Scientific and Technical Research Council, University of Buenos Aires, Buenos Aires, Argentina

© The Author(s), under exclusive license to Springer Nature Switzerland AG 2021
A. Scribano et al. (eds.), *Cities, Capitalism and the Politics of Sensibilities*,
https://doi.org/10.1007/978-3-030-58035-3_10

and women crossing the Mediterranean Sea to escape from economic struggles and war in Africa. We also have hundreds of thousands of undocumented migrants looking for jobs, as well as millions of urban outcasts who inhabit cities around the world. Consequently, a wide range of relations, objects, and conflicts arise, which shape cities into spaces that divide the things, people, and relationships grouped inside their borders. Cities are complex socio-historical and economic constructs involving relations of domination, which, along with their effects, may be examined through the shapes and contents of the space conditioning them, and also through the various meanings that are the mediators and the backgrounds to the experiences of their dwellers (Lefebvre 1991; Harvey 2012; Sassen 1991; Castells 1996).

Along with class and gender, race is actively involved in the (re)production of current cities, even in those societies where race has been consistently overlooked as an explanatory factor for the processes of social structuring (Segato 2010). Racialization is a social, political, and epistemic process by which domination produces racialized subjects (Miles and Torres 2007; Banton 2002). Under the illusion of rigid, stable, and complete ontological categories, this production is contemporaneous with the neocolonial stage of capitalism that produces racialized subjects and experiences throughout the world, "beyond colour".

The present analysis rests on the following fundamental supposition: race is a key variable to understand the different shapes inequality adopts in the Global South (Santos 2011). In the intersection with class and gender, race allows us to observe comprehensively the types of oppression as well as the resistance that appears in answer to expansionist and predatory capital. From this viewpoint, cities become paradigmatic scenarios to observe how experiences are structured and how practices are moulded in relation to the pain, distrust, insecurity, and uncertainty entailed by racialization.

The (judicial, social, political, institutional, ethical, and epistemic) practices that are the day-to-day mechanisms of racialization are only possible (and effective) due to the action of the sensibilities that reinforce their origins and consequences. In daily life, these sensibilities reproduce the inequality and contempt for the other, which are, at the same time, promoted and maintained by the structures of power and domination. In other words, racialization (along with class and gender inequality), provides a foundation for neocolonial and imperial projects updated in the twenty-first century and becomes a way to live and coexist. Therefore, racialization constitutes an unavoidable vector of social structuring when studying urban experiences.

This chapter engages in a dialogue with the contributions of Frantz Fanon (1986, 1963), and critically discusses the notion of racialization in relation to spatial configurations and urban sensibilities. We implement the concept-figure of "black" defined in relation to the structuring processes of sensibilities. After reflecting upon the links between urban space and the practices of racialization, we define the dynamics of "racializing segregation". The unit of analysis is the figure of the "*negro villero*" (black from the slums) in Argentina. Finally, we underscore some analytic relations between racializing segregation and urban sensibilities reproduced by the logics of "exclusion", "surplus", and "exception".

RACIALIZATION PRACTICES
AND POLITICS OF SENSIBILITIES

In the nineteenth century, the processes of racialization served as political, economic, and moral arguments for the consolidation of Nation-States. These processes produced, explained, and naturalized the racial differences as an ontological foundation for new types of social inequality and injustice that were deep-seated in the regime of domination that is colonialism (Quijano 2000; Segato 2007).

In the name of "white and European supremacy", the global oppression suffered by racialized groups explains and upholds colonialism in, at least, four main ways: (a) articulating the "irreconcilable" differences between the colonist and the colonized; (b) defining these differences as absolute, insisting they are definitive and immutable; (c) fostering actions, rules, and institutions so that colonial differences and injustices are legitimately regarded as "real"; and (d) defining the colonial scene as eternal, i.e. a "natural" relation and not a cultural, economic, and political experience whose origins can be traced in history.

This chapter defines racialization as an ideological and political process of subjectivation and analyses racialization in relation to the politics of sensibilities that have historically produced and defined racial differences as "natural" and "necessary" to colonial domination. These politics are defined as: "the set of cognitive-affective social practices aimed at the production, management and reproduction of horizons of action, disposition and cognition" (Scribano 2017, 244).

From this viewpoint, sensibilities lie unnoticed when organizing the daily lives, preferences, and values of subjects. Likewise, sensibilities, which are also social structuring processes, determine the criteria for the management of space and time where social interactions take place leading to "natural" and "naturalized" ways of perceiving the hours, days, habits, customs, the public sphere, the spaces of intimacy, etc. Briefly, sensibilities, defined as politics that organize and enable classifying dynamics of the social world (re)produce power structures in connection to daily practices and emotions (helplessness, rage, hope, uncertainty, etc.).

Within this framework, sensibilities articulate with racialization processes that nowadays, in the twenty-first century, are updated as part of the experiences of city dwellers from various social groups. In general terms, through racialization—which constitutes an epistemic, political, and social process—domination produces racialized subjects framed within a structure of power that classifies, names, and distinguishes humans according to phenotypic, linguistic, geographical, and, hereditary criteria, among others (Miles and Torres 2007; Banton 2002). Racialization processes, unnoticed in day-to-day lives, define categories that name, distinguish, fix, and distribute social typologies of subjects in racial terms, which are granted a status of objective reality. This production, governed by the illusion of rigid, stable, and complete ontological categories, coexists with the advance of capitalism in its neocolonial stage producing racialized subjects and experiences.

The production of racialized bodies and subjectivities—whose ontological foundation a priori conditions and ossifies them in a position of inferiority in relation to dominant groups—is framed in a general process of production of radical otherness. Thus, the meaning of the *racialized other* can only be determined in its historical, relational, and dynamic co-production with the *non-racialized other*. This process, whose origin may be traced to the conquest and the discovery of the Americas, persists nowadays through the ways in which the dehumanization, exploitation, and disregard of certain subjects–explicitly or implicitly—assume expressions that can be found in common sense, in the spheres of work and production, in the academy, in segregationist cities, etc. (Quijano 2000; Mignolo 2003; Wacquant 2008; Harvey 2012). Therefore, studying the links between racialization and the politics of sensibilities becomes a proper analytical approach to examine conflicts and experiences imposed by the current colonial situation in the social world, in general, and in the cities, in particular.

Along with racism,[1] racialization comprises a notion that distinguishes the human from the non-human, and that assumes various degrees of humanity exist, leading to the establishment of suspicion as a permanent attitude adopted by the colonist towards the colonized. Balibar and Wallerstein (1991) have identified the existence of "racism without races" around the world. Having dismissed the scientific argument of the inferiority of certain races—contemporary to the geopolitical realignment in the aftermath of the Second World War, the independent processes of European colonies, and the rejection to the horror of the Shoah (Tijoux and Palominos Mandiola 2015)–, societies replace "biology" with arguments such as culture, religion, or language to restore the structures of discrimination and stigmatization, cornerstones for the definition of the subjects-objects of capitalist exploitation. Balibar (2007) argues that, as a consequence of *mondialisation*, we are witnessing a "return of the concept of race", expressed not only in racism articulated around skin colour but also in relation to antisemitism and various processes of "animalization" of social groups deemed inferior. In these terms, the creation of "internal enemies", involved in the advancement of capital, entails the systematic adoption of an ideology of security. Various phenomena support this ideology, such as the securitized State, the citizen securitization practices, and the consumption of goods particularly aimed at assessing and minimizing risks when faced with a virtual state of lack of protection and distrust felt as an inexorable logic in current societies (Mbembe 2016; Balzacq 2010; Lippert and Walby 2015; Scribano and Cervio 2018).

Mbembe (2017) adopts a critical position towards viewpoints exclusively constrained to the optical effect of race. The author argues that, apart from skin colour and certain phenotypic traits, race is a primal representation that sends us, above all, back to "surface simulacra". Besides appearances, the race has the fundamental characteristic of engendering a substitute, or a mask. As such, race deflects attention towards a scopic regime that cancels the subject with an illusory replacement of the "human essence" with the characteristics arising from their bodies:

The work of racism consists in relegating it to the background or covering it with a veil. It replaces this face by calling up, from the depths of the

---

[1] For an analytical distinction between racism and racialization, *Cfr*. Grosfoguel 2016, Hochman (2019), Murji and Solomos (2005).

imagination, a ghost of a face, a simulacrum of a face, a silhouette that replaces the body and face of a human being. Racism consists, most of all, in substituting what is with something else, with another reality. (Mbembe 2017, 32)

Consequently, besides governing the world, practices and experiences through the "truth of appearances", racism and racialization produce effects and emotions by way of detouring from the real. Introducing key concepts of psychoanalysis, Mbembe sustains that "race becomes a perverse complex, a generator of fears and torments, of disturbed thoughts and terror, but especially of infinite sufferings and, ultimately, catastrophe" (2017, 10). Therefore, fear, disgust, and distrust are, for instance, emotions incited when the other is defined not as a fellow human being but as a menace/danger from which one must be protected through radical indifference or literal destruction.

Along with the contributions of Mbembe and the sociology of bodies/emotions, we argue that race is not a genetic nor an anthropological phenomenon. Race is a socially and historically situated construct with a political and economic origin, tightly linked to structural contradictions and conflicts of capitalism and its colonial and neocolonial aspirations. In this framework, race is understood as a dialectical game between a) the group of (accumulated and historical) effects that the "other" (racialized by the colonial reason) *produces* with their (physical, distant, or imaginary) presence on the colonist and their institutions, and b) the current and future practice, cognitive, material, and affective effects of this social relation, which is asymmetrical and unfair, on the body/emotion that is and has been systematically an object of racialization.

Following the aforementioned contributions, we have defined racialization in other works as:

A set of practices that produce social effects, based on a *deviation from reality* that is inscribed in the body and emotions of racialized subjects. By raising bodily (scopic) appearances as guarantees of "truth," racialization practices are part of an *episteme* of coloniality that produces bodies and subjectivities, structuring an "objective reality" (allegedly infallible/indisputable) that separates/alienates the subject of the historical, social and cultural totality that defines him as a human being. (Cervio 2020, 24)

Focusing on the "productive" dimension (of subjects and experiences) that characterizes the practices of racialization, as we have previously defined them, leads us to understand that their action in various spheres (such as the judicial, political, ethical, institutional, and academic areas, as well as the one related to public policies, among others) can only occur with the aid of a complex set of sensibilities that (a) exhibits and defines as "natural" the differences between colonists and the colonized; (b) values and enhances differences in favour of the colonist and to the detriment of the colonized; and (c) turns normal the permanent and irreversible feature of those distinctions, legitimizing a group of practices and procedures so that said diagnosis acquires a status of undeniable truth.

As a result of this structure of feeling, disdain, fear, and distrust towards the *racialised other* become core characteristics of current sociabilities and experientialities. These emotions support, encourage, and reproduce the structures of domination and power, which lay the foundations for the practices of racialization. In other words, racialization, along with class and gender inequalities, is a way of living and coexisting that organizes, categorizes, and classifies the values, expectations, and preferences of subjects in relation to themselves and to others through the "naturalization" and "normalization" of a series of racial stereotypes (Hall 2010). In-corporated (though unnoticed) as part of the "natural" procedures, resources, and rules organizing daily lives, those stereotypes, at the same time, (re)produce typified, exclusionary, and antagonistic ways of feeling and perceiving, carrying profound political, economic, and affective consequences for racialized subjects.

RACIALIZATION AND URBAN SPACE

According to Lefebvre (1991), the political economy of space corresponds to the self-preservation of space as the worldwide medium of the definitive installation of capitalism, which is the economic regime "ordering" life. Given the mythical and fictional traits of race (Fanon 1986; Balibar and Wallerstein 1991), racialization is undeniably a social fact intertwined inextricably and intricately with the spatial dimension.

Following Lipsitz, "the lived experience of race has a spatial dimension, and the lived experience of space has a racial dimension" (2007, 11). Racialization is a process that produces "objectively" racialized groups (Miles and Torres 2007; Banton 2002; Fassin 2011). In consequence, racial meanings and stereotypes linked to those subjects shift—as an effect of the fictionalization of the race—to the spaces those bodies inhabit, occupy, consume, enjoy, or suffer. Said "shift" occurs against a background marked by a strong interrelation between race and class that dominates power relations in our societies. Thus, bodies and experiences intertwine in spaces that become racialized to establish the domination of some classes over others, leading to the definition of certain spaces and their dwellers as the "others" in terms of class and race. This process strengthens a dangerous fusion of racism and classism in cities leading to profound dynamics of socio-spatial segregation.

Examining the dynamics of segregation in our cities entails studying the link between space and the shapes adopted by the production and reproduction of social differences and inequalities on the urban scale. Consequently, the need arises to review the idea that cities are heterogeneous constructions that comprise homogeneous elements. Besides, we deem it vital to analyse the existing structural possibilities that foster (or not) links between segregated subjects and spaces.

Sabatini et al. define segregation as "the degree of spatial proximity or territorial agglomeration of families from one social group defined either by age bracket, ethnic, religious, or socioeconomic status, among other criteria" (2001, 27).[2]

Framing the abovementioned definition in a broader picture involving capitalist accumulation and its territorial metamorphosis leads us to claim that *spatial proximity* between "homogeneous" subjects results from the differential appropriations that each social class has historically made of urban rights, residences, infrastructures, and services. Socio-spatial segregation becomes apparent in two complementary ways leading to sociological effects on the city and the experience of its dwellers: (a) the *social homogeneity* of socio-spatial subdivisions that "fracture" the city, and (b) the *concentration*, on an urban scale, of residential spaces occupied by various social classes. Both of these characteristics intertwining reinforce social inequalities—of which segregation is only one expression—and foster the configuration of urban zones anchored in a deep class cleavage.

Focusing on the logic of *social homogeneity* and *spatial concentration* allows us to observe three concurrent dynamics surrounding socio-spatial segregation:

[2] Translation by the author.

1. The particular mechanisms of *social differentiation* that express, in spatial terms, the hierarchies of human groups defined by criteria such as class, race, gender, etc., which vary historically and contextually (Duhau 2003; Picker 2017).
2. A spatial expression of *social inequality* as shown by, for instance, the deep gulf between urban areas defined as homogeneous, or the restrictions on movement imposed upon certain city dwellers (Nieuwenhuis et al. 2020; Bayon and Saraví 2018).
3. A profound *social distancing* between subjects identified as "others-strangers". The spatialization of otherness promotes deep-seated distrust, fear, and insecurity. These emotions toughen the numerous walls, borders, and frontiers crossing and shaping the "segregated city" (Scribano and Cervio 2018).

In Argentina, similarly to other Latin American countries, the racialization of poverty constitutes a dynamic present in various social environments that shape practices and spaces. Socio-spatial segregation that we can observe locally entails undeniable ties between class and race, which, beyond racial fiction, differentiate, disconnect, and isolate spatially the impoverished population giving way to various scales and types of suffering (D'hers and Cervio 2019). In Argentina, "blackness" has pushed the limits of skin colour to encompass human groups who have witnessed their social and individual autonomy and power being reduced at the hands of the expansion of global capitalism.

In fact, since the nineteenth century, the adjective and noun "black" has become one of the terms most usually deployed to refer to subaltern groups in Argentina. Therefore, terms such as *"cabecitas negras"* (literally, little blackheads), *"negros villeros"* (literally, blacks from the slums), and the more recent *"negros del plan"*[3] (literally, blacks on social welfare), have become ways to *name the other* beyond colour. All of these notions share the figure of the *black* (in terms of race or class) understood as "excrescence" and social "surplus".[4] Therefore, the *"negrification"* of otherness has been established as an efficient device of subjectivation

---

[3] The term refers to the recipients of social welfare and state programmes.

[4] Since the mid-twentieth century, the term "black" has no longer been associated exclusively with African descent and has come to indicate (as well) a subaltern position linked to impoverished and popular classes of the country. For an in-depth analysis of this subject, *Cfr.* Frigerio (2006), Geler (2016), Cervio (2020).

that names, identifies, describes, and makes subjects perceive the other as someone who "has no ontological resistance in the eyes of the white man" (Fanon 1986, 83).

The author claims that the colonial system can only be upheld with the intersection of race and class. Both of these variables are profoundly inter-twined, to the extent that each one of them dialectically co-produces the other. "In the colonies, the economic substructure is also a superstruc-ture. The cause is the consequence; you are rich because you are white, you are white because you are rich" (Fanon 1963, 40).

Fanon defines race as a social organizer and shows how through history and culture the colonial system of domination has invented legends, myths, and tales about black populations giving way to the establishment of a historic-racial schema. Racialized discourses and narratives support said schema and define an *essence* of black people *turning them into* inferior beings.[5]

In this context, the colonial subject in-corporates and naturalizes the horizon of meaning dominating the white world, plunging themselves in a strong feeling of inferiority. Thus, the black suffers the risk of becoming the *non-being* because of the abovementioned ontological denial. To be and to feel incapable of opposing white people (of contrasting with them) places the black person in a *non-place*, confiscating—even to a greater degree—their autonomy and condemning them to inhabit a world of surplus, where they are superfluous: "He looks for appeasement, for permission in the white man's eyes. For to him, there is 'The Other.' (…) of having no place anywhere, of being superfluous everywhere" (Fanon 1986, 55).

Race becomes the criterion organizing the colonial world through the denial of ideas, such as the common and community, as a foundation of the processes of domination and exploitation. This order marked by class distinctions and a racial organization ontologically forces the black man into an unquestionable feeling of inferiority in relation to white people. Thus, the colonized becomes a superfluous/surplus subject, given that

---

[5] Debating openly with Merleau-Ponty's notion of "body schema", Fanon (1986, 84) shows that the "historic-racial schema" gives way to the "racial epidermal schema". The latter does not require any kind of legitimacy, given that it is part of the skin of the colonized. This schema includes a group of racialized stereotypes and indications that perform the bodies, and transform them into damaged, flawed, and incomplete bodies, which become, consequently, available for domination.

they are placed outside of the common and become available for the process of regulating life (their lives.) Following this idea, Fanon claims blacks do not exist in themselves, but that instead they are continuously produced by the colonist as part of their own strategy of domination. "Producing the black" entails developing a social tie based on submission and exploitation, by which the colonized lays completely bare in front of the will of the colonizer, who is striving to accrue the maximum profit from them. Colonial bodies, by definition, follow the logic of subjection, availability, and resources.

Fanon argues that the black exists thanks to the plan and projection (always fixed and essential) of the white based on an external (bodily, epidermal) mark. Following this idea, nowadays we can witness renewed ways of negrification of the world that materialize in space as the most despotic currents of capitalism unfold in its neocolonial stage. Migrants, enslaved workers, refugees, the undocumented, and segregated urban dwellers are examples of racialized and declassed humanities reproducing colonial dominion and exploitation in the twenty-first century.

From our point of view, the negrification of the subaltern world involves reflecting upon the radical distance and difference established between the colonist and the colonized by and through a specific material surface: body and emotions. This process comprises a notion of the human and the non-human leading to the establishment of suspicion as a widespread attitude of the colonist towards the "others" in terms of class and race.

Against this background, the "epidermalization of inferiority" and the "negrification" of otherness establish the limits and the densities of the subaltern experience. From our viewpoint, the coincidence of both processes leads to three consequences:

a. Inferiority, being an ontological trait of the colonized, entails the indisputable superiority of the white. Thus, Fanon suggests social and racial ontologization and hierarchization constitute the same process of domination.
b. The subject *is fixed* in an essence that is not theirs. This (stereotyped) shaping of the subject has been built historically and culturally to reinforce the "reasons" justifying the differences between "them" and "us".
c. The "other" carries in their bodies/emotions everything the colonist wants to expel from inside themselves (sins, impulses, flaws,

etc.). They become the "scapegoat" of a white society built on the myth of progress, civilization, and enlightenment (Fanon 1963). The *other* becomes the (brutal, savage, dark but necessary) force opposed, as Thanatos, to the triumph of Eros (and his myths) in the colonial society.

Given its fictional basis, race involves a group of social processes leading to its *"establishment"* as an (ontological, social, and political) guarantee of truth. In consequence, race *reveals* (similarly to a chemical product) its selective and exclusionary power in terms of social structuring. Spaces constitute one of these processes. In fact, in capitalist cities, space is not only a product and result of class inequalities. Space also projects and produces racial fiction as a means of codifying differences and inequalities between colonists and the colonized. Therefore, we argument that focusing on racializing segregation is vital when studying the dialectic of space, class, and race in contemporary cities.

Towards a Definition of Racializing Segregation

The "black" is a figure-stigma (Goffman 1963) functioning throughout Argentina's social history as a deposit of the "non-place" and, therefore, of the "surplus".[6] Alongside the negation and stigmatization of these abject bodies, the notion of "black" became the metaphor for an endless colonial experience. In other words, notwithstanding historical differences, in Argentina "black" may be understood as a noun/adjective which reinforces the subaltern condition in two ways. Firstly, as proof of people trapped in the webs of racial domination (and available to others). Secondly, as a synthesis of an estrangement process that confines individuals who can only do, feel, dwell, and narrate their lives from the "outside", i.e. recurring to repertoires built and provided by the colonist.

As mentioned above, the politics of sensibilities, the foundation of the relations of power and domination, explain the ways in which societies manage and govern bodies and emotions. Now, sensibilities would lack the effectiveness to organize "in a natural manner" daily life according to structural prescriptions without the assistance of the "politics of the

---

[6] Rephrasing Mbembe (2017), the "remainder", meaning an (unrepresentable) representation of the dissimilar, different, and negative, is the ultimate sign of existences purely seen as objects, i.e. restricted to their condition of things.

senses". Consisting of the essential nodes of sensibilities traversing and configuring the current situation of domination, the politics of the senses socially distribute, produce, locate, and signify particular ways of smelling, touching, hearing, seeing, and tasting within a society in a particular moment. Thus, the politics of the senses present a radical content where class, race, and gender intersect.

Translating this idea into the urban landscape, the black, as a *body-stigma*, is the quintessential depositary of the "non-place". In Argentina, and in other countries of the Global South, the meaning of the notion of black—in the same manner as the poor, the undocumented, or the immigrant—has pushed the limits of skin colour to encompass the popular and impoverished classes. The term "black" has become a semantic, cultural, and political field pointing to the dis-sonant, the ill-looking, the foul-smelling, and the disquieting. This leads to various sensations ranging from indifference to disgust, fear, distrust, and suspicion. In addition, these territorial enclaves inhabited by precarious and superfluous bodies accumulate prejudices and stereotypes that, in spatial terms, limit, essentialize, naturalize, and fix radical differences, building the outcasts as the "other". This is the case of the group of stereotypes projected on *villas de emergencia* (slums),[7] and on their dwellers, popularly called "*negros villeros*".

Common sense usually "depicts" "*negros villeros*" with repertoires linked to violence, degradation, and excess. These labels place subjects in the margins and define them as exotic, overlooking the sociological, historical, and economic conditions of social inequality. Simultaneously, said stereotypes determine pain as a strong organizer of the individual and collective experience of those subjects, limiting or restricting the appearance of practices that may subvert or, at least, disrupt the social order.[8] Slum-dwellers have to overcome unceasingly obstacles and difficulties due to poverty. These hardships also become permanent biographical markers conditioning the ways subjects feel, do, and position themselves

---

[7] These types of urbanization represent the "paroxysm" of poverty and precarious housing on an urban scale in Argentina. The urban planning of slums, located on public lands or private property, is irregular. Corridors lead to the houses that are usually occupied individually. Estimates show that 4228 slums and informal settlements exist in Argentina, inhabited by approximately 3.5 million people (RENABAP 2017).

[8] Fanon (1986) argues that rage, resentment, and even a deep desire for "revenge", are emotions aroused by the injustice and submission on which colonial domination rests.

in the world. Pain, anger, helplessness, and resignation are some of the emotions populating these urban cartographies, where poverty and socio-spatial segregation are intertwined in a concrete process that racializes class inequalities and differences.

Drawing on the dialectical relation between race, class, and space, this study defines racializing segregation as a process by which class distancing, inequality, and differentiation expressed on a spatial scale produce racialized subjects. In other words, these are subjects essentialized through fixed categories, which are relatively stable and charged with racial and classist stereotypes, reifying social and racial hierarchies that become "indisputable" logics of the capitalist city.

According to Lipsitz (2007), racialized experiences bear a spatial dimension, and spatial experiences bear a racial dimension. Thus, racializing segregation shows two concomitant dynamics. On the one hand, spaces reproduce racial and classist stereotypes and stigmas projected on subjects from the most socially disadvantaged positions. In this way, spatializing segregation strengthens the idea that racial categories precede structural inequalities. These categories produce/reproduce the social distribution of bodies in the capitalist city. On the other hand, social relations of domination define racial categories as an a priori rather than as consequences of their own social, political, economic, and cultural interventions. This trend fixes the categories of subjects, defining as natural the racialized world visions that are the foundations for discourses and practice s of social segregation. The "other" becomes the material and symbolic universe of the void, the absence, and the mistake. "Failures" linked to these subjectivities are projected into every sphere of the existence of subalterns (consumption, affections, ethics, morality, etc.). The space inhabited by these bodies, that are the "other", assumes crucial importance in this structure of submission and exploitation. This owes to the fact that said space accumulates, simplifies, fixes, and naturalizes "differences", and "inequalities", which become an integral element of the heterogeneous urban space, denying, thus, their undeniable social origin.

Conclusions

Racializing segregation shows that the articulation between race, class, and space constitutes a sociological problem fundamental for contemporary social theory. In the context of the current reconfigurations of imperialism, dependency, and colonialism, the dynamics of racialization and the processes of enclassment divide, classify, and radicalize differences. These dynamics reinforce the discourse of war that produces the "other" as a threat.

Cities, as epicentres of global capitalism, reveal strong and intricate links between racism, the criminalization of poverty, and the "negrification" of otherness. Therefore, the need arises to update the theoretical approach to the global urban order. Millions of displaced people, refugees, migrants, and other urban outcasts from various parts of the world participate in the current "social tragedies" that urge social sciences to rethink these issues from a critical viewpoint free from any type of romanticism or complicit miserabilism.

These humanities, considered a surplus by the current accumulation stage of capitalism, put a strain on political, economic, cultural, and social issues stemming from the transnational flow of people and extreme poverty. These human beings also unveil processes of differentiation, classification, and hierarchization of people aiming at them being socially excluded or expelled. The registers of pain and cruelty mark these processes (Mbembe 2017). Consequently, cities around the world are deeply conditioned and shaped by (physical and also imaginary) walls erected inside them to separate, differentiate, and stratify practices, experiences, subjects, and consumptions. In the current global order, said boundaries reveal a renewed impulse for the production of racialized and enclassed subjectivities boosting the circulation of, at least, two types of surpluses. On the one hand, there is the economic surplus value produced by the "new" bodies of extraction which are functional to the accumulation of capital. On the other hand, there are the surpluses from the consumption of social groups expelled (as excess) from society (Scribano 2015).

As shown in this chapter, in neocolonial cities in the twenty-first century the notion "black" is not simply linked to certain phenotypic traits or ancestry. "Black" constitutes a social, historical, and economic construct that brutally defines as subaltern certain differences, and carves bodies/emotions of the racialized subject, producing thereby exclusion, surpluses, and exceptions, "beyond colour".

Intersecting with class, "black" is an abstract notion instrumental in naming the *surplus*, i.e. that which is left on the outside, leading an existence as a mere object. In the ontological, political, social, and economic order that capitalism establishes as the governing regime of life, the category "black" enables classifying, naming, and positioning those lives in a place of submission and subjection (infralives), which may be consumed without restrictions by the colonists of the twenty-first century and their institutions. Against a background of a profound and renewed "negrification" of the global world, "black" refers to those lives that may enter the circuit of waste/consumption/destruction precisely because neocolonial, patriarchal, and capitalist power has built them as *objects*. Including those lives in the political and economic repertoire of racial domination enables stigmatizing, denigrating, despising, segregating, and even locking-up those populations that the neocolonial order has defined as the legitimate risk-bearers, and has associated mainly with what is considered different, alien, and strange.

Following Fanon through the viewpoint of the sociology of bodies/emotions, we argue that in seeking domination the colonist exercises twofold violence over the colonized. On the one hand, the colonist defines how the world is shaped, who holds the power, and who the "other" is. Capitalism in its colonial stage entails specific accounts and actions on the world that produce inequalities leading to numerous wounds and humiliations. Colonial violence begins with an *episteme* that produces bodies and subjectivities, structuring an "objective reality" (supposedly infallible and undisputable) that separates/alienates the subjects from the cultural, social and historical totality that defines them as human beings. On the other hand, and in close relation to the above-mentioned point, for colonial domination to be successful, the colonist enclasses and racializes the oppressed as utter otherness. The performative power of words acts barefacedly. Naming, categorizing and classifying the other, resorting to their (ethical, economic, psychic, emotional, etc.) debts, flaws, and deficiencies, the dominant discourse performs the ways of doing, feeling, and perceiving the world of the colonial subject. The convergence of these types of violence essentializes and turns the other into an inferior being, reduced to an object. Therefore, the other is condemned to become a *non-being*, opaque and marginal, stripped of the spaces/times of humanity in the day-to-day life in colonial spaces.

REFERENCES

Balibar, E. (2007). Le Retour de La Race. *Mouvements*, 2(50), 162–171.
Balibar, E., & Wallerstein, I. (1991). *Raza, nación y clase*. Madrid: IEPALA.
Balzacq, T. (2010). *Securitization Theory: How Security Problems EMERGE and Dissolve*. New York: Routledge.

Banton, M. (2002). *The International Politics of Race*. Cambridge: Polity Press.

Bayón, M. C., & Saraví, G. A. (2018). Place, Class Interaction, and Urban Segregation: Experiencing Inequality in Mexico City. *Space and Culture, 21*(3), 291–305.

Castells, M. (1996). *The Information Age: Economy, Society and Culture. Vol. 1: The Rise of the Network Society*. Cambridge, MA: Blackwell Publishers.

Cervio, A. (2020). Afrodescendants, Racialization and Politics of Sensibilities in Argentina. *Universitas: Revista de Ciencias Sociales y Humanas, 32*, 19–36.

Congress, E. (2017). Immigrants and Refugees in Cities: Issues, Challenges, and Interventions for Social Workers. *Urban Social Work, 1*(1), 20–35.

D'hers, V., & Cervio, A. (2019). Dolor social, conflictividad y pobreza: un abordaje desde las experiencias de inmigrantes limítrofes en la Ciudad de Buenos Aires. *Digithum, 23*, 1–13.

De Graauw, E., & Vermeulen, F. (2016). Cities and the Politics of Immigrant Integration: A Comparison of Berlin, Amsterdam, New York City, and San Francisco. *Journal of Ethnic and Migration Studies, 42*(6), 989–1012.

Duhau, E. (2003). División social del espacio metropolitano y movilidad residencial. *Papeles de Población, 9*(36), 161–210.

Fanon, F. (1963). *The Wretched of the Earth*. New York: Grove Press.

Fanon, F. (1986). *Black Skin, White Mask*. London: Pluto Press.

Fassin, D. (2011). Racialization: How to Do Races with Bodies. In F. E. Mascia-Lees (Ed.), *A Companion to the Anthropology of the Body and Embodiment* (pp. 419–434). Oxford: Blackwell Publishing.

Frigerio, A. (2006). "Negros" y "Blancos" en Buenos Aires: Repensando nuestras categorías raciales. *Temas de Patrimonio Cultural, 16*, 77–98.

Geler, L. (2016). Categorías raciales en Buenos Aires. Negritud, blanquitud, afrodescendencia y mestizaje en la blanca ciudad capital. *Runa. Archivo Para Las Ciencias Del Hombre, 37*, 71–87.

Goffman, E. (1963). *Stigma: Notes on the Management of Spoiled Identity*. New York: Prentice Hall.

Grosfoguel, R. (2016). What is Racism? *Journal of World-Systems Research, 22*(1), 9–15.

Hall, S. (2010). El espectáculo del Otro. In E. Restrepo, C. Walsh & V. Vich (Ed.) *Sin Garantías. Trayectorias y Problemáticas en Estudios Culturales* (pp. 419–445). Quito: Envión Editores/Universidad Andina Simón Bolívar.

Harvey, D. (2012). *Rebel Cities: From the Right to the City to the Urban Revolution*. London: Verso.

Hochman, A. (2019). Racialization: A Defense of the Concept. *Ethnic and Racial Studies, 42*(8), 1245–1262.

Iglesias-Pascual, R. (2019). Social Discourse, Housing Search and Residential Segregation: The Social Determinants of Recent Economic Migrants' Residential Mobility in Seville. *Housing Studies, 34*(7), 1163–1188.

Lefebvre, H. (1991). *The Production of Space*. Oxford: Blackwell Publishing.
Lippert, R. K., & Walby, K. (Eds.). (2015). *Policing Cities: Urban Securitization and Regulation in a Twenty-First Century World*. Abingdon: Routledge.
Lipsitz, G. (2007). The Racialization of Space and the Spatialization of Race: Theorizing the Hidden Architecture of Landscape. *Landscape Journal, 26*(1), 10–23.
Mbembe, A. (2016). *Politiques de l'inimitié*. París: La Découverte.
Mbembe, A. (2017). *Critique of Black Reason*. Durham and London: Duke University Press.
Mignolo, W. (2003). *The Darker Side of the Renaissance: Literacy, Territoriality, and Colonization*. Ann Arbor: The University of Michigan Press.
Miles, R., & Torres, R. (2007). Does 'Race' Matters Transatlantic Perspectives on Racism after 'Race Relations'? In T. Das Gupta, C. E. James, R. C. A Maaka, G. E. Galabuzi & Ch. Andersen (Eds.), *Race and Racialization: Essential Readings* (pp. 65–73). Toronto: Canada Scholar Press.
Murji, K., & Solomos, J. (2005). *Racialization: Studies in Theory and Practice*. London: Oxford University Press.
Nicholls, W., & Uitermark, J. (2016). Migrant Cities: Place, Power, and Voice in the Era of Super Diversity. *Journal of Ethnic and Migration Studies, 42*(6), 877–892.
Nieuwenhuis, J., Tammaru, T., Van Ham, M., Hedman, L., & Manley, D. (2020). Does Segregation Reduce Socio-Spatial Mobility? Evidence from four European Countries with Different Inequality and Segregation Contexts. *Urban Studies, 57*(1), 176–197.
Piker, G. (2017). *Racial Cities: Governance and the Segregation of Romani People in Urban Europe*. London: Routledge.
Quijano, A. (2000). Coloniality of Power, Eurocentrism and Latin America. *Nepantla: Views from South, 1*(3), 533–580.
Registro Nacional de Barrios Populares (RENABAP). (2017). *Relevamiento Nacional de Barrios Populares. Informe general del período 08/2016–12/2017*. Buenos Aires: Jefatura de Gabinete de Ministros de la Nación. https://zul etasintecho.files.wordpress.com/2018/04/resumen-informe-de-gestic3b3n-renabap-ac3b1o-2017-docx.pdf. Accessed 15 March 2020.
Sabatini, F., Cáceres, G., & Cerda, J. (2001). Segregación residencial en las principales ciudades chilenas: Tendencias de las tres últimas décadas y posibles cursos de acción. *EURE, 27*(82). http://dx.doi.org/10.4067/S0250-71612001008200002.
Santos, B. de S. (2011). Epistemologías del Sur. *Utopía y praxis latinoamericana, 16*(54), 17–39.
Sassen, S. (1991). *The Global City: New York, London, Tokyo*. Princeton and New Jersey: Princeton University Press.

Scribano, A. (2015). *¡Disfrútalo! Una aproximación a la economía política de la moral desde el consumo.* Buenos Aires: Elaleph.com.

Scribano, A. (2017). Amor y acción colectiva: una mirada desde las prácticas intersticiales en la Argentina. *Aposta, Revista de Ciencias Sociales, 74*, 241–280.

Scribano, A., & Cervio, A. (2018). Distrust and Proximity: The Paradoxes of Violence in Argentina. In A. Scribano (Ed.), *Politics and Emotions* (pp. 193–219). Houston: Studium Press.

Segato, R. (2007). *La Nación y sus Otros. Raza, etnicidad y diversidad religiosa en tiempos de Políticas de la Identidad.* Buenos Aires: Prometeo.

Segato, R. (2010). Los cauces profundos de la raza latinoamericana: una relectura del mestizaje. *Crítica Y Emancipación, 2*(3), 11–44.

Tijoux, E., & Palominos Mandiola, S. (2015). Aproximaciones teóricas para el estudio de procesos de racialización y sexualización en los fenómenos migratorios de Chile". *Polis, 42.* http://journals.openedition.org/polis/11351.

Wacquant, L. (2008). *Urban Outcasts: A Comparative Sociology of Advanced Marginality.* Cambridge: Polity Press.

CHAPTER 11

Gated Communities and Dormitory Towns: Between (Dis)Trust and (In)Security

Jeanie Maritza Herrera Nájera

The Metropolitan Area of Guatemala City has been characterized in recent years by growing and accelerated changes in the urbanization processes. Analysing the link between emotions, sensibilities, and the (re)construction of cities, allows us to understand the intentions and motivations in the acquisition of properties and the process of socio-spatial segregation.

Thinking, feeling, and dwelling in the city implies (re)thinking the ways of (un)inhabiting, based on the structuring of the policies of the sensibilities and the mechanisms of social support. Fear and (dis)trust are primary emotions that influence the selection and access to housing, in response to a State that reproduces conditions of social inequality, poverty, labour inequity, and centralization of administrative activities, as well as a high rate of informal economic activity. In recent years, private-closed housing complexes have been created as a response to the search for social homogeneity based on the identification of the "others" as

J. M. Herrera Nájera (✉)
San Carlos University of Guatemala, Guatemala, Guatemala

© The Author(s), under exclusive license to Springer Nature
Switzerland AG 2021
A. Scribano et al. (eds.), *Cities, Capitalism and the Politics of Sensibilities*,
https://doi.org/10.1007/978-3-030-58035-3_11

197

foreign to the cultural, social, and economic values considered "acceptable" by the owners, and especially to an instinctive response to the perception of (in)security and the consequent search for survival in an apparent concrete jungle.

This chapter aims to understand the "inhabiting" experiences of the residents of gated communities built in commuter towns in Guatemala City's Metropolitan Area. To achieve this objective, the following argumentative strategy is followed: (a) we summarize the theoretical point of view on the connections between emotions, sensibilities, and cities, (b) we synthesize the secondary data available on trust and security in Guatemala, and (c) we present the main sensibilities, experiences, and emotions in the city and the motivations for access to housing complexes. The latter is based on semi-structured interviews and participant observation with owners of the condominium "Hacienda Vista Hermosa", located in the municipality of Mixco, Guatemala City, as a continuation of the research project *"Sociability and gated communities: sociability relations between residents of closed neighbourhoods, a case study in the municipality of Mixco, department of Guatemala"*. This chapter analyses the notion of dwelling in the city and questions the processes of daily interaction in the gated communities based on the sociology of bodies/emotions.

CITIES, SENSIBILITIES, AND EMOTIONS OF INHABIT

Cities have been considered, from the beginning, as the field of action in which the individuals establish relations according to the constant change of stimulation, specialization, and rationalization (De la Peña 2003, 30). Dwelling in the urban space entails thinking and feeling cities, from the absence or lack of the societal structure, to reach a sustainable human development; from the functional necessity, emphasizing the daily dwelling in the city (displacements, education, work, etc.,); as product of collective demands and the consequent civic answer when taking care of the absences and needs of a common good. The city is presented as "a shared space, trodden, where spontaneous, fluid, fragmented relations are carried out (…) generated from codes and systems of interaction" (De la Peña 2003, 46).

The connection between emotions, sensibilities, and inhabiting the city, makes visible the role of the policies of sensibilities, the mechanisms of social support, and the devices of regulation of sensations, from the new forms of interaction, that the processes of (re)construction of the city establish, as well as the embodied intentions and motivations that are materialized in the acquisition of residential areas and/or the choice of dwelling places, starting off social triggers that mobilize the plots of feeling. The city becomes a product of social relationships and experiences built and transformed from sensations.

The social interaction arises from the relationship between individuals according to certain impulses, material or subjective motivations, and/or purposes that can revolve around material interests, religious impulses, purposes of defence and attack, play and lucrative work, provision of assistance, and teaching (Simmel 2002, 78). Therefore, to feel the city and to feel in the city involve a process of social interaction, endowing it with a signifier and a meaning, which is translated in socialization processes, sociability, and experientiality. The *experience of dwelling*, is like a place-meaning through the body in permanent intersubjective co-constitution (Scribano and Cervio 2010, 2).

To dwell-the-city and to dwell-in the city implies a continuous transit of the ways of perceiving the sensibilities, the conditions in which the processes of interaction occur, and the embodied experiences that are internalized and those structured ways of feeling and co-inhabiting; we know the world through the body. Experientiality is a way of expressing the senses acquired by being-in-the-body with others as a result of "experiencing" the dialectic between individual, social, and subjective body; and the logics of appropriation of body and social energies (Scribano 2010, 174).

Sensibilities, experiences, and interactions allow the analysis of reality apprehension criteria, based on the recognition of emotions (in constant change), and the acceptance of sensations as elements of (re)action for decision making, for proximities and avoidance. These are conditioned by factors external to the individual that are internalized, and establish patterns of behaviour based on social limits imposed or self-imposed, which are part of the topography of the society's structuring processes and guide the avoidance of social conflict through socio-spatial segregation, devices for regulating sensations, and mechanisms of social support.

Devices for regulating sensations consist of processes of selection, classification, and elaboration of socially determined and distributed perceptions. Regulation involves the tension between senses, perception and feelings that organize the special ways of "appreciating-oneself-in-the-world" that social classes and individuals possess (Scribano

2010, 173). In the case of the housing complexes, social domination is configured from differentiated forms of dwelling in the city, according to conditions of (in)equality and contexts of access that individuals have, according to socioeconomic conditions that permeate the transit/socialization/experiencing of the city, depending on the distances from the "others", with the populated centres, the availability of social/corporal energies, and the interweavings articulated from the bodies/emotions.

Likewise, social support mechanisms are structured around a set of embodied practices aimed at the systematic avoidance of social conflict (Scribano 2010; Scribano 2004), which are produced and reproduced in the social order, which is glimpsed and constituted in everyday practices and processes of acceptance and regulation of actions.

The differentiated ways of inhabiting the city, of naming and co-existing in public space, of giving meaning to urban space based on the transformations and (re)construction of the notion of residing/dwell in social space, involves knowing the daily reality of the residents and the character of closeness/approach/trust in "the public space" and appropriation of urban spaces.

From the analysis of the symptoms, messages and absences of a society in breakdown, within the framework of access to housing, as well as tolerance of "given" situations, a kind of acceptance/resignation is given based on the limitations of body energy to turn around the collective problems that motivate negative emotions such as aversion, avoidance, detachment, frustration and terror, shaping policies of sensibilities based on fear and (dis)trust as primary emotions, and waiting, submission and frustration as part of the management of the time given up in terms of the incentives achieved, which nurture social ghosts and social fantasies. Therefore, policies of sensibilities are the set of cognitive-affective social practices aimed at the production, management and reproduction of horizons of action, disposition and cognition (Scribano 2017, 244).

Private urban development projects are presented as the solution to the real or imagined needs of individuals and groups, who seek well-being, happiness, and hope, as a motivation for the transformation of urban space, believing they can "momentarily" solve the breaks and absences of the desired common good, consolidating closed neighbourhoods as a bubble, as opposed to the open city.

This abovementioned "open city" must be understood as those colonies or housing nuclei open to normal pedestrian and vehicular traffic, where the coexistence between people of different social classes, ethnic groups, and cultures prevails (Bravo 2007, 199). On the other hand, the closed districts have reduced extensions, a reason why they tend to be located near urban centres and the main communication routes. Most offer recreational areas, green areas, and sports facilities, which allows the development of a new lifestyle, advocating a "return to the neighborhood" (Svampa 2008, 69). They are oriented towards the upper and middle classes with access to credit, and seek to provide security for their inhabitants, this being the main incentive for the residents.

Among the negative effects of such complexes, there is the issue of socio-spatial segregation, which they generate by constituting exclusive enclaves that isolate themselves from the city and transform physical barriers into social barriers (Roitman 2003, 6). This is exacerbated to the extent that residents of the closed neighbourhoods have little or no relationship with the urban fabric of the city to which they belong (Reyna 2015, 4) and end up generating a symbolic violence between both spaces, in addition to promoting idealizations based on a bubble of "momentary" protection to the residents.

GUATEMALA: PUBLIC POLICIES OF SECURITY AND THEIR LINK TO TRUST AS A SOCIALIZING FORCE

Guatemala is a multi-ethnic and multicultural country, with a population of 14,901,286 people, where 48.5% are men and 51.5% women, 62% are under 30 years of age and only 6% over 65. Likewise, of the total population, 41.7% identify themselves as Mayan and 56% as Ladino. The country is divided into 22 departments and 340 municipalities. The department of Guatemala, with 17 municipalities, constitutes the metropolitan region (CRG 1986), concentrating 20% of the total population, of which 91% live in urban areas. Three municipalities of this department concentrate 60% of the metropolitan population: Guatemala City, Mixco, and Villa Nueva with 1,822,899 inhabitants, and are characterized by having higher indexes of urbanization, commerce, and infrastructure (INE 2019).

The demographic and population characteristics allow us to understand the urban dynamics and the processes of construction of the city, as well as to know how unplanned urban growth becomes a risk factor for disasters and collapse of the road systems, where a centralization of industrial and governmental development becomes visible.

Urbanization is understood as the spatial concentration of the population from certain limits of dimension and density (Castells 2014, 15). On the other hand, the processes of diffusion of urbanization in territorial crowns that surround the central nucleus or traditional city (Mallarach and Vilagrasa quoted in Cabello and Pascual 2014, 603), conform the Metropolitan Areas, which are established as a city, considered as an axis that establishes continuities with other geographical areas (con-urbanization), strengthening their relationship (Martínez 2011, 15).

Historical factors such as internal armed conflict (1960–1996), and natural disasters such as earthquakes, floods, landslides, and droughts, have led to internal migration (rural-urban), making inequalities and poverty visible, as a result of accelerated urban growth, and limitations in access to employment, housing, and higher education. The Metropolitan Area has a high population density and expands to municipalities around Guatemala City. It has blurred the separation between urban and rural, leading to a proliferation of precarious urban settlements with inadequate access to basic services, that increase the environmental vulnerability as a consequence of weak integrated disaster risk management, and the proliferation of socio-spatial segregation based on the grammar of actions and the geometry of bodies.

The municipalities of the conurbation are considered dormitory cities, with a high percentage of the population commuting daily to Guatemala City. Commuter towns are created by the growth of population in surrounding municipalities that would increasingly play a functional residential role, possibly linked to daily movements between place of residence and place of work (Mallarach and Vilagrasa quoted in Cabello and Pascual 2014, 604). The creation of residential neighbourhoods in commuter towns allows us to (re)think about the notion of (un)inhabiting in the city, as well as the intentions and motivations behind the acquisition and choice of residences.

Since the 1990s in Latin America, the construction of private residential areas has expanded, mainly as a result of fear of violence and high crime rates (Svampa 2004, 2008; Bravo 2007; Demajo 2011; Roitman 2003), opposing the notion of an open city and modifying the dynamics of its inhabitants, making visible processes of (dis)trust towards the "others", generating in many cases political sensibilities oriented towards self-enclosure, social isolation, submission to norms of coexistence, and disconnection from inhabiting the city.

The condominiums are constituted in the social imaginary of the residents, in forts articulated in networks, which present a great tendency to social and generational homogeneity and to the generalized practice of selective mating in all orders (Svampa 2008, 126). Dwelling/inhabiting in a condominium brings benefits to the residents, such as private security, recreational areas, and regulated coexistence, promoting interaction in a protected and homogeneous environment. However, this provides a particular solution to a social problem, such as insecurity and urban violence, without acting on its causes, but only on its effects (Roitman 2003).

In contrast, the open city is associated with violence, (in)security and anarchy, increasing the fear, and (dis)trust of inhabitants. In extreme cases, fear turned into panic shapes distorted thoughts, and residents can even prefer not to frequent public spaces for fear of being robbed or suffering some act of violence. There is a perception that private spaces are established as the only reliable place where one can be safe from crime, being protected by elements of private security.

The urban growth increase of population density, and centralization of actions in the conurbation, make visible the shortages in citizen security, as well as the housing and socioeconomic problems, that make it difficult to achieve social and sustainable development. In this framework, public policies are a set of objectives, decisions, and actions that a government makes in order to solve a country's social problems. Therefore, they are constituted as strategic courses of action of the State and government based on citizen participation and legitimacy, national and international legal and political frameworks, aimed at promoting the population's well-being and enjoyment of human rights in its diversity and at the different levels of organization of the national territory (SEGEPLAN 2015a).

The National Development Policy (2015–2032), created in 2015, has limited policy guidelines for housing. They are mainly oriented towards reducing the deficit in access to housing for the population in conditions of poverty and extreme poverty, environmental sanitation, and disaster risk management; and highlight the planning of urban centres as a significant challenge, displacing the responsibility of this last aspect to municipal governments (SEGEPLAN 2015b). Social and spatial segregation is not seen as a collective problem.

Guatemala has a framework of 72 public policy documents, nine of which are linked to security, addressing issues such as: sexual violence, open data, maritime security, prison reform, national defence, addictions and illicit drug trafficking. In addition, there are three policies aimed at addressing and enhancing citizen security, and reducing violence and crime: (1) National Security Policy (NSP) (2) National Policy for the Prevention of Violence and Crime, Citizen Security and Peaceful Coexistence 2014–2034, and (3) Democratic Criminal Policy of the State of Guatemala 2015–2035, the last one located within the framework of criminal justice, investigation and prosecution.

The NSP, through the socio-human axis, identifies as part of the elements that threaten citizen security, threats related to extortion, 11rgani acts 11rganisa by members of gangs, smuggling, 11rganisat, robbery and vehicle theft. The NSP noted that during 2008 and 2009, violence reached its highest point with a rate of 46.36 homicides per 100,000 inhabitants (STCNS 2017). By 2019, according to census projections in the Fourth Presidential Report (2016–2020), the country had a homicide rate of 21.7 per 100,000 inhabitants (INE quoted in SEGEPLAN 2019). Despite the decrease in homicide rates, Central America 11rgani of the most violent sub-regions in the world.

Guatemala's Prevention Policy recognizes violence as the intentional use of physical rgan or power, as a threat against oneself, another person, or a community group that causes 11rgan likely to cause injury, death, psychological transitory damage of development or deprivation (Galtung quoted in MINGOB 2014). It recognizes crime as a typical, anti-legal and culpable action that allows for the breakdown of the human will to want to violate or harm persons or property (MINGOB 2014, 26), classifying crime into categories of family violence, sexual crimes, injuries, homicides, robbery, and theft. This preventive policy seeks to influence the community environment through the creation of community ties, 12rganisation, and participation in neighbourhood committees for peaceful coexistence.

Perception of (in)Security

Guatemalans live in an alarming state of paranoia, with a high perception of insecurity and fear, even towards entities in charge of providing public security. The lack of spaces for recreation and leisure, added to the lack of cohesion and the growing loss of values, as well as the (dis)trust towards the "other", are factors that affect the action, disposition, and cognition of the city, and its habitability.

According to the public opinion survey conducted by Latinobarómetro (2018), the most important problems in Guatemala are crime/public security, followed by unemployment. These elements are repeated when analysed from a municipal perspective, indicating that at the local level the problem generating the greatest impact is the one associated with the economy, followed by crime. In the case of crime and violence, a constant can be observed within the perception of (in)security: women between 26–60 years of age feel most vulnerable to violence in the streets, and would be in favour of the installation of more drastic measures to control public space in order to guarantee tranquillity and trust.

The survey also identifies gangs as the type of violence most harmful to the country's development, followed by domestic violence against children and women, and thirdly, organized crime. With regards to the type of violence most frequent in the place of residence, gang violence stands out, followed by violence in the streets. Men between the ages of 15–40 feel most threatened by the first type of violence in the place of residence, and women between the ages of 26–40 by the second type. In addition, 84.9% of respondents indicated that they would agree or strongly agree with the installation of that cameras, drones, and sensors in public space to help prevent crime.

It is important to note that, of the total number of interviewees, 72.7% indicated that they had not been victims of robbery, assault, or crime in the last 12 months. However, 57.6% are sometimes or almost always concerned about becoming a victim of a violent crime, especially the women aged 26–40.

Likewise, according to data from 2019 surveys of the Barometer of the Americas, 45.5% say that security continues to be the most serious problem facing the country. In addition, crime victimization continues to affect 1 in 5 Guatemalans (20.4%), and the perception of insecurity in the neighbourhood has increased considerably since 2012, from 31.5 to 52.5%. At the same time, the economy and politics (including corruption) are beginning to be issues of special concern in the country (LAPOP 2019).

The public policies and indexes on access to housing and (in)security make visible the processes of social structuring in the country. Linking the notion of inhabiting the city with a change in the dynamics of social interaction, guiding a trend towards social homogeneity, to the detriment of socio-spatial segregation, elements that are expressed through the transformation of the open city and the formation of condominiums or private residential complex that seek to position themselves as solutions to the absence of the State in terms of security.

When the dynamic of (re)construction of the city is altered, there can be changes in the forms of social relationships with the people in urban space, in this sense, differentiated according to the capacity to isolate oneself from the open city (Alvarado and Jiménez 2014, 103). Nevertheless, this process is consolidated from the geometry of bodies, the possibility of the individual to have his own presence and his positions in front of the being/feeling/inhabiting and the grammar of actions; meaning his capacity for action, appreciation and classification of the external world, the availability of the bodies that the individuals have (Scribano 2004). This makes visible how closed neighbourhoods are constituted as an alternative preferred by middle and upper classes, making visible how the policies of sensibilities and the mechanisms of social support are shaped from inequality, labour informality and the management of unreal time, allowing a reconfiguration of the notion of habitability from shared experiences.

Trust as a Socializing Force
Trust makes social interaction possible, and social interaction enables the experiences that make up the notion of inhabiting the city. Trust is a state of favourable expectation regarding the actions and intentions of other people (Ovares 2018, 31), and is presented as a hypothesis on the other's future conduct, a hypothesis that offers sufficient security to found in it a practical activity (Simmel 1986); it constitutes an intermediate degree between the knowledge about other individuals and the ignorance regarding them. The one who knows, does not need to "trust"; the one who ignores, cannot even trust (Simmel quoted in Cervio 2019, 75). Trust manifests itself at all levels of society, based on inductive knowledge, faith in others, reciprocity, and moral obligation. It is developed in the family as a first level of socialization and in the role of the community as a space of sociability, where trust emerges as a socializing force.

Trust is that halfway point between knowing and not knowing. Hence, the reflective feature of trust is found, not in the fact of pondering what is known, but in the individual's capacity to put in parenthesis (suspend ignorance and contradiction), because for every reason found to trust, there is probably a reason not to (Möllering quoted in Cervio 2019, 76).

The construction of a private residential complex is considered as a space that allows trust in those who are considered "homogeneous" and leads to distrust of the "others". The development of private complexes encourages the stigmatization of the neighbourhoods that make up the open city, creating (dis)trust towards those who live outside the residential perimeters, marking them out as the cause of the problem.

When we talk about the "other", we can see the relationship between the open city and the closed neighbourhood, but also the link between the condominium owners themselves, with whom the residents do not have the desire to socialize, nor to establish bonds of sociability. There are two types of trust that affect the way of seeing/observing/looking at it and embodiment: particularized trust, that is, in people we know and, on the other hand, a generalized trust, that is, in people who are not connected to us (Montero 2008, 17). The "other" can be cata-logued as a second category inhabitant, either because he lives in a social space foreign to that regulated and controlled by the security of closed neighbourhoods, because the temporality of residence is different (new neighbours), or tenants who are automatically excluded from the feeling of societal homogeneity of the owners (outsiders).

Regarding trust categories, according to the Latinobarómetro (2018), 78.2% of respondents consider that people can never be sufficiently careful in dealing with others, a perception that increases in women between 26 and 40 years, followed by those between 15 and 25; this is an element that requires us to question the devices for regulating sensations that lead women to live/inhabit with even greater (dis)trust and distance from the "other".

With respect to trust in groups, institutions or individuals associated with security, the survey identifies that 72.9% indicated they have little or no trust in the police, and 63.8% indicated they have little or no trust in the armed forces, with women being the most distrustful. Institutions associated with the justice system generate more trust than the institutions of representative democracy.

Trust towards institutions is configured as a result of the legitimizing conditions that are created and recreated from the organs of power at their different levels (Tapia et al 2017, 7). Trust can be understood as a form of governance and positive expectations, especially towards the State's framework for regulation and the search for satisfaction of basic needs, such as citizen security, reducing the deficit of housing and inequality. Political trust in an institution implies the belief that it will not act in an arbitrary or discriminatory way that is harmful to our interests or those of the country, but it will treat us and other citizens in an equal, fair, and correct way (Listhaug and Wiberg quoted in Montero 2008, 21).

Trust is built from the knowledge that emerges from the experience of citizens towards the proper functioning of their institutions (Tapia et al. 2017, 9). Its absence presents a break and affects the regulation of sensations and mechanisms of social support that are articulated through the bond and citizen participation in order to complement/substitute/demand the action of the State in terms of security and watching over individual and collective integrity, ameliorating social conflict arising from the absence of the demand for the common good, and the search for alternatives through neighbourhood committees to address the needs of groups considered to be homogeneous.

Sensibilities, Experiences and Emotions Around the City and the Access to Housing Complexes: "Hacienda Vista Hermosa" Condominium

The "Hacienda Vista Hermosa" condominium is a gated community made up of ninety-two homes, located in the Pinares neighbourhood of Ciudad San Cristóbal (open city), whose main requirement for acquiring a property was job stability and economic solvency. It has a security checkpoint, perimeter walls, surveillance cameras, green areas, children's playgrounds, and parking for visitors. The neighbours are organized to form a Board of Directors in charge of the administration of the private residential complex. In order to analyse the sensibilities, experiences and emotions surrounding access to the housing complex, a qualitative analysis was conducted based on participant observation and semi-structured interviews, using non-probabilistic sampling and a "snowball" strategy to access information from the owners of the condominium, located in zone 8 of the municipality of Mixco.

Mixco has 11 zones, with 465,773 habitants and 118,506 households. Out of the total of households, 64.18% are owned houses, 32.78% are rented houses, and 3.02% are borrowed or communal houses. Of the total number of owners, 42.55% are men and 32.33% are women (INE 2019). In 2002, there were 13 colonies and 68 condominiums in zone 8 of Mixco, and that had increased by 339.7% by 2018, with 18 colonies and 231 condominiums (Munimixco 2019). Also, according to data from the Department of Security, zone 8 has a violence rate of 5%, with most of the phenomenon occurring in the commercial area of the zone, in addition to be the place where most professionals reside (Munimixco 2018).

In the areas surrounding the condominium, there are 29 businesses and services (automotive, food, education, personal image and health), and 35 private homes. However, the fear associated with the open city generates an imaginary division between both spaces:

> There's been talk of a robbery on that main street. And that it is quite busy and commercial. But it's become... I think it's become dangerous because of the commercial. (E.PC.1, personal communication, 14 October 2019)

> No, I don't like *going to the commercial area*. For safety. My concept of security is the same. So, the less you stop and get out of the car, *better* (*Italics added*). (E.PC. 2, personal communication, October 14, 2019)

Of the total number of interviewees, most of them moved into the condominium before 2009, the total of interviewees identify themselves as Ladino, middle-middle-high class, with a medium or high educational level, with an average age of 40 years and children of pre-primary and primary school age. More than a half come from inside the country or from Guatemalan's conurbation, and almost all the interviewees come from open cities. The main motivations for acquiring the property were security, followed by green areas and a reduced number of houses in the residential complex.

The total number of interviewees indicated that they had no contact networks prior to their arrival, they also specified that did not practice sports or social activities in the recreational areas of the condominium, nor with neighbours outside of the residential complex, and only one person mentioned having a group of church couples on a weekly basis, an activity that they do in their own home, not in the common areas.

Among the main results, (in)security and (dis)trust are identified as social triggers for understanding the network of sensibilities that are embodied, affecting the (re)production and management of forms of social interaction and (un)inhabiting the city, affecting the acquisition and selection of residential spaces.

Plutchik (2001) identifies eight basic emotions that make visible another advanced emotion and their potential interactions (including opposing emotions), based on the intensity and closeness of the individuals involved in an interaction process. An emotion is defined as a response or reaction to a significant stimulus that an individual evaluates, consciously or unconsciously, according to his/her objectives or interests and influenced by his/her ideology and socio-cultural context. The rationalization, reflection and- interpretation of emotions trigger the construction of feelings, which are, therefore, more reflexive and lasting than emotions (Damasio 2005 quoted in Beas et al. 2016, 55).

Two basic emotions are emphasized: trust and fear, in order to understand and analyze the sensibilities associated with the acquisition and choice of inhabiting spaces. Stimulations, evaluations, and personal or collective reactions are considered as structuring elements of the emotions. The stimulation is more or less relevant depending on the cultural context, the receptivity of each subject and their capacity to generate responses (Damasio quoted in Beas et al. 2016, 55), including the response by the State to the needs and demands of the population that affect the consolidation of policies on sensibilities and devices for regulating sensations, including security.

Plutchik analyses composite combinations of emotions he calls dyads, identifying more complex feelings. The opposite emotion of fear is anger, and depending on its degree of intensity it can lead from apprehension to panic. Within the primary dyads, the fear associated with acceptance entails processes of submission, in which the will of the "others" is accepted, even if this means sacrificing one's freedom; while the fear associated with surprise entails processes of dismay. It is presented as an adaptive reaction to the threats of the social environment (Ángel Montoya and Monsalve Burgos 2015, Beltiukov and Abbasi 2019). Inhabiting a closed neighbourhood configures processes of submission through the regulations of the norms of coexistence and the search for harmony and peaceful cohabitation.

The search for security in response to fear entails the loss of guarantees of interaction such as coexistence with the open city. However, private residential complexes transmit a sense of tranquillity through perimeter walls, surveillance cameras and private security that watch entry and exit of the "others". This also makes symbolic violence visible in the face of restriction and rejection of the "outside", the "other", the "unknown", and becomes a symbol of power, control and regulation of sensations.

Trust has the function of mutual support and facilitates participation in groups, and having friendships, while its opposite emotion is rejection and according to its degree of intensity can lead from acceptance to admiration (Ángel Montoya and Monsalve Burgos 2015; Beltiukov and Abbasi 2019; Plutchik 2001). Distrust leads to refusing and avoiding, the opposite of when a mutual interrelationship is established, one that can lead to the belief in acting without danger or harm, accepting and making bonds with the outside world based on experience, and helping to reduce distances in search of peaceful coexistence and mutual respect.

Despite the consolidation of closed neighbourhoods as "safe" spaces, condominium owners highlight a limited sociability within the closed neighbourhood, making visible cordial but distant relationships, with a particular interest or sporadic contact, contrary to what they make visible about experience in the open city or inside the country in the past. This element can vary depending on the time and experiences shared among condominium owners.

> "As a child, I only enjoyed the benefits of inhabit in an open neighborhood. Then we could visit each other, eat, and having friends all from the same ages" (...) "I could see that in the case of my mommy that she knew all the neighbours. We go through the earthquake together and supported each other almost all the block. In other words, there was a lot of solidarity because we knew each other. Because if today something happens, we must see how we go out of that situation, and no one else, because everyone does the same. We don't have any coexistence". (E.PC. 2, personal communication, October 14, 2019)

> "I say it's like a brotherhood, because we were all like brothers, practically *(Open City)*. If something was ruined, to give an example of the *(hurricane)* Mitch, we all went out, got together, went out to bring rations" (...) "The truth is that there was more union (*Italics added*)". (E.PC. 6, personal communication, 29 October 2019)

About social support mechanisms, time management stands out significantly. The high demand for closed neighbourhoods, and the increase in the population density in the conurbation, has led to the proliferation of vehicular chaos. Traffic has been one of the main motivations for people to move to another place.

This element has an impact on the articulation of sensibilities, experiences, and emotions, making visible feelings of frustration and waiting in long lines and for several hours to be able to start routines of work and study. That significantly prolongs the time of "absence" in homes and neighbourhoods. Commuting towns begin to move around at 4:00 am, modifying leisure/exercise times, personal routines and sleep hygiene habits, food and family life, because the "waiting" is continuously present, in many cases forcing condominium owners to stay away from the neighbourhood dynamics. Given the lack of public transport, commuting towns increase the number of vehicles per family annually, generating greater complications in circulation.

A WAY OF CLOSURE

(Un)inhabiting the city challenges the processes of daily interaction and the link between the response of the State and the actions of individuals and communities looking for the common good: security. The different problems associated with living/feeling/dwelling and having an experience in the city start from an appreciation of the practices that are embodied in the inhabitant's availability for action, and the response to the multiple needs of the society, which are often latent.

Gated communities (re)create bubbles of protection against the challenges of the city. The need of individuals to obtain greater freedom in their place of residence is glimpsed; however, it is opposed to the self-enclosure policy to which the owners and tenants of the closed neighbourhoods are submitted, and also the self-isolation linked to individuality, fear, and submission, as well as the (re)construction of a city based on an interaction of the segmentation process, with an unusual inter-district and internal socialization, based on the premise of being commuting towns.

(Dis)trust generates weak community ties, where closed neighbourhoods apparently resolve citizen (in)security, leaving aside other types of violence and solidarity, whose ties of collective construction are strained by the interweaving of long-term perceptions/sensations/emotions. Residential coexistence is not a priority, but rather a lifestyle where privacy and discretion prevail.

REFERENCES

Alvarado, A., & Jiménez, G. (2014). Acercamiento al estudio de las urbanizaciones cerradas en Costa Rica: Notas Metodológicas. *Revista de Ciencias Sociales, 145*, 99–108.

Beas, M., González, E., & Salmerón, A. (2016). Estudio de las emociones en las consignas de cuadernos españoles. Curso 1964–1965. *Revista Estudios Sociales, 58*, 52–62.

Beltiukov A., & Abbasi, M. (2019). Summarizing Emotions from Text Using Plutchik's Wheel of Emotions. *Advances in Intelligent System Research, 166,* 291–294.

Bravo, M. (2007). *Proceso de urbanización, segregación social, violencia urbana y barrios cerrados en Guatemala 1944–2002.* Guatemala: CEUR.

Cabello, S., & Pascual, N. (2014). De pueblos a ciudades dormitorio: El crecimiento de la corona metropolitana de Logroño (La Rioja). *Inguruak. Revista Vasca de Sociología y Ciencia Política, 53–54,* 603–621.

Castells, M. (2014). *La Cuestión Urbana.* México: Siglo XXI Editores.

Cervio, A. (2019). Desconfianza e interacciones urbanas. Un abordaje desde las sensibilidades sociales. In A. Cervio & B. Bustos García (Comp.) *Confianza y Políticas de las Sensibilidades* (pp. 71–105). Buenos Aires: Estudios Sociológicos.

Congreso de la República de Guatemala (CRG). (1986). *Decreto Nº70–86, Ley Preliminar de Regionalización,* Guatemala. https://www.congreso.gob.gt/detalle_pdf/decretos/1697#gsc.tab=0. Accessed 11 May 2020.

De la Peña, G. (2003). Simmel y la Escuela de Chicago en torno a los espacios públicos en la ciudad. *Revista Sincronía, 28.* http://sincronia.cucsh.udg.mx/pena03.htm.

Demajo, L. (2011). Barrios cerrados en ciudades latinoamericanas, *URBS, Revista de Estudios Urbanos y Ciencias Sociales, 1,* 151–160. http://www2.ual.es/urbs/index.php/urbs/article/view/demajo_meseguer. Accessed 5 May 2020.

Instituto Nacional de Estadística (INE). (2019). *XII Censo Nacional de Población y VII de Vivienda,* Guatemala. https://www.censopoblacion.gt/explorador. Accessed 20 May 2020.

Latinobarómetro (2018). *Resultados por Sexo y Edad, Estudio nº LAT-2018,* Guatemala. http://www.latinobarometro.org/latCodebooks.jsp. Accessed 10 May 2020.

Martínez, F. (2011). *Transformaciones urbanas en Guatemala 1950–2002, Reunión de Expertos sobre Población, territorio y desarrollo sostenible.* Santiago de Chile: CEPAL. https://www.cepal.org/sites/default/files/events/files/florentin_martinez.pdf. Accessed 22 May 2020.

Ministerio de Gobernación (MINGOB). (2014). *Política Nacional Prevención de la Violencia y el Delito, Seguridad Ciudadana y Convivencia Pacífica 2014–2034,* Guatemala. http://ecursos.segeplan.gob.gt/CAPP/documentos/17/POL%C3%8DTICA%20NACIONAL%20DE%20PREVENCI%C3%93N%20DE%20LA%20VIOLENCIA%20Y%20EL%20DELITO,%20SEGURIDAD%20CIUDADANA%20Y%20CONVIVENCIA%20PAC%C3%8DFICA.pdf Accessed 20 March 2020.

Ángel Montoya. L., & Monsalve Burgos, J. (2015). *Control de emociones en el trabajo, el juego de los sentimientos organizacionales.* Proyecto de grado para

Especialización en Alta Gerencia, Medellín: Universidad de Medellín. https://repository.udem.edu.co/handle/11407/2189. Accessed 9 May 2020.

Montero, J. (2008). Confianza Social, Confianza Política y satisfacción con la democracia. *Revista Española de Investigaciones Sociológicas, 122,* 11–54.

Municipalidad de Mixco (Munimixco). (2018). Conoce la zona 8 de Mixco, Plan de Ordenamiento Territorial, Guatemala. https://www.munimixco.gob.gt/wp-content/uploads/2018/02/ZONA-8.pdf. Accessed 20 April 2020.

Municipalidad de Mixco (Munimixco). (2019). *Datos estadísticos sobre la división urbana de la zona 8 de Mixco,* resolución de solicitud de acceso a la Información Pública, Unidad de Acceso a la Información Pública, Guatemala.

Ovares, C. (2018). La sociología de Georg Simmel y el Capital Social: La Confianza como fuerza socializadora. *Revista Reflexiones, 97*(2), 23–34.

Plutchik, R. (2001). *The Nature of Emotions.* EEUU: American Scientist.

Proyecto de Opinión Pública de América Latina (LAPOP). (2019). *Estudio de la cultura política de la democracia en Guatemala,* Barómetro de las Américas. http://www.asies.org.gt/wp-content/uploads/delightful-downloads/2019/05/Cultura-de-la-democracia-en-Guatemala-2019.pdf. Accessed 10 May 2020.

Reyna, M. (2015). *Fragmentación y segregación: el fenómeno –countries– en la Ciudad de Córdoba.* Tesis de Máster Universitario en Gestión y Valoración Urbana, Centro de Política de Suelo y Valoraciones (CPSV), Cataluña: Universidad Politécnica de Cataluña. https://upcommons.upc.edu/bitstream/handle/2117/80134/REYNA_TESIS.pdf?sequence=1&isAllowed=y. Accessed 23 April 2020.

Roitman, S. (2003). Barrios cerrados y segregación social urbana. *Scripta Nova, Revista electrónica de geografía y ciencias sociales, VII*(146). http://www.ub.edu/geocrit/sn/sn-146%28118%29.htm. Accessed 15 April 2020.

Scribano, A. (2004). Conflicto y estructuración social: una propuesta para su análisis. In J. Zeballos, J. Tavares & D. Salinas Figueredo (Eds.), *América Latina: hacia una nueva alternativa de desarrollo* (pp. 54–68). Arequipa: Editorial UNSA.

Scribano, A. (2010). Primero hay que saber sufrir…!!! Hacia una sociología de la "espera" como mecanismo de soportabilidad social. In P. Lisdero & A. Scribano (Comp.) *Sensibilidades en Juego: miradas múltiples desde los estudios sociales de los cuerpos y las emociones* (pp. 169–192). Córdoba: Estudios Sociológicos Editora.

Scribano, A. (2017). Amor y acción colectiva: una mirada desde las prácticas intersticiales en la Argentina. *Aposta, Revista de Ciencias Sociales, 74,* 241–280.

Scribano, A., & Cervio, A. (2010). La ciudad neo-colonial: Ausencias, Síntomas y Mensajes del poder en la Argentina del siglo XXI. *Revista Sociológica, 2,* 95–116.

Secretaría de Planificación y Programación de la Presidencia (SEGEPLAN). (2015a). *Guía para formulación de políticas públicas*, Guatemala. http:// www.segeplan.gob.gt/downloads/2015/Politicas_Publicas/GpFPP.pdf. Accessed 20 March 2020.

Secretaría de Planificación y Programación de la Presidencia (SEGEPLAN). (2015b). *Política Nacional de Desarrollo*, Guatemala. http://ecursos.seg eplan.gob.gt/CAPP/documentos/57/Politica%20Nacional%20del%20Desa rrollo%20(2).pdf. Accessed 2 April 2020.

Secretaría de Planificación y Programación de la Presidencia (SEGEPLAN). (2019). *Cuarto Informe Presidencial al Congreso*, Guatemala. https://www. segeplan.gob.gt/nportal/index.php/biblioteca-documental/biblioteca-doc umentos/file/1441-cuarto-informe. Accessed 15 April 2020.

Secretaría Técnica del Consejo Nacional de Seguridad (STCNS). (2017). *Política Nacional de seguridad*, Guatemala. http://ecursos.segeplan.gob.gt/ CAPP/documentos/76/Politica-Nacional-deSeguridad-2017-.pdf. Accessed 25 March 2020.

Simmel, G. (1986). *Sociología, Estudios sobre las formas de socialización*. Madrid: Alianza.

Simmel, G. (2002). *Cuestiones fundamentales de sociología*. España: Editorial Gedisa.

Svampa, M. (2004). *La Brecha Urbana: countries y barrios privados*. Buenos Aires: Editorial Capital Intelectual.

Svampa, M. (2008). *Los que ganaron: La vida en los countries y barrios privados*. Buenos Aires: Biblos.

Tapia, E., Alemán, J., & Sánchez, O. (2017). *(Des)confianza en las instituciones y corrupción. El Caso de México*. XXXI Congreso ALAS Uruguay Montevideo https://www.researchgate.net/publication/323525772_DESCONFIANZA_ EN_INSTITUCIONES_Y_CORRUPCION_EL_CASO_DE_MEXICO. Accessed 10 May 2020.

CHAPTER 12

Urban Spaces of Fear and Disillusionment

Felipe Hernández and Ángela Franco

While carrying out ethnographic research on the peripheries of Cali, Colombia, a local resident casually told us that he had once been asked about his greatest fear of living in Cali, a question he replied saying: 'my fear is to raise my son here [in this type of housing] and even worse, in this District'. The local resident was a male Afro-descendant, a social leader from the Pacific Coast of Colombia, who currently lives as single father in the *Aguablanca* district of Cali. The man received a 100% subsidised house from the government as part of a programme to accommodate a small portion of the millions of people who have been displaced by the country's multiple conflicts. According to the Internal Displacement Monitoring Centre (iDMC 2020) Colombia continues to have the second

F. Hernández (✉)
Department of Architecture, University of Cambridge, Cambridge, UK
e-mail: fh285@cam.ac.uk

Á. Franco
Department of Architecture, Universidad del Valle, Cali, Colombia

© The Author(s), under exclusive license to Springer Nature Switzerland AG 2021
A. Scribano et al. (eds.), *Cities, Capitalism and the Politics of Sensibilities*,
https://doi.org/10.1007/978-3-030-58035-3_12

217

largest number of internally displaced people in the world after Syria.[1] It is also important to recognise that the majority of those displaced are Afro-descendants, a population that has suffered historically from multiple forms of abuse, exploitation and discrimination, starting with colonial slavery through to contemporary racism.

That Afro-descendants represent the socio-ethnic group hit most hard by the long-lasting conflict in Colombia is a well-known fact. In 2010, the *Observatorio de Discriminacion Racial* (Racial Discrimination Observatory), based at Universidad de los Andes in Bogotá, reported that 22.5% of the total displaced population in Colombia were Afro-descendants (Rodríguez et al. 2010). Their statistics imply that 12.3% of the overall Afro-descendant population of the country live currently in conditions of forced displacement.[2] In a different report, published in 2013, the Observatory confirms the existence of 'large scale residential segregation, where the areas of Afro-descendant concentration in cities correlate directly with the worst living conditions' found among peripheral urban residents in cities throughout the country (Duarte et al. 2013) This is alarming considering the existence of specific laws, such as the *Ley 387* of 1997, which set the principles for the restitution of housing and property to internal refugees and displaced people, as well as the subsequent *Decreto* 250 of 2005, which creates a national plan for the support and protection of people displaced by violence.

It is in this context that the government created the '100% subsidised housing programme' in 2012 to provide free housing for 200.000 extremely poor families, including those that had been displaced by the conflict and were left with no other alternative than to search for accommodation in cities, or large towns, across the country. In this paper we will examine the conditions in which many Afro-descendants live when they become 'beneficiaries' of government free housing. These conditions are: permanent fear, loss, vulnerability, rejection and inadequacy.

---

[1] According to statistics obtained on 18 April 2020 from https://www.internal-displacement.org/database/displacement-data, there are 5,761,000 displaced people in Colombia.

[2] The observatory reports evidence of mass displacement of indigenous communities, forced out of the 'territorios colectivos' (collective land constitutionally granted to them based on historical records of territorial occupation), but deplores the lack of precise data. Given that only 4% of the Colombian population is registered as indigenous, displacement statistics are often marginal. The presence of indigenous groups in cities is also small compared to Afro-descendant groups. As such, displaced indigenous groups do not have the same impact on cities as Afro-descendants.

We argue, following the Martiniquais psychiatrist and political philosopher Franz Fanon, that 'being Black' has complex psychological implications and, also, that the historical disparaging treatment of Afro-descendants causes insurmountable emotional trauma. The violence they suffer at the hands of right-wing paramilitaries and left-wing guerrilla groups who force them out of their rural lands and into the city enhances that trauma. And if it were not enough, once in the city, many displaced Afro-descendants have to endure poor housing conditions, lack of governmental support, unemployment, aggression by drug trafficking gangs, and everyday exclusions by an inherently racist society.

The feeling expressed by the single father in the *Aguablanca* district of Cali epitomises both the trauma of being displaced and the psychological implications of being Black in urban Colombia. In this chapter, we present several more statements like this, and reveal how a psychological landscape overlaps with the physical fabric of the city in neighbourhoods designed by the government.[3] If the '100% subsidised housing programme' was designed to offer sanctuary to those who have suffered the cruelty of war and displacement, then, the programme failed completely. We show how these neighbourhoods intensify the anxieties of a population that arrived to the city in search of tranquillity and opportunity, only to find further hostility and grater rejection. All these experiences determine the relationship that Afro-descendants establish with 'the city'.

ANXIETY AND DISILLUSIONMENT IN *LLANO VERDE*

The origin of the *Aguablanca* district dates back to the early 1970s when poor people, mainly Afro-descendants from the Pacific coast, began the extra-legal occupation of flood risk areas on the banks of the River Cauca without any access to public utility networks (Alcaldía de Cali 2016). The process is often described through the figure of the 'invasion': when people settle illegally on land that does not belong to them. However, the physical fabric of the neighbourhood since the 1970s shows great regularity in the distribution of plots, as well as the rectilinear arrangement of streets. As such, it is unlikely that rural immigrants alone developed these lands without the support of external agents, including landowners who wanted to push the city's expansion to the east. The fact that the

---

[3] All statements have been translated into English by the authors.

City Council quickly initiated a process of regularisation (i.e. legalisation of property and provision of services and utilities) following the gradual occupation of the area suggests that *Aguablanca* did not develop spontaneously but that it was, at least partially, the product of private economic interests, with the support of the municipality. Indeed, by the 1980s, the government had launched a massive programme of social housing construction in the area which, in turn, initiated a circuit of formal-informal development: the regularisation of informal housing and the construction of new housing encouraged new informal settlers from rural areas to move in, so that their ramshackle structures had to be regularised and more new housing had to be provided. This circuit was intensified in the 1990s due to an increase of paramilitary violence on the Pacific Coast of Colombia, which forced an even larger number of Afro-descendants to move to Cali. Many of these rural migrants set home in *Aguablanca* where they had family and support networks.

By the 1990s, the provision of housing had been privatised, and between 2012 and 2013, the neighbourhood called *Llano Verde* was the last private development built in *Aguablanca*. It was planned as a social housing complex by a private construction firm, and sold in its entirety to the national government for the '100% subsidised housing programme', and to the municipality for the *Plan Jarillón*.[4] The project comprised 4321 identical two-storey houses of 47 m^2 to accommodate 20,000 people. Of those, 3523 households were beneficiaries of the '100% subsidised housing programme', most of them (98%) victims of the armed conflict who had been displaced from their territories (Franco 2020, 55). Today, *Llano Verde* accommodates the most vulnerable population of Cali, concentrating Afro-descendant and indigenous communities in the District that has the highest rate of unemployment (Ministerio de Trabajo and Alcaldía de Cali 2013) as well as the highest rate of homicide (Alcaldía de Cali 2020).

Let us describe the physical fabric of *Llano Verde*, before entering a discussion about psychological effects of living there. Although *Llano Verde* complies with the required standards for public space provision such as parks and communal facilities, the spatial quality of the neighbourhood is unsatisfactory by all standards. In their plan, the construction firm set aside 'green spaces', as required by the city's Planning Code, but these

---

[4] Plan *Jarillón* was a parallel housing programme to relocate settlements from the banks of the River Cauca, an environmental reserve prone to flooding.

areas were never fully designed. Instead, these poorly designed, barren, and unlit spaces are often occupied by informal businesses, or controlled by gangs, all of which prevents the community from using them freely. Moreover, no community supporting facilities were built. Only in 2016 did the municipality secure funds for the construction of a school and two nurseries, but health support is still not fully provided (the health centre remains unfinished), and the neighbourhood does not have a community centre. Clearly, the focus was on the provision of housing units, not on the quality of space offered to the residents collectively, so they could integrate peacefully and productively to the city.

With public space unresolved due the designers' concentration on housing, one would expect the housing units to cater for the specific needs of displaced populations. That was not the case either. Careful inspection of the houses shows that they are small and inflexible, as well as ill equipped to deal with the variety of residents who occupy them. The architectural and structural design meets all the required standards for habitability and earthquake-resistance (Cali sits on an earthquake fault line), but residents often complain about the lack of space. One of the beneficiaries explains that even though she is grateful for having received a free house, the size of the house presents multiple limitations:

> Eleven people live in the house next door, and all the houses in the neighbourhood have two small bedrooms. There is space for only one small bed in each bedroom, and there is only one bathroom. I have to sleep with my little girl, so that my oldest daughter can have her own bedroom. We couldn't put two beds in one room; they just didn't fit. (Interview with local resident, August 12, 2017)

The size of the houses, coupled with the fact that they were handed over unfinished (i.e. incoming residents had to complete the construction, placing bedroom doors, painting walls, laying floor finishes and adding kitchen appliances), meant that residents did not have a sense of 'urban domestic normality' upon arrival. Instead, they were faced with hardship. Moreover, the government imposed conditions to prevent houses from being extended or modified, showing utter disregard for the need of the residents.

The house was not a home, and the city did not offer to them the benefits they expected after being expelled from their lands by the country's protracted conflict. Furthermore, structural and symbolic forms of violence quickly emerged in *Llano Verde*: drug trafficking gangs, petty crime, stigmatisation for being displaced, and generalised racism. In other words, the precarious notion that free housing would, on its own, enable the peaceful re-building of communities shattered by unimaginable suffering was not only naïve in the part of the government, it was also negligent in so far as it actually exposed those broken communities to further violence.

The residents of *Llano Verde* live in a continuous state of fear and vulnerability, where the experience of uprooting leads to feelings of rejection and inadequacy. Residents express these feelings and experiences in many ways. These are some statements:

> We, the victims living in *Llano Verde*, say that we want a better place for our kids. With our work, we can overcome this situation and give them a better life. But, while we are here we have to resist all that's happening [the violence and rejection]. (Interview with local resident, August 30, 2017)

Many of the residents aspire to find employment, and have the skills necessary to work in many industries. However, they are unable to get jobs either because they are Black or indigenous, or simply because being displaced generates distrust among potential employers. Moreover, the government imposed conditions to prevent houses from being extended or modified, and to block businesses from developing. Although businesses have indeed appeared in many of the houses, the government ban on commercial activity has inhibited economic opportunity, setting yet another hurdle for residents to adapt productively to urban life.

Disillusionment and despair prevail among the local population.

> As much as we want *Llano Verde* to be a model at the national level, we are not going to achieve this because the institutions and the government do not enable us to have the neighbourhood that we dreamed of. They [the government] believe that we are animals and believed the same when they built *Potrero Grande*: 'This is a pasture, go there and kill yourselves!' There was no social fabric. *Potrero Grande, Llano Verde*, what is the difference? Even the name is similar. (Interview with local resident, September 18, 2017)

Potrero Grande, which means paddock in English, was an earlier development in a different sector of *Aguablanca*. It became the most dangerous neighbourhood in the city, and *Llano Verde*, which in English means verdant field, also became a violent neighbourhood.[5] The reference to that earlier development, with the name paddock, is used here by a resident to express the frustration and impotence, the feeling that they are sent to paddocks, like cattle, to meander without purpose and eventually kill themselves.

Living with the Executioner and Segregation by Algorithm

Early in the process of assigning urban housing to rural migrants displaced by right-wing paramilitary and left-wing guerrilla groups, municipal officials detected many failures that were not corrected in time by the national government. In search for a method fairly to allocate the limited number of housing units to the millions of people who arrived and settled on the outskirts of cities, the government designed a ballot system to randomise the assignment—let us remember that less than 200 thousand units were built throughout the country for over 5 million forcefully displaced people. The system apportioned houses to both displaced people and former members of paramilitary and guerrilla groups, known as demobilised fighters in the same neighbourhoods. To be sure, as a result of this system, victims and perpetrators lived side by side, generating the resurgence of conflict, and placing innocent people at risk. As a resident explains,

> President Santos came and 'threw out' the victims together with demobilised former members of illegal armed groups because the peace agreement was going to be signed. We, the victims, have had to live in these blocks with people like them. (Interview with local resident, June 16, 2017)

Another resident indicated that:

> I was known for being a human rights activist and for supporting the victims of the armed conflict. When I came for the first time to my house in *Llano Verde* some men were waiting for me while chatting with my little son. They told me that they knew all my moves and that they came

[5] It placed 20th in the list of most violent neighbourhoods of 2019 in Cali.

to remind me that there were 'spaces' here that I should never enter. (Interview with local resident, August 30, 2017)

Right wing paramilitary groups circulate pamphlets, expelling community leaders from the neighbourhood and 'sentencing' others to death. In *Llano Verde* the law is not a singular system enforced by the government, but a multiplicity of evolving regimes each of which exercises its authority simultaneously and in competition with one another. This error in the part of the government exposed an immense lack of institutional coordination, as well as ignorance about the community that was going to arrive in the neighbourhood. In the words of a municipal official: 'in spite of the positives, the free housing programme became a "harming action" promoted and produced by the government itself'.[6] It arises that government officials became aware of these flaws, and the dangers they caused, but did not apply correctives timely. The result is a trail of death that renders the city void of its most basic elements of hospitality.

Another failure occurred when housing units were allocated according to markers of vulnerability. In this case, houses were assigned to individuals, or households, in relation to the degree of vulnerability, measured by an algorithm. For example, Afro-descendants are considered a vulnerable population. Women are also vulnerable, and more so if they are single mothers. It does happen that an Afro-descendant single mother has sufficient markers of vulnerability to gain priority in the allocation of housing. Indigenous people are considered a vulnerable population too. As a result, this system causes Afro-descendants and members of indigenous groups to occupy specific areas of the neighbourhood while other social and ethnic groups live in different sectors. Accidentally, the algorithm causes racial segregation, which in turn enhances the visibility of cultural difference, and this is used to justify racism in the form of stereotypes: Afro-descendants are characterised as lazy, noisy, over-sexualised and dangerous. Indigenous are ingenuous and reserved, which makes them easy targets of city-savvy gangs.

Previous struggles are accentuated by relegation (both spatially and socially) when the beneficiaries of the '100% subsidised housing programme' moved into *Llano Verde*, a neighbourhood that quickly

---

[6] Interestingly, the Ministry of Housing had compiled a detailed database of the beneficiaries of the programme and, therefore, had the information necessary to prevent this deadly overlap.

turned into an isolated space at the local scale, in a District already isolated at the urban scale. Relegation had negative consequences that affect the wellbeing of the residents. Instead of a place of sanctuary, far from the rural conflict they have fled, the city has become site of fear and disillusionment for all residents.

Twenty-First Century Spaces of Urban Coloniality

Before continuing with our analysis of *Llano Verde*, we consider it neces-sary to take a theoretical excursus to define urban peripheries in relation to the people who inhabit them, and the political mechanisms that have been deployed in order to locate those people there. Positioning bodies on the land in strategic geographical relations to the city has been a central prac-tice in Colombian urbanism since the foundation of cities during colonial times. In his insightful studies about Spanish colonialism in the Amer-icas, the Peruvian sociologist Anibal Quijano contends that race has been deployed since the seventeenth century as a way to sustain the newly emerging model of capitalist power. He argues that 'race became the fundamental criterion for the distribution of the world population into ranks, places, and roles in the new society's structure of power [capi-talism]' (Quijano & Ennis 2000, 535). In the Americas, and particularly in Hispanic America, indigenous populations were confined to serfdom and the Black were confined to slavery, while the Spanish (white), estab-lished themselves as the dominant race and could receive wages, be independent merchants, artisans or farmers. These were no clear-cut clas-sifications, yet they formed the basis of a complex distribution of rights, and also land, with significant impact on the consolidation of the colonial city.

The argument we strongly want to posit here is that such a spatial configuration persists in Colombian cities today. It is no coincidence that Afro-descendants (Black) and indigenous populations remain poor, under-represented and excluded from the dominant economic system. Moreover these are the most likely residents of urban peripheries. That is why we propose that urban peripheries in Cali are spaces of coloniality: they demonstrate the prevalence of colonial principles expressed on the urban fabric of cities in the twenty-first century, even though colonialism per se came to an end more than two hundred years ago.[7]

In his assertion that 'race' provided the basis for a classification of the world's population in such a way that it supported the emergence of a new model of global power, Quijano alludes to the constitution of modern biopolitics. Even though Quijano does not refer to Foucault directly—the French philosopher more closely associated with the concept of biopolitics—he maintains that people were stratified according to the colour of their skin in order constitute efficient administrative structures to control labour, resources and products. More importantly, by associating different groups of people to specific forms of labour, their lives acquired a value within the emergent modern capitalist system. Indeed, Black lives acquired the lowest value, being reduced to bare life.[8] That is why we maintain that the concept of biopolitics lends itself to undertake a revision of the terms in which certain techniques were created to regulate and control local populations in order to sustain a system of economic accumulation in the Americas. As such, the concept of biopolitcis enables a critical understanding of the inherent and ineludible connections between colonial techniques of administration and the morphology of Colombian cities.

In a similar vein as Quijano, the Cameroonian philosopher Achille Mbembe, maintains that the formation of mercantilist thought in the west coincides with the creation of two key administrative techniques: colonisation and the slave trade. For Mbembe, modernity, capitalism, and colonialism are also intrinsically linked and the three are articulated around racial stratifications that cause Black lives to lose their value. In this own words,

> [In the New World] life came to be shaped according to an essentially racial principle. But, thus understood, race, far from being a simple biological signifier, referred to a worldless and soilless body, a body of

---

[7] Hernández (2017) argues that urban peripheries in the Americas, not only in Colombia or Latin America, are spaces of coloniality, where the uneven distribution of resources, services and utilities, corresponds largely with racial classification whose origin is colonial.

[8] We are referring here to 'bare life' in the context of Giorgio Agamben's book *Homo Sacer: Sovereign Power and Bare Life* (2017), where he sets out to establish the function that the figure of the *homo sacer* plays in modern politics: the man 'who may be killed yet not sacrificed'.

> combustible energy, a sort of double of nature that could, through work,
> be transformed into an available reserve or stock. (Mbembe 2019, 10)

Since then, Black bodies have occupied what he calls 'third spaces' where
unimaginable cruelty was applied on the slave to maximise productivity.
The plantation is one of those third spaces, and indeed a relevant one
in the region of which Cali is capital: Valle del Cauca. Ever since the
late seventeenth century, the flat lands of the Cauca Valley have been
used for the plantation of sugar cane. Later in the eighteenth century,
mills started to appear and have remained central to the local economy,
playing a central role in the process of regional modernisation. Black
African slaves were brought in as labour to plant and harvest sugar cane,
and this brought about a segregated society with white-mestizo landlords
on the one hand, and African slaves on the other. As such the history
of Cali is strongly rooted in the tradition of slavery, a fact that needs
to be included in the study of the city's socio-spatial distribution—the
relationship between the urban form and the city's residents. It is here
that we see the appearance of a hierarchical spatialisation based on race,
which determined the geographical position of the African in relation to
the white-mestizo. Instead of lessening, this segregationist distribution of
space intensified after the abolition of slavery in 1851. Precisely because
former African slaves were unable to acquire property in the city, they
were forced to set up home along the banks of rivers, on the peripheral
wetlands, a third space between the city and the plantation, and indeed a
position they have occupied ever since.

In his work about the birth of Caribbean nations, Fanon describes how
the abolition of slavery did not improve the living conditions of former
slaves but, instead, rendered them 'peripheral' to the nation.

> [I]n the face of the extraordinary power of white planters, the abolition of
> slavery in the nineteenth century proved ineffective in bringing about a real
> improvement in the situation of Black workers. The later had to remain
> agricultural labourers on the plantations, and even today, their miserable
> huts sit side by side with the luxurious house of the master. (Fanon 2015,
> 584)

In his immensely insightful study of the abolition of slavery, Fanon points
out not only the position that former slaves occupied in local systems of
production, but also the socio-economic impact such a position would

have on them for many generations to come: descendants of slaves would live in poverty and beside the white master. It is worth mentioning that he wrote in the mid twentieth century (1958), and, nonetheless, the expression 'even today' continues to have the same effect. It is this aspect of his work that we want to refer to, what he calls the after-effects of slavery, namely poverty and racism. Fanon maintains that the struggle against poverty is particularly difficult 'because of the idiosyncrasies created by four centuries of colonisation', one such idiosyncrasy is, of course, racism. Thus, despite independence from direct colonial control, and in spite of their freedom, Afro-descendants continue to occupy a peripheral position in the structures of the nation, not only socio-economically, but also geographically in relation to the white-mestizo groups.

In this context, Mbembe's idea that the colonial plantation emerges as a 'third space' makes perfect sense. He uses that powerful concept in postcolonial theory, third space, to describe a site of legal opacity, somewhat (but not entirely) outside the law, where the Black—and other minorities like the indigenous, who were almost entirely eliminated by colonisation—were dehumanised, and continue to be discriminated against today. The conceptual third space is located besides the space of capitalist opulence, but not inside it, the third space is peripheral to capitalist wealth, and the wealth is in fact colonial.

We hope to have established that the racialised peripheries of Cali are not a product of twentieth-century economic disparities brought about by an uneven industrialisation that caused large sections of the population to remain on the margins of development—as is often argued. The origin of the periphery is colonial and, as such, it constitutes an inherent element of the Colombian city: there is no way of understanding Colombian cities without reference to its periphery because it is one of its constituent parts. The fact that peripheries continue to be occupied by the two ethno-racial groups most largely affected by Spanish colonialism makes them spaces of deprivation and struggle. That is why we contest vehemently Teresa Caldeira's enthusiastic celebration of the periphery as a site where 'residents engage in processes of construction that constitute them simultaneously into new kinds of urban residents, new kinds of consumers, new kinds of subjects, and new kinds of citizens' (Caldeira 2017, 4), and where 'new modes of politics' are produced, generating 'new kinds of citizens, claims, circuits, and contestations' (Caldeira 2017, 4). Some forms of cultural creativity may exist, and many strategies of resistance are developed, rather in order to cope with oppression not as a deliberate contribution to society. Our research shows that residents of the periphery do not see themselves as protagonists in the production of a new urban politics that contests anything. They hardly see themselves as citizens, and have very little to consume. Instead we propose that urban peripheries are spaces of coloniality because they reveal the prevalence of colonial mechanisms of exclusion, which for the past four hundred years have condemned racial minorities to poverty, exclusion and perennial violence.

Therefore, the selection of a deprived periphery to build housing for displaced people both ratifies and perpetuates colonial exclusions which prevent ethno-racial minorities from gaining full access to the benefits the city could offer to them, forcing them to remain subject to multiples forms of violence. In order fully to grant urban citizenship to rural minority migrants displaced recently by internal conflict in Colombia—who have also withstood historical forms of displacement and aggression—it would be necessary carefully to study the position of social housing schemes in such a way that they do not reiterate (colonial) exclusions, thereby facilitating, if not directly encouraging, the perpetration of crimes against minorities, whose lives are considered expendable. For as we have seen, in *Llano Verde*, violence translates into death, a death administered with unacceptable complicity by the government, the planner and the architect alike.

DEATH AND THE CITY

Our analysis of *Llano Verde* shows that the practicalities of 'accommodating' people 'displaced' by violence in order to meet housing targets—thus satisfying international expectations on human rights—supersedes considerations about the well being of the citizens. People are distributed across the national territory, and given a place in cities—a free house in poorly planned neighbourhoods—irrespectively of their origin, or the reasons why they have arrived in the city. The situation greatly disrupts basic principles of social justice. The distinction between victim and executioner, for example, is blurred in conditions where both occupy the same space under the auspices of a government programme whose intention was to seek justice through housing restitution; housing as a means to support and protect people displaced by violence. The unresolved coexistence of these two groups perpetuates a cycle of hatred and intolerance that results in further violence: it translates a rural conflict into an urban one, subjecting everyone to greater tragedy.

Rivalry between competing groups turns the city into a battlefield, a space of endless territorialisations that bring about a multiplication of boundaries segregating populations on the basis of race, class, income, origin, political affiliation and each time one of these identities emerges, another has to be spatially excluded. An 'imagined community' united by their national affiliation no longer exists, and with it the idea of nation-state falls rapidly under question. The presence of the state diminishes under the pressure of a proliferation of groups, all of which aspire to establish their own territory, control it, set their own rules and, indeed, impart justice in their own way. The government is forced to respond in uncoordinated, misinformed, and entirely inefficient, manner. The question about responsibility evades the authorities that admit failure, but fail also to implement corrective measures to prevent further loss of life. Without full acceptance of responsibility there is little room for justice and, therefore, the cycle of violence and death multiplies itself indefinitely. The free housing programme, created as a reparation to those affected by the longstanding national conflict, exacerbates hatred, intensifies divisions and, hence, injustice becomes not merely unavoidable: injustice is the norm.

Walking through the neighbourhood with local residents one is constantly reminded of the prevalence of death: 'in this corner someone was killed'; 'that is where someone else was left to die'; 'my life was threatened here'. The tragedy of death is so indelibly engraved in the physical fabric of the neighbourhood that it no longer feels tragic. Moreover, assassinations are often legally unresolved; even though residents know who the perpetrators are, as do the authorities, only rarely is someone tried in a court of law or imprisoned. Death and injustice are part and parcel of everyday life in *Llano Verde*, where local residents expose the complexity of the situation in many ways, yet always revealing an emotional rejection of their neighbourhood, and the city more generally.

> One of the most difficult things a mother, or a father, in this neighbourhood has to experience is the burial of their own children. (Interview with single mother, Afro-descendant displaced from the Pacific coast, September 5, 2017)

That is how a mother explains the experience of death as a fact of life in the neighbourhood, one she has to get used to, even though she finds it unbearable. Life itself has lost value in the continuous territorialisation of the city by competing groups displaced from the countryside.

Rather than a 'biopolitics' whose aim is to administer life, we witness a 'necropolitics', a concept which in the words of Achille Mbembe 'stands for organised destruction, for a sacrificial economy, the functioning of which requires, on the one hand, a generalised cheapening of life, on the other, a habituation of loss' (Mbembe 2019, 38). Loss is the condition of everyday urban existence on the peripheries of Colombian cities. Each corner of the neighbourhood brings memories of loss:

> A stray bullet killed a child here. The boy was playing with a ball in front of his house. Two young men, members of the football team were killed too. We thought we were going to live well here [peacefully], but it was a lie. We came here to experience war again, and we continue to see our children die. (Interview with single mother, displaced from San Vicente del Caguán by the FARC guerrillas, September 18, 2017)

The story told by a local male single father at the start of this chapter, begins to make sense along so many testimonies offered candidly by parents and residents of *Llano Verde*. The anxiety they express about the future of their children occludes their own fear, the fact that they themselves could be killed and, therefore, their children would not have anyone to look after them.

Conclusion

At the start of this chapter we set out to explore the psychological effects that living on the periphery of Cali have on members of minority groups who have been displaced from the countryside by the protracted internal conflict in Colombia. We also addressed the subsequent rejection of the city, which is no longer perceived as a place of safety, but rather as a site of fear. We argued that the unimaginable violence suffered by Afro-descendants and indigenous people in Colombia at the hands of right-wing paramilitaries and left-wing guerrillas finds it roots in colonial structures which rendered their lives expendable. We then proceeded to demonstrate that accommodating displaced populations—the majority of whom are Afro-descendant and indigenous—on the periphery of Cali

perpetuates their exposure to violence, this time at the hands of drug trafficking gangs, or simply as a result of everyday exclusions by an inherently
racist society. We showed through dramatic testimonies that government
housing schemes have not achieved their objective but, instead, often
intensify the anxieties of a population whose arrival to the city brought
further hostility and grater rejection.

The construction of poor-quality urban spaces to accommodate the
most vulnerable groups on the periphery of the city reveals an attitude of
disdain towards minorities groups. The charity of providing free accommodation is undermined by the lack of attention paid to the conditions of
live provided, the lack of institutional support, and, ultimately, the avoidance of responsibility. Subject to conditions of deprivation and violence,
constantly under the threat of death, we invoked the notion of necropolitics, insufficient as it is on its own, in order to argue that neglectful
government attitudes confirm the low value assigned to the life of the
Afro-descends and indigenous minorities. The irony of the '100% subsi-
dized housing programme' for vulnerable and displaced populations is
that it condemns them to living where they have always lived: in poor-
quality housing on the periphery, where, in the view of the residents
themselves, they are left to die.

That is why we propose that urban peripheries are spaces of coloniality,
that is, spaces where colonial mechanisms of exclusion and inhumanity
remain in place, even though colonialism as such has ended. Moreover,
we maintain that, as such, the peripheries expose the disintegration of
the nation-state in so far as it makes visible the proliferation of evolving
regimes that contest the authority of the government by exercising their
authority simultaneously and in competition with one another.

That the study of urban peripheries in Cali, and many other cities in
Colombia, exposes underlying and longstanding inequalities is an enormous understatement. Much has been said about structural poverty and
violence, where poor-quality social housing conditions, such as those
found in *Llano Verde*, deepen social exclusion and reduce social mobility
opportunities. Social housing with minimum standards solves the problem
of accommodation, and occasionally facilitates access to public services,
indeed it turns displaced people into home owners. However our analysis proves that these housing schemes do not foster peace, nor do
they improve living conditions for poor communities of rural migrants
displaced by conflict. Quite the opposite, at least in Cali, the '100%
subsidised housing programme' translated a rural conflict to the urban

space, where it has become more acute. That is why we question simplistic arguments about structural poverty and violence, for they may both be structural indeed, but the structures belong to a politics of neglect that cannot be resolved through equally simplistic practices such as the provision of social housing, be it free or subsidised. For as long as there is an abyss separating the giver from the receiver of housing, government housing schemes will continue to perpetuate the exclusion of minority groups and the violence they currently experience in Cali. Only a radical revaluation of the concept of the city would bring to and end the circuitous repetition of socio-spatial exclusion. Politicians, government officials, planners and architects need radically to reconceive the city from the perspective of the excluded, the Afro-descendant and the indigenous, whose experience and expectation of the city is different from that of the white-mestizo. In other words, for as long as government officials, planners and architects continue to conceive the city from their perspective, expecting the migrant to 'assimilate', they will continue to reproduce the exclusions that perpetuate the current conflict.

REFERENCES

Alcaldía de Cali. (2016). *Plan de Desarrollo Comuna 15, 2016–2019*. http://www.cali.gov.co/documentos/1569/plan-de-desarrollo-decomunas/genPagDocs=2. Accessed 12 May 2020.

Alcaldía de Cali, Observatorio de Seguridad. (2020). *Informe de Homicidios*. https://www.cali.gov.co/observatorios/publicaciones/147590/observatorio-de-seguridad-delitos-contra-la-vida/#dcv. Accesed 18 May 2020.

Agamben, G. (2017). *Homo Sacer*. Redwood: Stanford University Press.

Caldeira, T. (2017). Peripheral Urbanization: Autoconstruction, Transversal Logics, and Politics in Cities of the Global South. *Environment and Planning D: Society and Space, 35*(1), 3–20.

Duarte, N., Villamizar, S., & Rodríguez, C. (2013). *Raza y vivienda en Colombia: La segregación residencial y las condiciones de vida en las ciudades*. Bogotá: Universidad de los Andes.

Fanon, F. (2015). In the Caribbean, Birth of a Nation. In J. Khalfa & R. C. Young (Eds.), *Franz Fanon: Alienation and Freedom* (pp. 583–590). London: Bloomsbury.

Franco, A. (2020). *The Production of Marginality. Paradoxes of Urban Planning and Housing Policies in Cali, Colombia* (Doctoral Dissertation). University of Cambridge, Cambridge: UK. https://doi.org/10.17863/CAM.50138.

Hernández, F. (2017). Locating Marginality in Latin American Cities. In F. Hernández & A. Becerra (Eds.), *Marginal Urbanisms: Informal and Formal Development in Cities of Latin America* (pp. 1–48). Newcastle upon Tyne: Cambridge Scholars Publishing.

Internal Displacement Monitoring Centre. (2020). *Global Internal Displacement Database.* https://www.internal-displacement.org/database/displacem ent-data. Accessed 29 April 2020.

Mbembe, A. (2019). *Necropolitics.* Durham: Duke University Press.

Ministerio de Trabajo & Alcaldía de Cali. (2013). *Encuesta de Empleo y Calidad de Vida para el municipio de Santiago de Cali.* https://planeacion.cali.gov. co/amda/index.php/catalog/1. Accessed 16 May 2020.

Quijano, A., & Ennis, M. (2000). Coloniality of Power, Eurocentrism, and Latin America. *Nepantla: Views from South, 1*(3), 533–580.

Rodríguez, C., Orduz, N., & Berrío, J. (2010). *El desplazamiento forzado de los afrocolombianos: Evaluación del cumplimiento del Gobierno colombiano del auto 005 de la Corte Constitucional.* Bogotá: Universidad de Los Andes.

CHAPTER 13

Cities, COVID-19 and Sensibilities: A Kaleidoscope of Experiences

Adrián Scribano, Margarita Camarena Luhrs, and Ana Lucía Cervio

At the same time as the writing of this book, the COVID-19 pandemic broke out across the world. The entire planet shook and the most important cities in the world radically changed their daily lives. From Shanghai to New York, from Madrid to Rome, from Berlin to London, from Buenos Aires to São Paulo, time/space twisted and the planet "entered" into a new band of the multiple Moebius strips that usually contain it.

We could not ignore the subject. We couldn't keep quiet. We could not stop expressing what we are living, seeing and investigating in these contingent, indeterminate, complex and planetary contexts. That is why we decided to write this last chapter three-handed, under the figure of the kaleidoscope. A figure linked to metaphor, to play and also to beauty,

A. Scribano (✉) · A. L. Cervio
National Scientific and Technical Research Council, University of Buenos Aires, Buenos Aires, Argentina

M. Camarena Luhrs
Institute of Social Research, National Autonomous University of Mexico, Mexico City, Mexico

© The Author(s), under exclusive license to Springer Nature Switzerland AG 2021
A. Scribano et al. (eds.), *Cities, Capitalism and the Politics of Sensibilities*,
https://doi.org/10.1007/978-3-030-58035-3_13

235

which allows us to write three chapters in one, from where the reader can draw his or her conclusions and literally finish the book.

Kaleidoscope is an expression that refers to a tube that has various mirrors inside, which are tilted. At one end of the kaleidoscope there are two sheets of glass: between them, different irregular objects of different colours. By rotating the tube and looking at the opposite end, the images of these objects located between the sheets of glass multiply symmetrically. These gadgets usually contain three mirrors, arranged like a prism, with a triangular shape that reflects towards the internal sector.

In his work "The Kaleidoscope in Spanish Literature", Dorde Cuvardic García (2018) states:

> The term to designate the kaleidoscope was proposed by David Brewster himself. It is made up of the Greek words χαλός, bella, εἶδος, form, image, and σκοπέμ, see, observe, etymological provenance that is responsible for reeling at the beginning of the book that he published on the subject –until not translated into Spanish– entitled *The Kaleidoscope. Its history, theory and construction with its application to the fine and useful arts* (Brewster, 1858, 1) 4. Etymologically, it means the action of "observing a beautiful image" (Cuvardic García 2018, 66).

In this context, this final chapter is a three-part device that seeks to allow the reader to capture some fragments of the sensibilities of cities in the pandemic. It is an irregular look, diverse across each of the three elements, which reflects the feelings of those who have looked through these three mirrors, constituting them. It is a playful ending: the reader can start and end with any of its parts and also borrow its metaphorical force from the kaleidoscope to reach unknown terrain by known means. They are reflections open to dialogue and multiple endings, to multiple images, to multiple observations. It is a chapter where beauty will be a matter for the reader, since it will be his or her eye that validates, denies or rewrites the policies of the sensibilities of the cities today.

In this framework, the chapter has three sections that operate as three "chapters". The first, written by Margarita Camarena Luhrs, is "*In the face of the COVID-19 pandemic, emerging mutual aid practices inspired by values of protection and care for life*". The second, "*Cities in silence. A global response to fear of the other*", is offered by Ana Lucía Cervio. And, finally, "The Pandemic City: between lack and possibility", is authored by Adrián Scribano.

We have decided to claim authorship of each section separately, for having had the experience in different cities, for being impacted by dissimilar practices of being in the city, and for valuing how the collective does not eliminate the personal, hence the selection of the title of the chapter as a whole.

IN THE FACE OF THE COVID-19 PANDEMIC: EMERGING MUTUAL AID PRACTICES INSPIRED BY VALUES OF PROTECTION AND CARE FOR LIFE

As it is currently unknown how and when the COVID-19 pandemic will end, everyone experiences a different degree of risk, threat, even danger of death. Even so, the uncertainty that this causes is an unprecedented social force that moves us equally. Under these conditions, different valuations of life itself emerge. These can be seen from responses that range from indifferent indolence on the part of some authorities, to the most practical, massive and compassionate forms of mutual aid.

Inseparable practices of values emerge that exceed the economic priorities of the market: reciprocity and trust, bravery and courage, generosity. Above all, it is essential to protect life, to take care of oneself, which suddenly turns out to be everyone else. For this "I" that could no longer be known multiple, from the *status quo* the collective individualism that we felt as something so crystallized, immovable and safe, something suddenly happens: the pandemic and, once again, the feeling that We are lost.

Doubt, hesitation and indecision are seen everywhere. Something lurks behind immediate contact. The possibility of being infected dilates the encounter, it affects us passively. There is, again, that old known presence of fear; a catalyst that we had tried to forget. With the COVID-19 pandemic other emotions come into play, another state that mixes the imperative to "stop feeling" with "regain feeling (yourself) in others".

The normalized amalgam of conflict networks before the pandemic cannot be rescued. It seems that it will no longer be possible to return to the former. What will change? It is not foreseeable, beyond the fact that they will try to endure the experience in the best possible way, with a grace that empowers women with much love for all people. For this reason, the situation that threatens world health opens up unprecedented opportunities that may shake capitalist structures through possible adaptations. It is clear that previous needs emerge in full force, that there are newly affected in addition to those that already existed within the prevailing social order. Controversial dilemmas appear, and not all decisions in the face of events manage to leave behind well-known authoritarian and unsustainable ways.

"New Normal"

This crisis of certainties has been prolonged more and more. It seems that the world will face a "new normal" in response to COVID-19, as evidence shows that the majority of the population remains susceptible to the virus. As the situation stabilizes in Europe, the numbers begin to rise in Latin America where, according to experts, there is still time to avoid massive outbreaks (UN 2020, 1). Have there been in history or today more conflict networks materially and emotionally virulent than those now experienced with the spread of the coronavirus?

If they may have been longer in duration due to the outbreak of contagion, even with the tremendous hope (lessness) and fear shared today with other devastating historical episodes, there are emerging practices inspired by (re) appropriated values of unedited ways. So it can be alluded to that this pandemic is as virulent as the best known of antiquity.

It can be seen this way not only because it exposes structural historical conflicts that seemed immutable, but because it complicates them by adding to these conflicts multiplied by expressive networks of pain and suffering, of death that has no reparation, that is pure destruction. While what we are currently experiencing is a cathartic conjuncture of unprecedented consequences and difficult to measure, even so, we witness the over-institutionalized violence, too many attempts to maintain control of what had managed to be normalized in all areas of social life; trying, probably fruitless, to successfully instal a "new normal" everywhere.

Along this spectrum, other possibilities for structuring social reality are suggested. Although it would be too soon to confirm it, if the emergence of other practices related to the protection of life is not observed, other responses that go beyond the previous lines of possibility are beginning to be evident: the care of victims in different ways and in different measures; on this occasion we all live in anguish, in isolation, feeling helpless, unprotected, afraid, in the midst of a helplessness that even silence and weather cannot break.

Memories of fatal epidemics that transformed societies and states remain from the depths of history. Ravages of its consequences are still expressed in the bodies/emotions of people everywhere. Alive, perhaps less fatal, are the traces of high-risk contagious diseases such as smallpox, measles, polio, malaria, tuberculosis, amoebiasis, cholera, dengue, viral hepatitis, typhoid, dysentery and other food poisoning infections. These and other diseases are present throughout the history of despair that has plagued the world with health crises at different times, as seen in the following Table 13.1.

This comparison between COVID-19 and other major historical health crises caused by previous pandemics helps us to remember how much they altered world history and, above all, to state that there may now be a possible lesser degree of devastation because it will end, to a great extent,

Table 13.1   Major health crises that influenced the course of history, according to estimated data

Pandemic	Years	Places	Deaths
Plague Antonina (by measles or smallpox)	AD 165–180	Byzantium (current Istanbul City)	5 million
Justinian's Plague	Successive outbreaks lengthened the ailments from 165 to 750 AD	Byzantium, Mediterranean ports	35 million
Japanese smallpox	735–739	Japan	1 million
Black plague or death	1347–1353	Eurasia, Europe	Between 75 and 200 million
Smallpox	1520	Europe	56 million
Third plague pandemic	1855	Europe	12 million
Cholera epidemics	1833–1834, 1855, 1863–1873 and 1885	Spain	800 thousand
Spanish influenza	1918–1919	Europe	40–50 million
Influenza H1N1virus (IAV)	1918–1920	United States and the world	50 million
SARS	2002	29 countries	770,000
HIV/AIDS	1981–2020	World	32 million
Ebola	2014–2016	World	11.3 miles
MERS	2015–2020	World	850
Swine flu H1N1	From 2009 to	Mexico2010, world	12,469
COVID-19	2019 April 2020	China, world	160,000

Source: Own elaboration based on Carrión (2020), Garrido (2020), and Opazo Sáez (2020).

thanks to the fact "that modern science and medicine can be rationally used to stop it" (Opazo Sáez 2020, 4).

Still, the events of death remain part of the common denominators of all these epidemics. Like famines or wars, the COVID-19 pandemic makes evident correct measures or great failures experienced in each place and on each of the occasions mentioned. The truth is that measures implemented have not yet been sufficient to completely contain it. In fact, it is difficult to have sustainable public health programmes when priorities change according to what happens at any given time.

One difference with what happens with the COVID-19 outbreaks now is that public health measures are beginning to be effective in some way to control the "spikes" of maximum incidence, delay the spread of germs and thus reduce the level of deaths worldwide. Current epidemiological surveillance is an important historical difference in knowing who is affected and who is not. Knowledge about the spread of germs is decisive. However, it is massive physical distancing and voluntary quarantine measures that work the most.

Emerging Mutual Aid Practices That Are Life-Inspired Values

The need is known and felt to protect goods and services essential for social life (e.g. health, food, water, energy, work, housing, transportation, communication, education, etc.) as well as access to all this in economic conditions that, although not completely paralyzed, are necessarily restricted by sanitary measures that seek to selectively contain the contagion nuclei.

If income and payments should be equal for everyone simply by being alive, the reality is that they are not the same. Asymmetries in income, or depending on what is done in different jobs, generate very different profits and wages, and salaries do not correspond to profit margins. These differences in spending capacity, combined with the informality of 56% of the economy and unemployment, force jobs to be carried out in extremely unequal ways. So the information and protection resources to face the pandemic are also very different.

> This is evident when we see that, for example, 17% of Parisians (Greater Paris) have left the city to take refuge in their temporary residences in the

countryside. That is something that the poor cannot afford. The Covid-19 drama in New York, a city with crowded morgues and field hospitals (Paredes 2020, 2).

Thus, we know that huge sectors of supermarket and warehouse employees, those who distribute basic products, cannot be quarantined, nor are those in charge of their transport, drivers and storekeepers, or hospital staff. As criticism of government actions around the world shows, very different perceptions emerge about what care and protection measures need to be put into practice. "People die because circumstances compel them to continue working. This generates fear and anger at the same time, because many feel abandoned. It is as if the life of the poor had no value" (Paredes 2020, 4). Thus, different perceptions also arise about what is considered urgent.

We are experiencing a cultural change that is not only worldwide, which, if it forces isolation, not only has with it very harsh introspective effects of an overwhelming silence. The normality that with all the difficulties and tensions of the day-to-day was already lived with difficulty until before November or December 2019, was left behind. When we felt more or less safe, this happens with COVID-19. And the feeling grows that we are lost again. Now, something else haunts us everywhere.

We are reaching this future very quickly, because in order to care for and protect life, the forces of society are mobilized and those of the State are questioned.[1] "We have governments that do not know how to handle the crisis and who constantly change their minds. These actions have taken human lives" (Paredes 2020, 3). The causes are many: that if one acts well and for good or, on the contrary, that the action put in place corresponds to authoritarian and petty interests, that hospital medical capacities are not enough, that small groups cannot mobilize everything necessary, etc.

---

[1] We certainly have to consider how our own reactions to COVID-19 exercise influence, because "deeper effects may have nothing to do with (the behavioral immune system), but more directly with the perception of how well government officials respond or not to the situation... Whether we express a conformist opinion, judge the behavior of another, or try to understand the value of different containment policies, we might ask ourselves whether our thoughts are really the result of rational reasoning, or whether they might have been molded by an ancient response that evolved millennia before the discovery of germ theory" (BBC 2020, 2).

Among the facts, opinions, and recommendations reported by serious mass media and authorized global health institutions, the need to protect life itself constantly emerges. At the same time, in order to achieve this, mutual aid is constantly breaking through. With this common value, support is organized within housing units, some prevention of contagion is being achieved, and there emerge even broader and more effective responses with support networks to stop the spread of the disease.

Realizing with COVID-19 that life itself is valuable is leading to the recognition of many other substantive values of social coexistence. What matters is the emerging solidarity practices of generosity and piety. Above all, practices that reintegrate doing with what has been done, saying consistent with acting. Practices that are showing that, with the emergence of the value of mutual aid, trust is also emerging as a common good. Between fear and these hopes, perhaps a better society will flourish.

To cope with the pandemic, errors or failures of state responses can be pointed out. It can also be seen that people are giving themselves a practical, compassionate response to the current crisis of world development. As the social values put into practice to take care of one's life grow, because it depends on everyone's life, another value is achieved that is quite far from the market.

Taking Care of Life Is Essential for the Pandemic City

Inside and with the other, something comes up that reconnects us. A particular connection emerges so as to be able to keep in touch in these abnormal conditions. Perhaps this is a peculiar experience of forced isolation to avoid infection. The fact is that it resizes the essential, makes it evident, leads to the choice, forces us to decide between different paths to take. If we never go back to the exact same place, these decisive practices taken at each moment of the pandemic, in each place and city, raise different meanings. The slightest choice made by and with others reverberates immediately across the entire planet.

The cultural change we are experiencing right now comes from many different experiences, places and influences that reiterate the need to reconnect with the earth. The pandemic declares a period of change not without violence and death in which unmentioned proposals emerge. It is possible that what we are experiencing heralds radically changing timesof transition towards another order that is not patriarchal but, fundamentally egalitarian and free.

Realizing this multiple revaluation that we are implementing in favour of life and mutual aid is key for all of us because it comes from another ethic "that values care, life and democracy. The central political task at this time of crisis is to live and organize around those values" (Mair 2020, 12). Therefore, in the face of the COVID-19 pandemic, it will seek to encourage inseparable emerging practices of values inspired by the care of life.

Cities in Silence. A Global Response to Fear of the Other

Saint Peter's Square without faithful or pilgrims on Easter Sunday; the Roman Colosseum without tourists; Tiananmen Square in Beijing empty; the Plaza de la Revolución deserted and without the traditional parade for Workers' Day in Havana. A similar picture, of silence and stillness, is observed in the Obelisk in Buenos Aires, in the Paseo de la Reforma in Mexico, on the Copacabana beaches, in the centre of Beirut or on a Panamanian highway. These and other images of a world "without people" resignify to "silence" as part of the urban cartographies inaugurated by the global pandemic of 2020.

In the framework of hyperdigitalized societies, in which information and interconnection through technological innovations make up a good part of the macro and micro-social dynamics, silence is undervalued. It is hardly supported in a face-to-face interaction and is usually uncomfortable in a video call or in a conversation on WhatsApp. It is only admitted as a prayer and protest against death. At most, silence is considered as what "remains" after the passage of sound, or as a mere backdrop for noise.

Le Breton (2001) argues that observing the social situations in which silence appears constitutes a privileged analytical way to examine the social order. With this, the author defines the "transgressive" character that silence has in today's societies. From our perspective, far from being a discursive abyss or a void between noise and noise, silence is an activity crossed by a body/emotion. As such, it constitutes an opportunity to initiate the active listening that is necessary for collective action. Understood as the starting point of any form of social interaction, silence opens worlds. Hence, in the connections between "knowing how to listen" and "making silence", all possibilities of dialogue with the context and with others begin (Scribano 2019).

Silence. It is what prevails in the avenues, neighbourhoods, factories, schools, shopping centres, stadiums and monuments of most cities on the planet. Silence. This condition that seemed to be in danger of extinction in large cities is one of the great "miracles" that the COVID-19 pandemic has unexpectedly offered to billions of the world's inhabitants. In the framework of the current confinement of populations, silence is not only a state that denotes an absence (of sound). Fundamentally, it points to the presence of new (and not so new) social relations drawn up to respond to the demands of capital that the virus brought with it. The home office, e-learning, e-commerce and even sexting are some of the trends that have spread massively with isolation, causing the world's homes to become—overnight—exclusive areas for working, learning, consuming, loving and enjoying in times of Coronavirus.

Out of fear, starting in March 2020, the entire world had to slow down. For physics, deceleration is the negative variation of speed, that is, it expresses the passage of a body in motion from one speed X to another lower, always following the same path. In the current context, the irruption of this social, economic and affective "pause" that seeks to contain the spread of the virus means, as a derived effect, the establishment of a novel urban silence. In addition to the decrease in noise pollution that several cities have verified in recent months (Zambrano-Monserrate et al. 2020), which has favoured, among other aspects, the reappearance of sensations such as hearing the trill of the birds or that the people manage to improve their quality in rest, remembering Melucci (1996) we can affirm that this "new" silence is a "message" of structural social processes.

As such, the silence that accompanies the compulsory and/or voluntary confinement of populations as a result of COVID-19 testifies to the forms taken by the social relations of production—especially between capital and labor—and the functions that States assume in their articulations, with the global agendas and actors and, in particular, the pre-existing social inequalities that the pandemic illuminated and deepened in a virulent way. Indeed, there are millions of human beings who do not have adequate housing to "comply" with isolation; urban agglomerations that do not have sanitation services and lack basic facilities for hand washing; thousands of hospitals in the world without resources or basic supplies to care for those infected with COVID-19 (and other conditions); precarious health professionals with pictures of stress and emotional exhaustion linked to their working and salary conditions. These and other snapshots are part of the silent urban postcard that materially and symbolically unfolds "outside" the interiors of our houses and that the passing of this health and economic crisis does nothing but aggravate.

In the framework of the race initiated by the health and executive authorities of the countries to "beat" the virus, seeking to "flatten" the curve of infections and deaths, a social experiment of unprecedented mass seclusion of people has been carried out, that not even the most visionary mind could ever have imagined. Taking care of yourself and confining yourself at "home" has been approved worldwide as the best "vaccine" to prevent the spread of the virus. In practice, this implies making the private, domestic and intimate environment a kind of "trench" to contribute to one's own and the community's health. In this scenario, the idea of the common has been resignified as a compulsive virtuality, with no escape: we are and, therefore, we contribute to the community by staying "inside". Meanwhile "outside", on the outside, the other (the unknown, but also the neighbor, friend or relative) is installed as a threat (Korstanje 2019). That is, as a suspected virus carrier and potential contagion agent, capable of breaking with the possibilities of a healthy future, outdoors and in freedom. It is precisely this fear of the other that has established silence as one of the most extraordinary consequences that cities exhibit today.

In this compulsion for life and health "entrenched" at home, the street has become—more than ever—a mere place of transit, moderate, limited and monitored by the security forces, and also by security prac tices assumed by the citizenship from their windows, balconies or terraces. All in all, social isolation has reinforced the erosion of the political and creative possibilities that the street houses as a place of information, social exchanges, entertainment and stimulation. In urban terms, the pandemic has further radicalized the "colonization" of public space historically undertaken by capital in its expansionist drive. In the streets, the place par excellence of the public, change and exchange value dominate over use and use value, limiting themselves to being reticules organized by and for consumption (Lefebvre 1991). For example, with the mandatory isolation imposed in several countries of the world to contain the spread of COVID-19, city streets have become solid passages that allow people to move around (on foot, or with the aid of the car or transportation) in public to local shops or hospitals and then return, rigorously, to "home". This cadence makes public space not a collective product but rather the effect derived from the sum of individual body movements delimited and monitored according to the guidelines that govern the extension of displacement and the length of stay abroad imposed by the authorities to control the contagion.

The abrupt change between density and emptiness, between noise and silence, has established a new social order that forces social sciences to reformulate the traditional approaches to the city and its dynamics. With the advance of the pandemic, the noises, sounds, music and voices begin to resignify in the great urban void. This supposes an evident alteration of routines and daily lives, as well as a drastic reformulation of the space-times of the interactions that originate new ways of conceiving the hours, the days, customs, public life and the spaces of intimacy. In particular, the generalized silence imposed by the pandemic has broken with the "previous urban normality" and has become a sign of suspicion and mistrust in the face of all things, people and relationships that are "outside" the personal area of confinement.

In this scenario, the virus is foreign. Its "invisible" presence involves risks, uncertainties and mistrust that are projected onto others, configuring them as latent threats. In this table, mass seclusion in the private sphere appears as the fastest and cheapest way for individual defence and protection. So, in the face of fear of the other, the answer is confinement and an expectant silence. Something like the scene that is repeated in any thriller where the hidden victim, in the dark and in silence, awaits the (inevitable?) stalking of his victimizer.

But just as silence is a necessary condition for interactions, urban mutism caused by the massive confinement of populations reveals the nullification of all possibility of listening to the other, of looking into their eyes and of opening other worlds. When the noise, the sounds and the voices are confined in the private space and the cities are silent, everything that happens outside the walls bears the exclusive mark of suspicion and threat. Thus, in the face of the individuation, differentiation and social fragmentation that accompany, as features, the current phase of capitalism—and that the fear of COVID-19 has deepened to the extreme—distrust is a feeling that permeates much of the experiences of the life, consuming, sharing and enjoyment that take place in cities day by day (Scribano and Cervio 2018). Immersed in a sanitary rhetoric that defines interpersonal distance and self-care as social responsibilities necessary to face the emergency, the aforementioned structural conditions are deepened still further, drawing limits and manufacturing (socio-sensible) borders that regulate the contacts that are "allowed" and the "adequate" distances between bodies that are recognized as strange, dangerous, threatening.

In short, we are facing an uncertain social scenario, full of paradoxes and contradictions, haunted by the pain caused by deaths and infections, cornered by the collapse of health systems and by the collapse of world economies. In this context, mistrust expands as a bastion of urban social interactions. To distrust is instituted, then, in a sensation and form of socialization to which the subjects resort to continue acting in the world (in their world), hoping to find "there", in the stubborn and routine construction of inter-individual borders, some opportunity to reduce the risks and uncertainty that inexorably accompany the spread of the pandemic.

The Pandemic City: Between Lack and Possibility

The City as Lack and Absence

The COVID-19 pandemic has produced an amplification effect on several of the most complex and negative edges of cities and, at the same time, has brought forth diverse potentialities. Here we want to refer to the city as a lack, trying to highlight the limits and deficiencies that quarantines and isolation have "emphasized", and also as a possibility, pointing out the practices and sensibilities that appear increased under pandemic conditions.

I have named the set of spatial/temporal features of the cities affected by the spread of the virus and subjected to public policies to mitigate its effects as a "pandemic city". This is not a different city, which brings with it the inheritance of what was discussed in Chapter 1, but it is a different time/space that is expressed in a feeling of "being suspended in the air", "being in parentheses", in a timeless way of being.

As faults that are increased and reproduced, we systematize the following: hunger, "roof", education and distraction. As possibilities, we present the redefinition of the indispensable and the look on the next paragraph

Hunger

One of the aspects that the pandemic city reveals is that not all citizens, the neighbours, have enough to eat. One of the first sources of tension is in this new way of organizing the city around food procurement, not only because shops are closed, not only because shops are concentrated (they are concentrated in the sense that they are the big chains), and those that are benefited, but also by the attention/tension that emerges with the "senses" of local businesses. This relationship is redefined between waiting in line, "keeping distance" in the supermarket and buying in the store (where the stores are) in the Chinese supermarket, in the smaller local supermarkets. A tension is redefined between waiting and patience, such as civic virtues, and food. In the neighbourhood there is a tension of what it means "not having to buy", "not being able to buy" and "not being able to produce an activity to buy".

The pandemic city is a city of lack. When productivity stops, when trade ceases, when transfers freeze, what appears is what is missing and the first thing that is missed is the possibility of constituting that triangle so difficult to capture between food, meal and satisfaction. The pandemic city demands that we keep in mind the regular satiety indices; the purchase is made between what it takes to feed, between food to fill up with, and the possibility of doing it.

The pandemic city shows very clearly that capitalism has constituted a social fantasy of what it means to be satisfied, what it means to be satiated, what it means to "be eaten". This city of lack reveals that in front of the veneer of normality there is a large mirror that reflects that there were many human beings without food, hidden in a bazaar of frivolity of consumption, in the corners, on the margins, on the edges. Paradoxically, the city that provided everything was reduced to having the possibility and the disposition to acquire it; and it becomes more radical when those possibilities/provisions refer to food. That is why the structure of that dialectic, of that triangle between food, meal and satisfaction, is revealed, it is seen pornographically when the city empties, when silence occurs, when lack constitutes the structure of what was always bustlingly complete. It is very clear who eats every day in this city where food begins to be a central problem of the day-to-day for most of those who have to stay at home: it is already more clearly seen that it was not a city of all, that it was not a city for everyone, that everyone did not eat.

Roof
Another of the features of this city of lack, of the pandemic city, is to make present, to put under the magnifying glass, a problem that is structural for the capitalist city and which is precisely the lack of a house. When you look at a city what you see are houses, buildings, shopping

malls and, for that same reason, you cannot clearly perceive that there are thousands of people who are not included in the social fantasy of the house. They do not have a room to stay in, they do not have a house in which to isolate themselves because the roof is an object of dispute, not a given natural condition. There is no fantasized homogeneity of the public/private structure of a "type" of house in the spaces of these cities, understood as a room for a certain number of people, a place to eat for a set number of people, places for sanitizing for a specific number of people: the fantasy of "having a house" is collapsed in the pandemic city by the ghost of "not being able to stay at home", due to the impossibility of being in a house. This is not only experienced by those who are on the streets, this is not only experienced by those who wander in the parks, but those thousands of people who literally live "outside the house", who go to sleep in a small place that is constituted simply in a "place to arrive", but they do not have the class conditions implied by the fantasy of being able to stay at home, they do not have the water to wash their hands, they do not have the conditions to have social distancing. If we add to this the sanitary measure called a "face cap" it is very interesting to observe its ineffectiveness because its effectiveness is related to the fact of "having" distance, proximity, the logic of being close together, implies the impossibility of defending against the pandemic. But also, there is no mask because there is no cash, because there is no money, because there is no work, because they have lived in informality for decades. So there is no way to mediate an instrument between the subject and the other subject. The device, the thing called a "face cap", is the result of the uneven distribution of the possibilities of self-administering that device. In short, the pandemic city clearly states that not all of us have a place to stay, not all of us have shelter, not all of us have that "natural border" against the virus: house/roof.

Education
A third element that the pandemic city brings to the table is the unequal distribution of access to educational opportunities. If people are to stay at home and education is going to be virtual, they need, on the spot, at home, the internet connection and the device to connect with it. Beyond all the logic of the structuring that has resulted in the digitization of the world, beyond this continuum between digital/mobile/virtual that has occurred globally, the pandemic city puts inequality under the lens, the lack of that which you really should have access to: the plan to manage

gigabytes, to connect. Whether through WhatsApp or any other platform, connecting with the other involves spending money and there are multiple varieties of access. The pandemic city revealed that neither the material conditions of existence, nor the organizational forms of information distribution, nor the material structure of connectivity, are distributed more or less equally. The necessary consequence was then that educational inequality was reinforced by amplifying another lack of the city. To be able to watch a video on WhatsApp or Facebook, the person needs money and what stands out as a possibility of equality ends up being a new inequality. I cannot stay at home and I do not have internet access and, in that sense, I am condemned to not having an education precisely because the pandemic city reinforces the pre-existing faults. One of the most radically suggestive aspects of this absence of possibility and condition is that it is also experienced by teachers, those who have to teach, not only the children, young people and/or adults who receive these classes; which shows very clearly that this exposed lack, this exposed breakdown of education in the pandemic city, is the product of a structural movement prior to the pandemic itself. This is an exposed breakdown generated by the structural inequality of both students, teachers and those who have to receive education.

Distraction / Enjoyment

Finally, the pandemic city highlights the close link between the social fantasy of a city for all and the enjoyment of the means of entertainment and distraction that keeps people happy. The means of containment involve a contained citizen, that is, one who is not ready for conflict, who is prepared for collaboration with the city and its system. That is, precisely, a distracted citizen, that is, entertained. It is a distraction from that radically important thing that was hunger, which was the roof and education, and that is why the first three offences increase, grow, in pandemic conditions. Now these faults are seen because there is no longer organized enjoyment, because there is no longer organized distraction. The social magic stops, that is, producing an event with one hand while the other hand is the one that distracts the attention of the public. Magic involves the fact that people "relapse and repeat" what is seductive in fantasy: disconnection from the real world. At the end of football, at the end of the cinema, at the end of the walks, at the end of the bars, at the end of the theatres, at the end of everything that is ready to distract and provide enjoyment in the city, he asks himself once again what is essential: that also brings with it the fact that there is another city, that there are other features of the pandemic city.

The City as a Possibility

Opening interstices between the structural flaws that the pandemic city makes visible and puts under the magnifying glass, we find other consequences that deny the value of totality that the regime of truth pretends to have: the indispensable and what is next.

The Indispensable

The pandemic city lets us see the other side of social organization because it challenges us, and once we have found ourselves facing hunger, homelessness and lack of options, in a context of non-distraction we begin to think the indispensable. We begin to reflect on what we really cannot stop doing; we begin to think about what it would be impossible to continue living without, and in this context, the pandemic city confronts us with the decision to continue immediate enjoyment through consumption slowed by the closure and emptiness of the pandemic city. As a consequence of the measures of confinement, of the same measures of defense against the virus, conditions are structured to decide "another way", and not just to continue wildly in consumption. The pandemic city confronts us with the possibility of selecting those things that seem important to us, that are indispensable, that without which we could not produce the coordination of action, the reproduction of life and the elaboration of the fabric of the social. The pandemic city puts us in the predicament of having to re-decide just what indispensable means.

For the coordination of the action what is indispensable is that which has no aggregate, that does not depend on any fiction, that which is not only set for the other to see me, that which is above the purely instrumental. In this sense, what is indispensable is not an "as if": it is that for which the coordination of the action is not possible. That is why the pandemic city, has written on its frontispieces: it leaves out everything that is a weight, that is a ballast, that will not serve to meet the other, to relate to others. The pandemic city opens the door to concentrate on that without which action is impossible. But what is essential is also what allows us to reproduce: to sleep, eat, breathe, walk, "be in the world", last, relate the present with the future, take advantage of what we learned in the past. All these things are indispensable, that is, they cannot be absent, we cannot stop doing them, because they have to do directly with our own reproduction. In the pandemic city, the urban fabric is rewoven, the set of threads that weave the urban structure, new networks, new paths, are knotted again: because those indispensable paths appear.

The Proximity

This pandemic city leads us, once again, to think about what otherness means and with this gives us another possibility for that which is shared. Who is the other? Who is my neighbour? Who am I with? These are all questions that in the context of uncertainty, fear and the slowdown in life, the pandemic city allows us to ask. It allows us to configure these dimensions as radical questions.

The pandemic city allows us to think about proximity, the distance that differentiates us from each other, what separates, what connects, what is at a time-space that allows to be easily found others persons and that allows to be identified as similar person.. The pandemic city gives us the possibility to stop thinking about the abject, to stop thinking about the discriminating, to stop thinking about domination in the face of the different, because the other, the proximity and the distance are redefined according to silence and emptiness of these threatened cities rebuilt and rearmed by the violence of a humanity that crossed all limits with other species, with itself and with the entire planet. The pandemic city allows us to think the other and the Other with a capital letter, allows us to think again that taking care of myself I take care of the other, that taking care of the Others I take care of myself. The self is not defined by its capacity for isolation but for its ability to care for the other, to meet another at a distance, to allow that which redefines who I am isolated constitutes the starting point of the common, of the communal.

The spatial temporal unpinning that allows a city to be lived at a distance leaves the doors open to radically think of the other as someone who is necessary and indispensable to me in order to narrate myself in an individual and community history. The one next to it becomes this one that allows me, when taking a distance, to take it into account; the crowding is radically transformed into the possibility of seeing the other. Those two metres allow us to identify faces, not in the mass that walks disoriented in search of a consumption that allows self-centred enjoyment. The next one at a distance recovers the possibilities of redefining what is next, who is my neighbour, who are our next ones.

Thus, if we connect the indispensable with the next, we can draw a new geometry of the bodies; we can rethink the new normality that does not throw us into the emptiness of being mere objects of enjoyment for others. In the pandemic city, others are indispensable, neither luxuries, nor fantasies, nor phantoms. What is indispensable is the common that can only be produced by and with others.

Conclusions

By the reader.

References

BBC News Mundo. (2020, April 12). Coronavirus: Cómo el Miedo a la Enfermedad Covid-19 Está Cambiando Nuestra Psicología. *BBC News Mundo*. https://www.bbc.com/mundo/noticias-52191660.

Carrión, M. (2020, March 27). Infografía. Las Pandemias de la Historia. *El Ágora, Diario del Agua*. https://www.elagoradiario.com/open-data/infogr afias/las-pandemias-de-la-historia/.

Cuvardic García, D. (2018). El Caleidoscopio en la Literatura Española. *Káñina, Revista Artes Y Letras XLII, 1*, 65–87.

Garrido, A. (2020, April 19). Precedentes al Coronavirus. De la Peste al Sida: El Impacto Social de Otras Pandemias Históricas. *Periódico El Mediterráneo*. https://www.elperiodicomediterraneo.com/noticias/sociedad/peste-sida-impacto-social-otras-pandemias-historicas_1290214.html.

Korstanje, M. (2019). Disasters in the Society of Fear. In *Terrorism, Technology and Apocalyptic Futures* (pp. 123–141). Cham: Palgrave Macmillan.

Le Breton, D. (2001). *El Silencio*. Madrid: Sequitur.

Lefebvre, H. (1991). *The Production of Space*. Oxford: Blackwell Publishing.

Mair, S. (2020, March 31). How Will Coronavirus Change the World? *BBC Future*. https://www.bbc.com/future/article/20200331-covid-19-how-will-the-coronavirus-change-the-world.

Melucci, A. (1996). *Challenging Codes. Collective Action in the Information Age*. Cambridge: Cambridge University Press.

ONU. (2020, April 22). La Pandemia de Coronavirus va Para Largo, Los Contagios a la Baja Pueden Volver a Dispararse. *Noticias ONU*. https://news.un.org/es/story/2020/04/1473272.

Opazo Sáez, P. (2020, April 20). Enfermedades. Comparación Entre COVID-19 y Otras Pandemias Históricas. *Nación Farma*. https://nacionfarma.com/comparacion-covid-19-otras-pandemias-historicas/.

Paredes, N. (2020, April 12). Coronavirus. El Confinamiento es un Concepto Burgués: Cómo el Aislamiento Afecta a las Distintas Clases Sociales. *BBC News Mundo.* https://www.bbc.com/mundo/noticias-internacional-52216492.

Scribano, A. (2019). A Modo de Prólogo. El Silencio Como Punto de Partida. In A. Cervio & V. D'hers (Comp.) *Sensibilidades y Experiencias: Acentos, Miradas y Recorridos desde los Estudios Sociales de los Cuerpos/Emociones,* (pp. 11–13). Buenos Aires: Estudios Sociológicos.

Scribano, A. & Cervio, A. (2018). Distrust and Proximity. The Paradoxes of Violence in Argentina. In A. Scribano, *Politics and Emotions* (pp. 193–219). Houston: Studium Press.

Zambrano-Monserrate, M., Ruano, M. & Sánchez-Alcalde, L. (2020). Indirect Effects of COVID-19 on the Environment. *Science of The Total Environment,* Vol. 728. https://doi.org/10.1016/j.scitotenv.2020.138813.

Index

Printed by Printforce, the Netherlands